Wild Camping

STEPHEN NEALE

Wild Camping

EXPLORING AND SLEEPING IN THE WILDS OF THE UK AND IRELAND

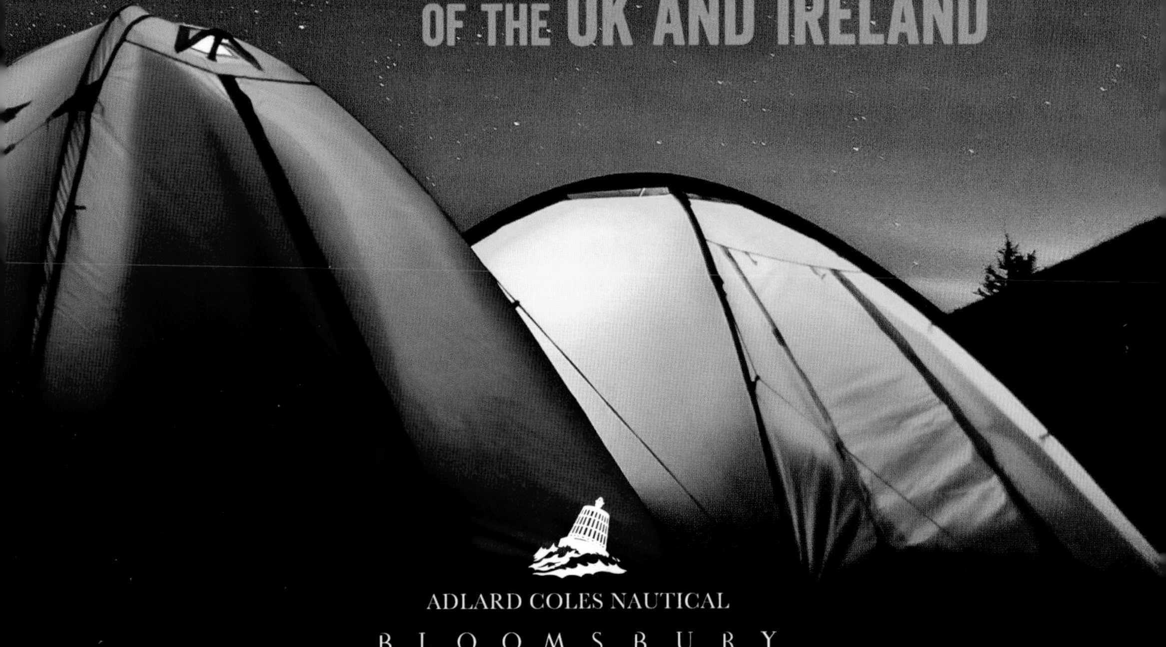

ADLARD COLES NAUTICAL

BLOOMSBURY
LONDON · NEW DELHI · NEW YORK · SYDNEY

FOR ROMI

Adlard Coles Nautical
An imprint of Bloomsbury Publishing Plc

50 Bedford Square
London
WC1B 3DP
UK

1385 Broadway
New York
NY 10018
USA

www.bloomsbury.com

ADLARD COLES, ADLARD COLES NAUTICAL
and the Buoy logo are trademarks of
Bloomsbury Publishing Plc

First published 2015

British Library Cataloguing-in-Publication Data
A catalogue record for this book is available
from the British Library.

Library of Congress Cataloguing-in-Publication
data has been applied for.
ISBN: PB: 978-1-4729-0034-0
        ePDF: 978-1-4729-0036-4
        ePub: 978-1-4729-0035-7

2 4 6 8 10 9 7 5 3

Typeset in Bell Gothic
Designed by Austin Taylor
Printed and bound in RR Donnelley Asia Printing
Solutions Limited

Bloomsbury Publishing Plc makes every effort
to ensure that the papers used in the manufacture
of our books are natural, recyclable products
made from wood grown in well-managed forests.
Our manufacturing processes conform to the
environmental regulations of the country of origin.

To find out more about our authors and books
visit **www.bloomsbury.com**. Here you will
find extracts, author interviews, details of
forthcoming events and the option to sign
up for our newsletters.

CONTENTS

Going into the outdoors, alone or with company, can be hazardous. Foreshore, rivers, mountains and other areas should be approached with extreme caution at all times of year. Seek expert advice and proper training. Always alert people to where you are going and take particular care in winter when locations, including hills and mountains, can become particularly hazardous.

Distances of trails throughout often have multiple sources. Most paths included within have been associated with distances recorded by the Long Distance Walkers Association: http://www.ldwa.org.uk.

KEY TO SYMBOLS

WILD   MIDDLE   FORESHORE   MOUNTAIN
      EARTH

contents continued overleaf

PART TWO

ENNERDALE WATER

HOW TO USE THIS BOOK

SLEEPING OUTDOORS is one of the most liberating things a person can do. Peaceful sleep in the wild epitomises freedom. Rolling out a sleeping bag at dusk and rising with the dawn makes us feel alive.

Part One explains where I'm coming from when I talk about 'wild camping'. An expression we didn't know about when we were kids. We just wanted to have fun camping in the garden after dark. But once we grew into adulthood we got scared. Because of a 1,000-year land grab.

Part Two explains where to go. Walk under the stars and into an unenclosed space, far from any road or building, lie down and sleep. It will change your life forever. There are four 'bedzones' in Part Two. They are: Wild, Foreshore, Middle Earth and Mountain (see page 5 for key to symbols). Secret zones that sailors, mountaineers, hikers, cyclists, canoeists and pilgrims have been using for centuries.

● The first is the Wild bedzone: Scotland. Where sleeping outdoors only became a legal right under the Land Reform (Scotland) Act 2003. There's the first clue that something needed fixing – a law reform.
● Second is the Foreshore zone. Salt creeks and coasts mainly in South and East England. The space below the high tide mark that was stolen from us, but then given back as a communal, 24-hour larder under concession of Magna Carta. Another legal right returned.
● The third zone is Middle Earth. Central England and Ireland are the regions I've chosen to explore: a Middle Earth of trails, canals and freshwater rivers, where there's no burden in 'asking'. Wild camping isn't a right, but no shame in asking for salt with the chips.
● The Mountains are the final zone: Wales and North England. Where we can climb onto the peaks and ridges.

Wild camping can be a safe, fun way of getting out into the outdoors – an adventure that's better than legal. Because it's free.

PART
ONE

SCOTTISH
HIGHLANDS

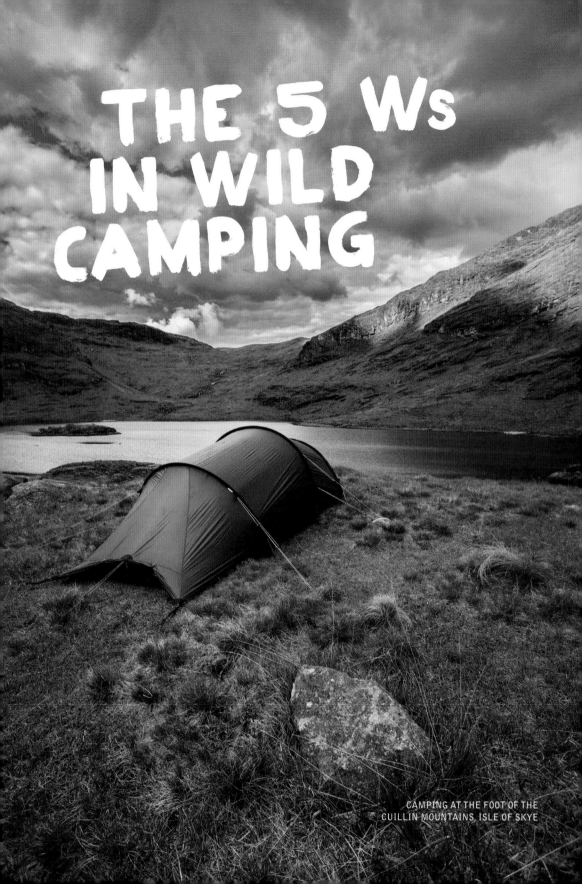

THE 5 Ws
IN WILD
CAMPING

CAMPING AT THE FOOT OF THE
CUILLIN MOUNTAINS, ISLE OF SKYE

I SLEEP ON MOUNTAINS.

We all have natural rights. I believe one of them is the right to dream at night on hilltops.

Most of our rights are written down in law. The right to breathe clean air. To pick and eat fruit from the wild tree or bush. To fish in the sea. To drink water from the stream. Others aren't written down. Like the right to sleep on a mountain.

Wild camping in any unenclosed place – far away from roads, buildings and towns – is one of the most precious things a person can experience. Walking, cycling or canoeing into the outdoors, bedding down at dusk and waking with the dawn, contains a magic ingredient that rebalances our body clocks, re-syncs our minds, and makes us feel alive.

I know. All sounds like pseudo science from a snake oil salesman, doesn't it? But the only catch here is a historic one. A 1,000-year land grab so cleverly PR-managed that it has allowed us to lose touch with who we are. Alfresco sleep, which helps reconnect us with an ancient tradition of free movement that we enjoyed for tens of thousands of years, was forcibly removed from us. That change was like being handed a lifetime ban on walking the pavements for no other reason than someone said, 'Stop!' So we got angry at first, but then we forgot. And now no one notices anymore. This part of the book explains how that happened, the history of British land laws, and why we can use a little knowledge to wild camp and explore secluded locations in the British Isles – 100 of which are listed in Part II.

Our ability to get outdoors – let alone sleep in the wild – is increasingly threatened in the 21st century. Partly because our footpaths are disappearing at the very same time public lands are being sold off. But mostly because we have one of the most unequal landownership systems in the world. Old traditions of camping in forests and on moors have almost vanished. And

that's crazy, because no one should have to be told how much fun it is to snooze under the stars while listening to the dry rattle of a grasshopper or the hoot of a tawny owl. We all knew that from our childhoods. Only we've been encouraged to forget.

During the mid 1980s – between the age of 19 and 27 – I hitchhiked from London to Zurich, to Athens and Israel, to Egypt, and then back into Istanbul, to the Londra Mocamp – the largest lorry park in Europe – out into eastern Turkey and on across Iran, Pakistan, India and Nepal. Down into south-east Asia, Timor and across Australia from the Northern Territories to Perth via Townville, Brisbane,

THERE IS NO statutory right of public access to woodland in England and Wales.

Melbourne, New Zealand, Los Angeles, Fiji, everything in between; and back home. Then I did it all over again.

Ditches, gardens, car parks, cemeteries, doorways and bus stops provided a bed. It was a means to an end. A way to keep going. Longer, further. It never felt like hardship, and it never felt wrong.

I mostly worked or looked for jobs. In Israel, in Tel Aviv and Eilat, by day and night, in the restaurants and nightclubs, milking cows in Lahore, selling carpets in Cairo, tomato picking in Bowen, Australia. After work, I'd join fellow campers, asleep on the beaches. Strangers for a few minutes, sometimes friends for a lifetime. You learned to make acquaintances quickly. We'd get our stuff stolen occasionally. But more gear went missing when we lived in workers' accommodation than was ever lost bivvying down in a doorway or park.

Fellow workers or the bosses on the farms, hotels and shops would ask what it was all about. The living under wet skies. I'd tell them about the cold, the fear, the rats and the police. Then how people would come to leave us food in the mornings. The workers and bosses said, 'You're mad,' but they didn't say it with any conviction. It was as if they knew what we knew. That sleeping outdoors contained an esoteric truth so profound it could not be challenged.

We're not talking about homelessness here. That's something very different and very sad. Homelessness is about having no choices. As young, penniless backpackers we were always making choices. There were times when paying for a night's accommodation was simply wonderful – even if it did involve selling a good watch or a pair of walking boots. Often, renting a room came after having a bad feeling about a place. Perhaps I'd arrived late, well after dark, and safe didn't seem realistic. It was just a feeling, and maybe it meant nothing. Just peace of mind. A sense of well-being based on choice, not confinement.

If you believe a person does not have a right to sleep unless he has paid for a room, this book is not for you. If you believe that only a person who owns a mountain has a right to sleep there, this book is not for you. Those who think that way are not selfish. They're frightened. Worried that we sleepers might want to hurt or steal from them. They are wrong. Sleepers are static ships of the night. They are just regular people: climbers, cyclists, travellers and walkers. They pitch up after dark when everyone else has gone home. Not just hidden from view, but hidden from the public consciousness.

Invisible aliens crossing over the landscape by day, hanging from hammocks in trees, or bivvying down under bushes by night. We are free to join them; only held back by the false claims that we're committing a crime or doing something that's very bad. Fenced in by the fear and ignorance we grew into when we left childhood and adolescence.

After travelling I became a journalist. Not a brilliant one. There was no graduation out of local newspapers on to Fleet Street. I remained a regional hack covering the courts, council meetings and charity fun days for almost 20 years. I learned to enjoy it. Writing about 'home' replaced tramping abroad. But newspapers taught me something about the world that was just as important: every story begins with an idea. They call it an intro, and it has 5 Ws:

WHO – Every person
WHAT – has a natural-born right to sleep outdoors without paying...
WHERE – in the British Isles
WHEN – right now
WHY – because wild camping is too much fun to be wrong.

Oh yeah, I forgot; there's a 'how'. That's the thing with formulas. Remembering them.

HOW – Abandon your car, abandon your fear; abandon everything you have learned to believe in since leaving childhood. On a warm, clear night, go and walk under the stars and in an unenclosed space, far from any road or building, lay down and sleep. It will change your life for ever.

GREAT GABLE, CUMBRIA

QUESTIONS
AND ANSWERS

ONE OF MY FAVOURITE parts of being a journalist is asking questions. So I thought I'd insert a Q&A here. It goes like this:

So no one has a right to sleep outdoors wherever they want?
Errrr. No.

Wild camping is illegal then?
Not when you follow the A, B, C, D rule – that makes it all legal and good.

What is the A, B, C, D rule?
Ask the landowner's permission.
Be discreet – camp away from roads and buildings.
Clean up and leave no trace.
Don't stay more than one night.

OK, so apart from when following the A, B, C, D rule, wild camping is illegal?
Well... except when you're in a place where permission is not required, like:

a) Scotland
b) Dartmoor
c) upland areas of Lakeland, north-west England
d) upland areas of Wales
e) upland areas of north-east England (the Pennines etc)
f) staying in or outside a bothy in England and Wales.

OK, apart from when you're:
1) following the A, B, C, D rule
2) sleeping on top of a mountain
3) sleeping in most of Scotland
4) sleeping on most of Dartmoor
5) staying in or outside a bothy in England or Wales...
wild camping is illegal?
Except when you're overnight fishing on the foreshore (that's below sea level – usually when the tide is out) of a tidal river or beach, and you want to climb into your bivvy for some sleep until the tide returns. This is especially good for people who are nervous about heights (mountains and very high hills).

*Right, so to summarise – apart from
when you:*
1) ask permission
2) sleep on a mountain
3) camp in Scotland
4) hike over Dartmoor
*5) rest up in an English or
Welsh bothy*
*6) or fish on the coast or a tidal river...
wild camping is illegal?*
Mmmmmm? Not when you're navigating
tidal waters (including rivers) in a kayak,
canoe or small boat and you need to
overnight on the foreshore until the high
water returns.

OK! OK!! Apart from:
1) mountains
2) Scotland
3) Dartmoor
4) bothies
5) foreshore
6) tidal rivers
*7) and when you have permission...
wild camping is illegal?*

Nope! Wild camping is not illegal.
It used to be, back in the 1930s.
But it was decriminalised by Section 4
of the Vagrancy Act 1938.

*So if it's not illegal, why do
people keep petitioning Parliament
to make wild camping a right
enshrined in law?*
Because most people – including
officials and landowners – are unclear
about the law. That's because it's all
a bit too fragmented and confusing.

So why doesn't someone explain it?
OK. Good idea.

*Then can I go sleep on a mountain
without worrying about the law?*
Yes.

PROLOGUE

BUTTERMERE,
CUMBRIA

The first rule about fight club is you don't talk about fight club.

The second rule about fight club is you don't talk about fight club.

You don't say anything because fight club exists only in the hours between when fight club starts and when fight club ends...

TYLER DURDEN IN *FIGHT CLUB* (1999)

MY MUM USED TO slap me when I was a baby. It wasn't that she didn't love me. Of course she did. She still does. It was just that I slept a lot and it worried her. Slept so long and so deep, she told me how sometimes she thought I was dead. How she would nervously but quietly call out, 'Wake up, baby! Wake up!!! Waaaaaayyyyk uuup!!' And then she would nudge me. And push me. 'C'mon. Wake! Up!!' ... while gently tapping the jowls of my chops with her soft fingers. Until eventually, I did; wondering what all the fuss was about. And then I went back to sleep again, happy.

Sleeping into childhood was good, too; so much so that I could doze anywhere. Even standing up. The opportunities were endless. In school lessons; at the dinner table. Then on into adulthood, between serving drinks to diners who didn't want the night to end; on buses and trains. Once asleep, that was it. Gone. Even when my wife went into labour at night she couldn't wake me. There is not a shred of spin, mischief or malice in that story. She had to drive herself to the hospital. Thank God it was a false alarm. I'm as ashamed now as I was back then. I still tell her I'm sorry. But I digress. Because in between sleeping is living. And that's even better.

Like most kids, I grew up playing imaginary games. Outdoor games morphed into overnighting under canvas in the backyard. It was so terrifying we were usually indoors by 10pm. When we left school at 16, we slept out on the beach at Chalkwell, Southend-on-Sea. In the mid

1980s we grew wings and went backpacking. 'Wild camping' wasn't what we called it back then. We called ourselves 'travellers'. Pretentious hobos, who did most anything that didn't involve getting arrested.

Then in 1990, when I was 26, I met my wife. I was at home in England on a sabbatical before returning to start another new life, on a road to somewhere else. But one dream ended, and another began: a companion, a home, a dog, a baby daughter whom we called Romi (pronounced roam-me) and a new career as a local newspaper reporter.

The next two decades had more ups than downs, and passed quicker than a condemned man's last supper. And we suddenly arrived in the year 2010. I had a teenage daughter who didn't want to go on camping holidays any more, and a wife who had grown to love horse-riding more than kayaking. So I started looking to recapture my youth. A midlife crisis bound up with a nomadic existence from my past that had aged and almost died. I returned to walking, cycling, and even more canoeing. And in particular, looking for somewhere to sleep outdoors. But something had changed in those 20 years. It was as if the world had become more serious. Yeah, OK, it was great in the sense that there were these things called 'the web', 'forums' and 'YouTube' where I could meet up with like-minded blokes with beer bellies, grey beards and a penchant for reruns of Jack Hargreaves' *Out of Town*.

But whenever some dude or young dad came along asking for advice on locations for 'wild camping' or 'bushcraft', forum moderators would interject to warn that the thread would be closed down because such talk was 'illegal'. Other sites and forums chose to offer no practical advice on 'where', but instead their members seemed to want to pass on their stories in secrecy via personal messaging on a need-to-know basis, as if the entire countryside was one giant ecstasy-fuelled rave that the cops would swoop in on with gnashing dogs, taser guns and batons, if only they could discover the whereabouts of the bearded offenders and their disciples.

It seemed absurd. Was it really possible that the stuff we enjoyed as teenagers and young adults on the roads abroad, less than two decades ago, had suddenly been outlawed in Britain? Yet still to be tantalised with what we once had, by TV celebs like Ray Mears and Bear Grylls because they had 'special permission'? Like boy scouts attached to a secret society; an underground fantasy that had more in common with Tyler Durden in *Fight Club* than the *Easy Rider* I thought epitomised the youth I grew up in. How did it come to this? I asked myself. Why were some people so nervous about the 'dreamers'?

THE UK has the lowest forest cover in Europe, at around 13 per cent. France is second with 29 per cent. Finland and Sweden have 73 per cent and 69 per cent respectively.

The science of sleep is a puzzle, because no one truly knows why we do it. But without stating the obvious, it only seems to fulfil the most basic of human needs. Humans can function for weeks without food. Days without water. But they can do very little after 48 hours without sleep. This calling to sleep is a basic human need for anyone – especially when outdoors. But as I looked for some answers, more questions were popping up. So for instance, unlike breathing, walking, eating and drinking outdoors, 'sleeping in the wild' wasn't protected as a right like it was in so many other countries (Scotland, Norway, Sweden). I just found it incredible that apart from Scotland, the British Isles had been a virtual sleep-free zone for quite some time. How did this happen?

OLDANY ISLAND

ON THE BEACONS WAY, OVER LLYN Y FAN FACH, BRECON BEACONS

A TRADITION OF PILGRIMAGE

THE TRADITION of overnight travel and outdoor sleep seems to have existed in some limited form until a few hundred years ago. It was commonly known back then as a pilgrimage. A holy trek; a homage to an ancient past: a time when we lived a nomadic lifestyle before our ancient forefathers gave it up around 10,000 BC – give or take a few thousand years. Pilgrims (or travellers) experienced the nomadic journey along a simple track or road – while sleeping in bushes and secluded verges – for a reason. Without getting too philosophical about it, it was the 'discovery of self', a spiritual journey that awakened some inner sense of oneness with the wider world and perhaps the past.

There was inevitably a destination (perhaps to replace the nomadic search for food and a new home), often a church or holy shrine. The destination often served as a virtuous justification for passage that could be offered up after any suspicious challenge from locals as private lands

were crossed, to convince them that the strangers were not criminals. These walks or tours were carried out over many days or weeks, coinciding with holy days or the anniversaries of saints.

The link between the holy day, travel and a final destination was the precursor to the modern Holi Day. Pilgrims who once gave up the pleasures of the home for simple living on the path to self-discovery were replaced by secular holidaymakers in search of something that was not necessarily wrong, but very different. The Holi Day resort became the popular interval to everyday living – a place where traders and property owners capitalised on the influx of visitors, providing them with a warm bed, fine food and trinkets to remember their stay by. Eventually it became known as the 'package holiday', and Holi Day ceased to be about 'the journey' (the trip is often now seen as burdensome) and was everything to do with the 'arrival' and the Holi Day resort. We had forgotten its raison d'être.

Memory loss is not the defining factor here. A combination of law changes introduced by the invading Normans in 1066, the 16th-century Reformation under Henry VIII and the Enclosure Acts of the 18th and 19th centuries conspired against our right to sleep outdoors. The feudal system the Normans introduced and the new systems of landownership set up a pattern of enclosure; the loss of access. New land laws didn't include former rights of passage over the countryside. 'Roaming' was eventually forbidden under the new vagrancy laws of the early 19th century. These were partly aimed at restricting the medieval 'Pass' laws (similar to modern passports but for internal passage) that granted 'approved travellers' limited permission of free movement throughout the countryside.

The Vagrancy Act 1824 made the pilgrimage even more difficult. Losing the freedom to sleep in a forest or on a trail or mountain was tied up with these changes. The Norman land grab started it all.

Recovering those old rights may not be on everyone's 'A' list of priorities for the coming decades. Many people I speak to tell me they have no particular interest in sleeping out on a beach, in the forest or on a mountain. But there's a good reason why a 'sleeping revolution' represents more than a romantic night out in the wilds. Most of our existing access to the land is defined by more than 146,000km (90,000 miles) of footpaths in England alone. That was the deal previous generations made when they realised the land had been stolen and fenced off: 'Give us access.' But the funding required

to keep those paths open into the next decade is being withdrawn, which is why they are vanishing at an alarming rate. Tens of millions of pounds are being cut from government budgets. And it's happening at the very same time as successive government attempts to sell off more and more public-owned forest and upland.

That's very bad news because more than 90 per cent of the countryside is already in private hands. If public trails continue to be lost as a result of government budget cuts, we'll be left with nothing more than domesticated parks and gardens. Yes, 'the wild' will still exist beyond the boundary wall, but we will be excluded from it.

To keep the gatekeepers out and the outdoors open requires a sleeping revolution. We need to slide under canvas after a long day's trek, canoe or cycle. Then just keep going in the morning. Further, deeper, longer. Enjoying and exploiting our 'natural right' to overnight in the wild pushes back the boundaries, the budget cuts, the sprawling undergrowth and the landowners who know no better with their fences and their ploughs.

The gatekeepers argue that Right to Roam legislation is granting unlimited access to moors, making the paths redundant. It's a lie. This 'unlimited access' only covers 10 per cent of the UK, but it's being introduced to the detriment of the old 'rights of way' network that criss-crosses

UNLIKE MOST of Europe, the UK does not have a tradition of community-owned forests.

the other 90 per cent. Public money is being diverted away from the 90 per cent towards signing, managing and mapping the new Access Lands. This means councils on limited budgets are being forced to renege on their statutory obligations over paths.

I attended a quarterly meeting of the Essex Local Access Forum (ELAF) in 2013. An independent body – made up of ramblers, landowners, bridleway groups and council officials – that advises the County Council on how to make the countryside more accessible via the footpath network. The meeting was devastating. It was effectively a debate about which footpaths should be allowed to grow over. I spoke to the council rights-of-way officer after the session and asked if there was any way to save all the paths. He shook his head and stated that the aim was simply to maintain those that were commonly used each day around towns and villages. The majority, navigating the denser parts of the countryside, would likely be lost.

ROUGHLY 25 PER CENT of EU citizens live in the countryside. More than 90 per cent of people in the UK live in towns and cities – the largest urban density in Europe.

This is from the minutes of that meeting in October, 2013: 'X asked Essex Local Access Forum members if they had noticed deterioration to the network. All agreed deterioration is evident.'

I couldn't bring myself to go to another Local Access Forum meeting. It was too depressing listening to a discussion about managed retreat from paths and the debate over which ones should be left to grow over. There was nothing on how to increase and 'improve' access.

But if the government's priorities are shifting, it's fair to say society is changing,

too. I wonder whether the concept of 'slow passage and sleep' is drowning in a pool of triathlons and speed. We are increasingly obsessed with doing things quickly: fast cars, fast cycle tours, fast hikes across the countryside. Sometimes, it's not so much that we aren't getting into the outdoors. It's just that we want to do everything so quickly. We want to cover more and more ground before getting back, rushing home and crossing the next achievement off the list: the next Munro climbed, the river trail cycled, the path walked end to end in record-quick time. The obsession to cover and cram more and more into our relatively

SNOWDONIA,
OVER LLYN OGWEN

short lives denies us the pleasure of taking things slowly.

There are exceptions; the best I can think of is a canal holiday on a barge, where the pace and peace of the slowly rising lock epitomises a calmer lifestyle. Modern canals are restful places, and the opportunity to enjoy their surreal-like slowness is, I think, intrinsically linked to the ability to sleep. On board a vessel; inside a loosely constrained narrow, moving, floating bedroom. In a sense, it's the nearest thing we have today to a modern pilgrimage. Temporal, moving homes floating towards the old pilgrims' consciousness of virtue, where the shrines and churches are now secular attractions of wonder: the Pontcysyllte Aqueduct, in North Wales: Bingley Five Rise Locks, in West Yorkshire; the numerous waterside pubs and restaurants all along the way, a canal-side view of the Pennines. But we can do better than that. As great as these watery arteries and their towpaths are, there is an even bigger maze of open tunnels that lead down into a rabbit warren of undergrowth; the tens of thousands of miles of creek, footpath, bridleway and greenway – most of which don't see a single cyclist or walker from one year to the next, and are already disappearing. OK, they still show up on the

OS map. But there's no point being able to read a map if you can't trek through brambles and nettles faster than a mile or two a day.

The outback and its trails need to be explored from the source to sea, in the way that the great British explorers of the 17th and 18th century navigated central Africa. It's more important than uncovering a new plant, lizard or lost tribe. It's about keeping the land open for the next traveller. Tramping down the bramble, stamping back the thistle, re-establishing the path with another clod of the boot.

To do that we must become modern-day pilgrims of the outback by carrying a sleeping bag, tent, a map, a compass, food and water on our backs. The hook is the peaceful sleep at the end of the trail that allows us to go further into the wild. I won't lie. It's as much a feature of the mind as geography: penetrating a little deeper into the unknown as dusk approaches. But it's so exciting. The upshot is we are helping to keep the land open. By making a choice to be out there. Choosing not to return home, or diverting off towards the city or town where the B&Bs and guest houses offer warm welcome, fried breakfast and Sky TV. Because by 'choosing' to stay out there, by tramping even further along the path, we are reinforcing our right to the outdoors. Sure, it's good to walk the trail all day. But how much better to sleep on it; getting into our bag at dusk and then rising with skin tingling in nature's dawn, to just keep going the next morning? Climbing over into the thousands of virgin paths within 50 yards of the canal towpaths and national trails. Beyond the mountain track that gets pummelled on sunny, summer weekends is a tangled mass of under- and overgrowth that can be unpicked, unzipped and beaten back. To tramp, camp and sleep over the parts of the outdoors that those Local Access Forums have already given up on.

So what's the plan?

CAIRNGORMS

THE PILGRIM BURGER SOLUTION

WELL, MY PLAN involved researching where I could find peaceful, outdoor sleep while staying within the law. That meant studying our modern-day rights, and then mapping them against the geography of the British Isles with access via water and land trails. I did this for three years between 2012 and 2014. My journey started in the Highlands, at Glencoe, and finished at the River Eden, in Cumbria (a doff of the cap to Wainright, whom I see as the Bruce Lee of walkers; a martial artist who believed that everything was possible and no single path was right or wrong). Sandwiched in between was almost every county in England, Wales, Ireland and Scotland. Call it a pilgrim burger.

As sleeping wild inevitably means walking, cycling or canoeing into the outback (there are no buses, trains or car parks), my search for a bed involved creating a map of where I was legally allowed to sleep. I chose 100 places, each of which linked to at least one trail (a path, river, canal, track, bridleway, or drovers' road), and I refer to these throughout this book. Specifying an exact place to wild camp is daft, a bit like directing someone towards a particular oak tree in a forest. Although it works legally, it sort of negates the beauty, the romance and the freedom of being able to choose somewhere by yourself; with no signs or anyone telling you, 'Here is an official place to camp.' What I've done instead is pinpoint your natural right to find sleep in a given location and then give you the access points into that sleeping/wild camping area.

For instance, the Thames is listed as one of the 100 places where sleep is especially wonderful, and perfectly legal. The river's legal rights for 24-hour fishing, 24-hour canoeing and 24-hour walking – each justifies the need to camp outdoors. Typically, there are places to hang a

LEEDS AND LIVERPOOL CANAL

hammock in the willows or to pitch a tent on a grassy lock, and the river manager – the Canal & River Trust – is mostly sympathetic to requests from walkers/ canoeist/ramblers/cyclists on where to bivvy, or moor for the night in a canoe.

What's important about each of the 100 locations is how their trails divert campers off and away to explore the tens of thousands of miles of 'off piste' paths and waterways that link to the surrounding countryside. These diversions might be half-mile dead-end paths to nowhere. Where they will take you: who knows? Only sleeping out makes that freedom of exploration, movement and the senses truly possible; a journey where you can choose when and where to camp, before continuing the next day at your own pace and direction.

Just before setting off, I decided to research the historic demise of outdoor living in the British Isles. I didn't have to go back very far. One thousand years.

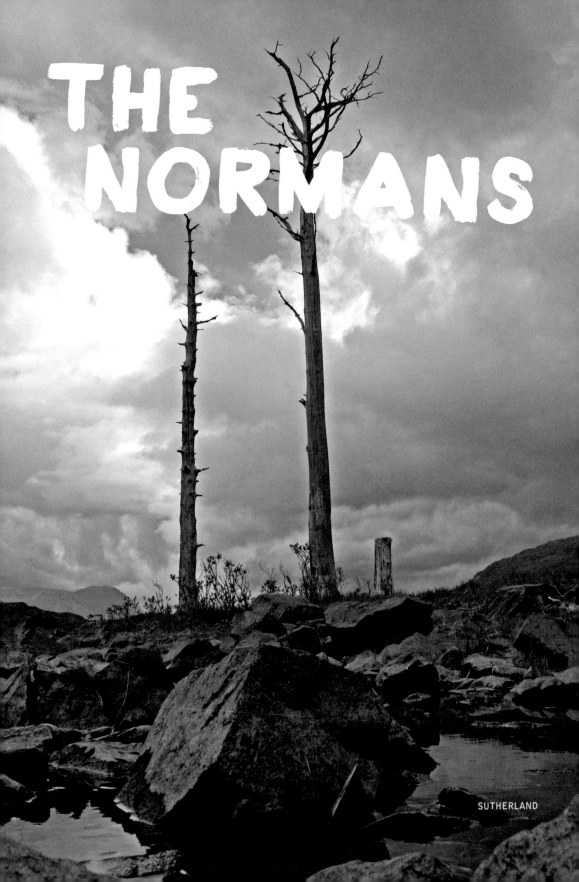

THE NORMANS

SUTHERLAND

THEY CAME, THEY SAW, THEY STAYED.

Sleep is so important it could start a revolution. But it means more than that, because revolutions change nothing. People do.

William the Conqueror invaded England in 1066 and then made himself king. It was like any other invasion or conquest, in any other time or realm. King Harold II was dead. Long live the King. Life goes on. But there was a difference. New laws saw all of the land seized by the Crown – a relatively unique development in the history of conquest. Saxon barons were replaced by the Norman lords and their allies. The Domesday Book – the most definitive land registry document ever devised – was produced on William's orders in 1086 to identify the new owners and their land holding and what they might owe, in tax, favour and loyalty, to the king: the sovereign Landlord.

Landownership had worked broadly in the same way ever since our ancestors abandoned the nomadic life, and took up the shovel and plough about 10,000 BC. What the Normans changed in Britain was the communal right of access over the land. That system of non-communal access is still very much in force today among the modern-day descendents of the Normans. Which is why William's 1086 census – the Domesday Book (and its modern version, the Land Registry) – remains so important. It serves as a legal document that establishes ownership by the legal holder of the title.

My research into where I could roll out a sleeping bag today meant looking at landownership. I discovered that very little had changed since the Norman invasion.

Just 0.6 per cent of the population still owns 50 per cent of the British lands, and most of this elite are the descendants of the 11th-century Norman aristocracy.

A report – 'Who Owns Britain?' – by *Country Life* magazine in 2010 was said to be the most detailed survey of its kind in over 100 years. The research claimed that just 1,200 aristocrats and their families own 20 million of Britain's 60 million acres of land. The top private landowner in Europe was the Duke of Buccleuch and Queensberry, who owned 240,000 acres in England and Scotland. Research by the London School of Economics in 2013 claimed that the Normans who conquered England – with surnames Baskerville, Darcy, Mandeville and Montgomery – still dominate the student rolls for Oxford and Cambridge universities, still make up a large proportion of the elite that holds the prime positions in professions such as medicine, law and politics. They also control a good number of the political agencies, public bodies and charitable organisations that oversee rules regulating land management and access.

But 1066 was about more than Saxon lords losing their holdings. It was how it affected the peasants that mattered most. The common rights over common lands like Sherwood Forest and the Kentish Weald were gone. Those rights included the right to roam over woodlands, marshes, moors and coasts of many common areas; to graze animals, collect wood for fuel, tools and buildings, to eat fruits, to collect water from rivers and streams, to catch fish and generally to do all the things that made it possible to live off the land.

FOREST LAW

BUT THE NORMANS didn't just take the land. They created brutal laws to protect their estates. Old communal and tenanted strips of farmland became 'forest estates'. The French word for 'forest' (*forêt*) does not mean trees; it means 'outside of law', an occupied status where the indigenous population had no rights. Countryside areas were cleared of people, who were replaced with game animals that the Norman royalty wanted to hunt. The countryside became a 'game reserve' for the pleasure of the new elite. Almost all of Essex was defined as 'royal forests'. But the 'reserves' were less about safeguarding the wildlife, and more about protecting the holdings of the new landowning classes who wanted to keep many of the indigenous serfs and peasants off their land.

Forest law resulted in people being criminalised for camping, trespass, catching fish or deer to feed their families. 'Offenders' were often executed. About a third of England was under this control, mainly in the south and in East Anglia. Essex and the surrounding counties became renowned for revolts against the forest laws. The stories of Robin Hood are partly based on tales of those who lost their lands and took up with rebels, forced to live illegally in the 'forest' areas.

The brutality of 'forest law' didn't last for ever. Like all great pendulums in life, it swung too far. The oppressive 'royal' controls over land became so harsh they eventually began to impact on the new landowning barons who needed trade in order to sustain their estates. Crown control of tidal waters, for instance, was considered by the barons to be an infringement of their natural rights to engage in commerce.

Peasant discontent, combined with opposition by the landowning hierarchy towards the royal house, resulted in the drafting of the Magna Carta in 1215.

RIVER SOAR

The document was presented to and then signed by King John somewhere near the banks of the River Thames, and was an attempt to re-establish some of the traditional rights over the land (although it never went far enough). The feudal barons hoped to force the king to award them a right to control land, businesses and trade. It had very little to do with popular justice, but it did highlight important crimes against the people. Clauses of the Magna Carta still on statute, 47 and 48, directly refer to abolishing most of 'evil' forest law.

The new charter reintroduced rights that existed pre-1066, such as tidal navigation, the right to fish on tidal waters and access over land and even 'forest'. But it failed to get the non-tidal rights returned, which is why there are still no public rights to fish

THE UK has no natural forest left.

or navigate on non-tidal freshwater rivers in England and Wales (there are in Scotland).

Magna Carta was, in many ways, a failure for the things it left out. But for our purposes today, Magna Carta is more important for what it allowed than what it didn't; because Magna Carta granted rights in the hills, mountains and the foreshore that pertained to 24-hour access, day AND night. That meant sleeping in the wild becomes at times a necessity, if not a right per se. Despite the oppressive vagrancy laws of the 18th century, we're no longer classed as criminals for sleeping in the forests that our peasant forefathers were forced to leave. Magna Carta had a lot to do with that because it undermined some of the old forest laws. Trespassers can no longer be prosecuted. But understanding what constitutes a trespass – and what it means as a civilian offence – requires studying the new rule guide. Because although we can now sleep in our own bed, and many

of us 'own' our own strip of land or garden we believe is ours (until we get served a compulsory purchase order in the name of the Crown), we are still too restricted to staying exclusively on the footpath when we go outdoors. Almost 1,000 years after William the Conqueror we still have no legal entitlement to sleep in the forest or on the mountain beyond the path or tidal river.

There's an old cliché about knowing stuff: follow the money. It's a lot easier than that. Follow the law: the law of the land, an old history lecturer once said. His advice about life's puzzles was that they are bound up in law.

'Never stop asking, "why?",' he said. 'And when you want answers, go to the law. It's how our rulers justify doing whatever they want.'

I bought a copy of the *Gentle Art of Tramping*, by Stephen Graham, written in 1927, and read it in virtually one sitting. Then I reached for the law books.

THE LAW

Notice

These ponds are
dangerous
keep off

Notice

Trespassers
will be
prosecuted

MY HISTORY LECTURER was fascinated by North America.

'Do you know why America is the most powerful country in the world?' he'd ask us.

'Military power?' we'd reply.

'Nope.'

'Wealth?'

'No.'

'Resources?'

'Nope. It's the lawyers,' he'd say. 'American power is based on law. America has the best lawyers in the world. So they win, even when they're wrong. With legal knowledge they can do almost anything, however morally obscene or unreasonable the outcome might seem.'

He ordered us to study media law, to know it, to learn it, to understand it and to keep updated on it. Because he said if we learned it, we could do anything, too. Not the bad stuff like Guantanamo Bay and Drone strikes in Pakistan. But the good stuff. He wanted us to expose the fallacies in society, the misunderstandings, the injustices; by legally navigating around the laws of contempt, libel, official secrets and common law.

He could have included the laws around land use and communal rights. One of the misunderstandings in law is that wild camping (or sleeping outdoors) is illegal.

The confusion is where people get lost in between something that is a 'right' enshrined in law – to walk safely in the street – and something that isn't – like laying a bath towel on the beach, or swimming in the sea, or parking a car in the street. They are as different as giving a present to someone you love on Christmas Day or a birthday, or a surprise gift on any random day. One is akin to law, the other isn't. But none are illegal.

And just because something is not enshrined in law as a 'right' doesn't make it legally wrong either.

Legal rights are codes that have grown up out of concessions, often granted by the ruling elite to their rich friends throughout our history. Sometimes large numbers of people protesting and making a fuss can effect change. Protesters from all walks of life have fought for individual and collective rights: some they won, others they lost. We have a right to catch fish in the sea, but not to swim in it. We have a right to pick fruit and eat it from a private tree, but no right to sleep under the tree.

Every square metre of our British Isles is owned and managed by either an individual, a family or a collective of people representing a charity, trust, group or company. The rules these owners and managers must observe regarding sleeping rights over their lands fall into four categories:

1) Wild camping enshrined as a legal right, and no permission required from owner or manager (eg Scotland, Dartmoor etc).
2) Wild camping allowed under a presumption of historic use, but not as a 'right' (eg hillwalking in upland areas of Wales and northern England, bothies, fishing on canals or 50 per cent of foreshore owned by the Crown; vessels that become marooned on Crown-owned foreshore by the tide as part of a tidal navigation; on board or next to moored vessels/canoes on the network owned and managed by the Canal & River Trust).
3) Considered on a case-by-case basis, but only on request from the individual (the majority of landowners outside of 1 and 2), sometimes with a presumption against permission, sometimes not.
4) Byelaws or policies introduced that make wild camping an offence because of the

potential threat to the environment (much of the Forestry Commission land, some highly vulnerable and sensitive areas owned by English Heritage, the National Trust or other private landlords and owners).

There are many places in Britain where we don't have to ask permission; there are many places where asking permission is polite. But in most cases where asking permission is polite, it is unpractical – usually because finding the owner at dusk is unrealistic. In a tiny proportion of cases, wild camping is out of the question without written permission, because byelaws (usually indicated by signs) have defined specific actions as constituting a criminal offence.

There are several differences between criminal and civil law. Trespass is civil law and is not a crime. No one can be prosecuted for trespass. A crime is an offence against the state: murder, robbery, theft, assault.

Breaking a civil law is an offence that only an individual can bring to court for damages. A civil wrong is known as a 'tort'. There is no civil or criminal wrong aligned with sleeping. But the act of wild camping and being inside a structure such as a tent can be defined as 'trespass' if the landowner has not granted permission.

Although the act of trespass is actionable in the courts, the landowner will only be granted nominal damages of a few pounds if there is no loss or damage. The question, really, is whether it is worth it if someone is moving on soon.

The most obvious way to avoid court action is not to damage anything and to move on if asked. Don't break trees, don't cause criminal damage and don't light fires unless you have permission to do so.

In my experience, over more than 30 years, most landowners are reasonable when it comes to travellers sleeping out on their land while passing through. There are times when an owner will insist the camper moves on. Negotiating a small fee is an option, but a refusal to leave after that, or an angry outburst, means the civil 'trespass' can become more serious. Acting in a threatening or abusive manner is criminal. There's no excuse to remain on private land to sleep once asked to leave, unless in an emergency. Common sense should always prevail, although a landowner can use 'reasonable force' if his or her request to leave is ignored.

I've wild camped since I was 17, and have only been asked to move on a few times. Once I pitched up my bivvy too early, at 4pm, on a sunny day, and decided to boil a brew. A few hours later I was off the owner's land, and pitched in a hammock between two trees. Happy, safe and legal. You will almost never have to explain yourself. Although signs that say 'Trespassers will be prosecuted' are rare and inaccurate, they're a good indicator that this is not a good place to sleep.

THE WEST HYLAND WAY, NEAR GLENCOE

THE SPIRIT OF THE LAW

EVERYBODY HAS a God-given right to sleep, whether they have cash in their pocket or not. It's better to have rights enshrined in law, like Scotland. But we have to work with what we've got; and it's not at all bad. When debating the rights and wrongs of wild camping, and what the law of trespass means in relation to sleeping, common sense is a good rule to follow.

Laws are not drafted for the sake of being followed. They are designed, crafted and written to serve a specific purpose. This is sometimes referred to as the 'spirit of the law', and is more important than a literal or fragmented interpretation of wording. An 11-year-old cycling on a pavement is committing a criminal offence under Section 72 of the Highways Act 1835 as amended by Section 85 (1) of the Local Government Act 1888. But, if not risking danger to pedestrians, there is, for common sense reasons, almost zero risk of any action by police. On the other hand, a mountain biker has a 'legal right' to cycle on a bridleway in a park. But if a child runs out in front of the bike, while chasing a squirrel, and is struck and injured, it may be that the cyclist is liable for a criminal prosecution because he has allegedly – in pursuing a hobby enshrined in law as a right – failed to have regard for the safety of others due to his speed and the time of day when others

were in the park. The child cycling on the pavement was facing less risk of prosecution because he was not undermining the spirit of the law: pedestrian safety.

Civil laws intended to protect the rights of landowners, tenants and other legitimate land users are not there to stop a person in transit from sleeping while causing no damage or harm. The knowledgeable wild camper is unlikely to break the spirit of the law.

THE VAGRANCY ACT

'WILD CAMPING' or sleeping outdoors has been a feature of travel over private land for thousands of years in Britain, and was decriminalised in 1935.

The Vagrancy Act 1935 allowed sleeping outdoors and wild camping (subject to other criminal laws – eg criminal damage by making a fire or cutting down trees – not being broken in the process).

Originally, Section 4 of the earlier 1824 Vagrancy Act stated that 'every person wandering abroad and lodging in any barn or outhouse, or in any deserted or unoccupied building, or in the open air, or under a tent, or in any cart or waggon, not having any visible means of subsistence, and not giving a good account of himself or herself' was classified as a person committing an offence to be deemed a rogue and vagabond. The punishment was three months' hard labour.

But a crucial amendment made in the Vagrancy Act 1935, Section 1(4), now reads: 'The reference in the said enactment to a person lodging under a tent or in a cart or waggon shall not be deemed to include a person lodging under a tent or in a cart or waggon with or in which he travels.'

It's an important change that effectively legalises 'the traveller'. The Vagrancy Act is still very much in force today when it comes to rough sleepers and homeless individuals – who are non-travellers – with many hundreds of 'offenders' prosecuted each year in magistrates' courts, particularly in London. But as long as you are en route, you are within the law.

CAT BELLS, CUMBRIA,
LOOKING OVER
DERWENTWATER

SQUATTERS' RIGHTS

SQUATTERS' RIGHTS can be used to prevent a landowner from insisting an individual leaves an area. However, the existing traditions, codes, laws, and good practice between landowners and travellers almost certainly negate the justification for ever using these rights.

Section 6 of the Criminal Law Act 1977 protects squatters defined as the 'occupiers' of properties, but possibly undermines everything that a wild camper is intent on doing: sleeping in transit while travelling between two locations. More importantly, it reinforces the case of the landowner who fears that allowing a traveller to sleep might facilitate a claim over his land.

I enjoyed a game of golf several years ago with 11 friends at an old course called St George's Hill, at Weybridge, in Surrey. It wasn't cheap at £80 for two rounds. Before we arrived, I looked at an OS map to see where the footpaths and rights of way existed. There were none.

St George's was the scene of a famous trespass and peasant revolt in April 1649. Back then the hill was common ground, under the control of freeholders. The peasants were known as The Diggers and they claimed that, since 1066, commoners had been denied access and use of their land by the Norman invaders. The Diggers camped and began growing vegetables on St George's Hill in the hope that others would occupy similar common areas in the name of 'the people'.

The protesters were evicted by the courts and the landowners a few months later. The action has some significance today among modern-day campaigners for land reform. But perhaps more importantly, St George's became the UK's first gated community. The cheapest of the 400 houses was valued at £4,000,000 in 2014. It is officially the most exclusive private residence in Britain. The private golf course, tucked away within the 3.9sq km wooded estate, can be played by visitors paying a green fee. Just for one day, we were members. But we couldn't plant anything in the ground other than our size 10 spiked shoes. All visitors must leave the grounds by the time the bar closes. Unless you have a good lawyer, or a copy of this statement (based on Section 6 of the Criminal Law Act 1977, as amended by the Criminal Justice and Public Order Act 1994, which applies to non-residential buildings):

TAKE NOTICE

THAT we live here and intend to stay.

THAT one person will always remain in this property.

THAT a summons for possession in the County Court or in the High Court, or the production of a written statement or certificate relating to S.12A Criminal Law Act 1977 (as inserted by Criminal Justice and Public Order Act, 1994) is required if you want to get us out.

THAT knowingly making a false statement to obtain a written statement for the purposes of S.12A is an offence under S.12A (8) Criminal Law Act 1977.

THAT we are opposed to any entry without the permission of one of us who is in physical possession.

THAT we will prosecute you for any attempt to enter by violence or by threatening violence.

THE OCCUPIERS

PUBLIC LAND

SNOWDONIA

THE WOODLAND OFFICER from my district council in Essex was a kind person. She was running bushcraft courses in the park for teenagers. The newspaper advert read, 'Come and learn bushcraft. Discover how to build dens, carve wood and start fires.'

I rang the number printed on the page, excited at the thought that the advert might be for real, but suspicious too that it was a fraud. It was neither:

ME: I'd like to sign my daughter up for the bushcraft course.
COUNCIL: OK, sir. What's her name?
ME: What will she be learning?
COUNCIL: How to make and light a fire. How to build a shelter. How to carve wood.
ME: That's great. Will she be allowed to make a fire in the woodland once she's learned how to do it properly and safely?
COUNCIL: No. We have byelaws in place preventing it.
ME: Oh. OK. Will she be able to make a shelter and sleep in the wood at night?
COUNCIL: No, we have byelaws in place preventing sleeping out in the woods.
ME: Will she be allowed to remove fallen logs from the wood to carve, though?
COUNCIL: No, that's not allowed either.
ME: Are there any woods in the borough where bushcraft skills are legal?
COUNCIL: No.
ME: Why are you teaching them then?
COUNCIL: Because your daughter might enjoy the course and then want to find somewhere where she can go and practise her new skills, outside of the borough?
ME: Do you know the name of any districts or boroughs that approve of bushcraft in public woodland?
COUNCIL: No.
ME: Did you know that the Forestry Commission in England does not allow fires in its woodland?
COUNCIL: Yes.

ME: So where can she go when she's learned her skills?
COUNCIL: I don't know. Perhaps do it at school?

The warden was trying to do her job. But she struggled with the context. Although she had a passion for the skills she taught, she couldn't reconcile her romantic view of an ancient past with her perceived reality of what the UK had become. A tiny group of islands with too many people all wanting to start fires and hang from trees in urban woodland. Ironically, it's a fear based on a fact that she didn't know: too much land, in too few hands.

There are broadly three types of terrain that are typically owned by the state in countries around the world: forests, national parks and foreshore. In Britain and Ireland, most of all three are owned by private individuals and estates: the elite.

More than 65 per cent of UK forests and woodland – which account for less than 10 per cent of the landmass – is in private hands. Public access to the majority of these forests is blocked.

About 50 per cent of the foreshore and tidal rivers is in private hands.

More than 90 per cent of national parks is in private ownership.

When it comes to dealing with government departments and officials, they are mostly passionate about encouraging people into the wild. They're rarely opposed to a lone walker sleeping out in the forest, as long as he or she leaves no damage and causes no one any offence. But there is sometimes a nervousness about how best to say that. What follows is a sample of what they say for the record, and what perhaps they may mean in practice.

MORE PEOPLE in Britain visit a forest than the seaside.

SANGO BAY,
DURNESS

THE LEGAL DEFINITION of the foreshore is the land that is left exposed to the air between high tide and low tide. Owners of the foreshore include the Duchies of Cornwall and Lancaster, local authorities, the RSPB, the National Trust, the MoD and private estates and individuals.

THE CROWN ESTATE

THE CROWN ESTATE is one of the largest landowners in the British Isles, and is – according to its officials – governed by the British parliament. The land it controls amounts to 144,000ha (356,000 acres) of farm, forest and roughly half the UK foreshore. Much of the Crown foreshore is leased on to local authorities and government agencies such as Natural England.

I first spoke to the Crown management team in 2012 to ask about wild camping and making fires. I was told verbally that although there was no 'right' to make fires or to sleep, and although the Crown retained the right to prevent certain activities, its officials would not necessarily do so. I emailed the same questions:

21 December 2012

I spoke to you this afternoon about fishing from the foreshore. You explained that subject to access across private land and/or byelaws, this was allowed.

As I usually prefer to fish at night, I also asked you about setting up a bivvy on Crown-owned foreshore. You explained that in certain areas this may be prohibited by council byelaws, but that if it was not, and if the area is not protected under Acts of Parliament or other legislation regarding protected status etc, the Crown Estate had no problem with the setting up of a bivvy within the context that I wish to use it (protection from the rain or perhaps to sleep and rest for a few hours if waiting for the tide to come in).

One last question. Can I make a small fire enclosed in stones on something protective to avoid danger? Subject to the issues you've already raised, I've been told by other fishermen that I can do this below the high-tide mark. Just wanted to check.

I received this response:

Dear Steve

My comments relate to the situation in England as it is different in Scotland and there may also be regional differences in Wales and Northern Ireland. There are, however, only two public rights over the foreshore in England and they are fishing and navigation.

It is also important to note that the Crown Estate does not own all the foreshore around the UK and much is owned by local authorities, other public bodies such as the MOD, nature conservation groups, and there are areas in the ownership of private individuals.

There is no right of public access over the foreshore in England, although the Crown Estate has a general permissive consent for access along foreshore that it owns and which is not subject to other restrictions, for example where there may be environmental designations or where it is leased and our tenant restricts access.

The MOD may do this, for example, if the foreshore is, or is next to, a firing range.

In terms of a fire, the land that the fire is being lit on will always have an owner who will be able to restrict the activities that take place on the foreshore.

I would imagine again that it would be of more interest and concern to the local authority in question.

A small fire close to the tideline is obviously likely to be of less concern than a large bonfire, but again there is no right to do so, so you may find yourself being asked to extinguish it, but a call to the local authority or council is likely to be a good starting point.

Most of the Crown Estate's foreshore is also leased to the relevant local authority allowing them to regulate activities as they see fit.

Hope this helps.

XXXXXXX
Xxxxxxx Manager

FORESTRY COMMISSION

TREES ACCOUNT FOR 1,215,000ha (3,000,000 acres) of the UK and Ireland, 10 per cent of the land, of which only about one-third is open to the public. Public forests are mostly managed by the Forestry Commission, Britain's biggest landowner.

Forestry Commission byelaws state: 'No person shall in or on the lands of the Commissioners... set up or place any caravan, tent, booth, stall or erection of any kind, including equestrian equipment.'

The reality is much more agreeable.

Seventy per cent of the Commission's land is in Scotland, where wild camping is enshrined as a 'legal right'.

The Commission website for Scotland states: 'Camping wild in the forest can be fun if you're hardy.'

In England and Wales, there is no mention in the byelaws of sleeping bags, bivvies or hammocks, none of which are traditionally classed as a structure (although lighting fires and stoves is restricted). The Commission allows wild

FORESTS AND WOODLANDS cover 45 per cent of Europe's land area. During the 1920s, woodland and forest cover in Britain was reduced to around 5 per cent and 1 per cent in Northern Ireland.

camping at a number of sites outside of Scotland, including along the River Wye at Biblins Youth Campsite, Whitchurch, Ross-on-Wye. Bushcraft courses can also be booked with wardens on this site (although there's a fee).

Wild camping, bushcraft, shelter-building and open-fire cooking events have been held by the Commission at Haldon Forest Park in Devon, Rendlesham Forest in Surrey, Hamsterley Forest in County Durham and many more.

Courses in bushcraft and shelter- and den-building are also organised for children and young people, and there is no formal ban on sleeping. The Commission's website states:

Woods are full of natural materials such as fallen branches, leaves and bracken and so are just great places to build dens.

Most children don't need guidance on how to build a den – they just do it. But we have produced a simple guide on what to do to make sure that dens are safe.

We make it clear that as long as they make their parents or guardians aware of what they are doing and where, and they follow the lessons learned, there is very little risk in den-building.

We are not actively encouraging sleeping out at night, although young people often do... Environmental risks are very low, with cold and wet weather being the biggest issue. The risk from strangers in a woodland is very low indeed.

The full report is here: http://www.forestry.gov.uk/forestry/ INFD-6PNDYF

CANAL & RIVER TRUST

IT'S A LONG ROAD, London to Greece. As backpackers, we would travel aboard the Magic Bus, bags on our shoulders, Victoria to Athens. £25 one way; almost 2,000 miles of road. That overland route fascinated me.

The Canal & River Trust does better than that. More than 3,220km (2,000 miles) of waterway and paths. The charity was set up as a navigation authority by the UK government to manage the canals and rivers of England and Wales. Most of the network is in public ownership.

People camp on these canals while fishing, canoeing and kayaking or as part of a long-distance hike or cycle. The Trust is progressive and actively encourages night-time fishing and bivvying outside

of the closed season (15 March–15 June inclusive), which protects the fish during the main breeding season.

An annual ticket for fishing, known as the Waterway Wanderers scheme, costs a few pounds and gives 24-hour access to 480km (300 miles) of waterway. Anglers are able to sleep at night in bivvies and even cook up drinks and meals, as long as they don't obstruct the towpath access for other users, including vessels. The list of all locations in England and Wales covered by the fishing pass is found here: http://canalrivertrust.org.uk/media/ library/1509.pdf.

Many of these locations are on the edges of towns, but they include areas of great beauty and seclusion, especially on

THE FORESTRY COMMISSION offers volunteer opportunities. You can't assume that providing free labour guarantees a right to sleep or camp in the forest at night, but what goes around generally comes around.

GALLOWAY FOREST

MARKET BOSWORTH,
LEICESTERSHIRE

the Ashby Canal, the Caldon Canal, the Coventry Canal, Hertford Union Canal, the Lancaster Canal, the Leeds and Liverpool Canal, Llangollen Canal, Monmouthshire and Brecon Canal, Montgomery Canal, Oxford Canal, Peak Forest Canal, Shropshire Union Canal, Stourbridge Canal, Tame Valley Canal, Trent and Mersey Canal, Waterworks River and Wyrley and Essington Canal.

Under general fishing guidelines, the Trust states that lighting fires is forbidden, but offers advice on where to bivvy:

Do not use a bivvy on the towpath unless there is sufficient space for other towpath users to be able to pass safely.

A recent article on the Trust website – featuring Carl Nicholls, Fisheries and Angling Manager for the Canal & River Trust – promoted night fishing and stated:

Many anglers use a bivvy bag (man-sized waterproof sack) and do nap throughout the night safe in the knowledge that if a nice chunky fish does bite, their alarm will startle them out of sleep.

Elton Murphy of the website anglersnet. co.uk is quoted in the same article:

Night fishing combines two of a boy's favourite things – fishing and camping! At times, the camping is just as important as the fishing.

Carl Nicholls is then quoted again:

Although angling can be a solitary hobby, it can be very social and many anglers who fish at night do so in pairs or small groups.

Sometimes it's just about getting together with your mates, enjoying the outdoor environment and eating and drinking in the fresh air. If they catch a fish, then it's a bonus.

There's a great feeling watching the sunset and then watching it rise again the next morning. Along with this you get to see the changing seasons and see many forms of wildlife that most people rarely if ever see. Generally anglers are quiet in their pursuit of the big fish and this also enhances the opportunities of the animals and wildlife they see.

BRITISH CANOE UNION

THE BRITISH CANOE UNION is a partner organisation of the Canal & River Trust, the Environment Agency and the British Olympic Association. It is the umbrella organisation for Canoe England, Canoe Wales, Canoe Association of Northern Ireland and the Scottish Canoeing Association.

A British Canoe Union annual membership grants a licence to the kayaker/canoeist to navigate almost the entire canal network for a few pounds.

I make a point of contacting lock officials to explain that I intend to moor at night as part of an overnight expedition. For £5 a key is provided for access to toilets, showers and even power points along the way. The community of boaters and barges is helpful and supportive of fellow travellers and I've spent many a night aboard a larger vessel enjoying stories, banter and beer.

The Canal & River Trust also promotes kayak fishing and training courses on its waters, all of which can be done day and night when a boat is moored to the bank, with the permission of the relevant fishery.

Wild camping is an important part of canoeing and kayaking. Training and qualifications in leadership often include the ability to camp from a canoe or kayak.

Canoe Wales, for example, includes this in its Memorandum of Association:

> *To encourage and help all, especially young people ... to acquire a greater knowledge, enjoyment and care of the countryside through the use of canoes and kayaks in competitive and recreational activities, especially when carried on in the open air, and including the practice of camping and kindred activities in connection with canoeing.*

Canoe England offers advice on its website for kayakers who want to wild camp around the coast. This sample – http://www.canoe-england.org.uk/waterways-and-environment/environmental-good-practise-/estuaries-i-marshes-i-land-masses/ – on building fires, dovetails with the advice I was given by the Crown Estate (see p 41):

> *Sea kayakers on multi-day trips will quite often have a fire on a beach*

OLDANY ISLAND

OLDANY ISLAND

as part of their overnight camping experience. Following a few simple guidelines should ensure that you don't cause any damage.

Check first to see if the local laws/byelaws allow fires. Fires below the high water mark are washed away by the next high tide, so this can be a good way of ensuring that your fire is cleared away and properly put out.

Before starting to build a fire assess the fire risk. Consider the wind direction and strength and think about the proximity of any dry forest or vegetation. If in doubt, don't have a fire.

Be careful on boulder beaches that there aren't any birds, such as storm petrels, nesting under the boulders.

If you have a fire above the high water mark then use established fire rings or mound fires on sand or soil piled up to provide a protective base for your fire.

Make sure your fire is well burnt out and that there is no risk of it spreading before you go to your tents and check there is no trace whatsoever of your fire before leaving in the morning.

The latter advice is as relevant to walkers as it is to kayakers.

NATIONAL PARKS AUTHORITY

THERE ARE 20 'national parks' in the UK and the Republic of Ireland. Ten in England, three in Wales, two in Scotland, none in Northern Ireland, and six small parks in the Republic of Ireland. They are almost entirely privately owned. The National Park Authority website states: 'Not ours – but ours to look after.' Read into that what you like.

The land covers almost 9 per cent of England, 20 per cent in Wales, 8 per cent in Scotland, and 1 per cent in the Republic of Ireland.

The English and Welsh parks are the Peak District, Lake District, Snowdonia, Dartmoor, Pembrokeshire Coast, North York Moors, Yorkshire Dales, Exmoor, Northumberland, Brecon Beacons, The Broads, New Forest and South Downs.

Scotland has Loch Lomond and The Trossachs National Park and the Cairngorms National Park.

The Republic of Ireland has Ballycroy in County Mayo, Connemara in County Galway, Glenveagh in County Donegal, Killarney in County Kerry, The Burren in County Clare and Wicklow Mountains, County Wicklow.

Virtually all the uncultivated areas of the parks have walking access (in England and Wales under the Countryside and Rights of Way [CRoW] Act 2000).

Each park has its own authority, which employs rangers and wardens. So while there's a tacit approval from the umbrella authorities in favour of wild camping, this changes from park to park and sometimes even from ranger to ranger.

The National Parks Authority website has a section on wild camping, which advises campers to ask landowners' permission, and also offers basic tips:

• Care for the countryside by leaving no trace of your visit behind you.
• If you pitch late and leave early, you'll cause less disturbance to wildlife and other people.
• If there are no toilets, use a trowel to bury human waste at least 30 meters away from running water or lakes.
• Move your tent after two nights to avoid damaging the vegetation underneath it.
• Keep to small groups of just one or two tents to keep noise and disturbance levels down.
• Try not to camp immediately beside a lake or river to avoid disturbing birds and animals.

The Authority also names 'parks' that allow wild camping and those where there are risks associated with campfires:

Some National Parks welcome wild camping, as long as you act responsibly and leave no trace of your visit behind you.

The Broads Authority provides free 24-hour moorings across the entire water network. Because demand for moorings can get high during summer, the Authority aims to provide more 'wild' moorings.

For those lucky enough to live within close range of any national park, the volunteering opportunities are endless and provide excellent access and camping opportunities.

NATIONAL TRUST

THE NATIONAL TRUST should probably be in the private section, but I decided to put it here as it operates under an Act of Parliament, which makes it close to a public landowner.

The National Trust describes itself as a conservation organisation. It owns almost 2,550sq km (1,000sq miles) of parks, moor, mountain, countryside and coast in England, Wales and Northern Ireland. The Trust controls almost 25 per cent of the Lake District and 12 per cent of the Peak District National Park as well as about 20 per cent (1,126km or 704 miles) of the coast.

The National Trust for Scotland is a conservation charity set up in 1931. It is the largest member organisation in Scotland and controls 808 sq km (312 sq miles) of Munros, coast, countryside and 400 islands and islets.

The National Trust promotes and actively facilitates wild camping at some of its sites. There are exceptions, particularly in areas like the Peak District where fire risk is considered a danger.

Although the Trust is able to introduce 'reasonable' restrictions around boating, bathing and fishing, The National Trust Acts 1907–1971 specifically prevent the Trust from 'mak[ing] any charge in respect of navigation in tidal waters'. This restriction on charges and fees clarifies the rights of navigation. It also restricts the Trust's occasional attempts to prevent the legal use of its foreshore, even when the area is considered an extremely sensitive or precious place for wildlife and plants. The courts are only likely to grant restrictions to access where public use is excessive rather than the occasional fisherman, bait digger or canoeist.

37 (7) states:

Nothing in this (byelaws) section shall be taken to empower the National Trust to make any byelaw prohibiting, restricting or interfering with rights of navigation in any tidal waters or in any waterway which is not tidal water.

Anglers and bait diggers have won court cases where the Trust has attempted to remove rights to fish and collect bait from the foreshore, where these rights were allegedly considered a potential risk to wildlife. The cases demonstrate how public rights are enshrined in law and sometimes cannot be removed, even where there may be a good reason.

An important part of the Trust's landholding for members is its 657 car parks. They might not make for good overnight places to leave a car, but they're a great place to be picked up or dropped off for a few nights out in the hills. These car parks are, in my experience, one of the greatest assets in the National Trust's portfolio. The National Trust does not publish its entire list of car parks, and when I emailed for the list as a Trust member my email received no reply. I phoned the Trust to follow it up and was told that no such list existed, but that one was planned and that other members had requested it, too.

The National Trust's wild camping policy is relatively clear and, contrary to what most might think, more in favour of wild camping than opposed.

The policy should not be confused with what happens on the ground when confronted by a Trust warden. Wardens have the power to deal with any given situation as they see fit, so it's wise to be discreet sometimes, to avoid being asked to leave.

The Trust pursues three potentially conflicting objectives, which require some subtle balancing:

1) Safeguarding areas of natural beauty and heritage.
2) Facilitating the 'wilderness experience'.
3) The need to generate a vast amount of revenue to meet objective 1.

Wild camping does not necessarily meet objective 3, although I would argue that if, like me, you are a paying member, you're a long way towards meeting all three.

This is what it says on the Trust's website about 'Recreational Activities at National Trust Properties: Guiding Principles and Good Practice':

> There is a presumption against camping on non-recognised sites without permission. This presumption is waived in certain circumstances and areas, eg in the Lake District in upland areas above 450m (1,450ft) out of sight of the public highway, to allow the wilderness experience to be enjoyed.

There's a lot to pick over there. The first sentence is left purposely vague. Notice it doesn't say 'no camping'. The dictionary says of presumption 'an idea that is true on the basis of probability'.

This can really only be interpreted to mean 'we probably won't allow wild camping without permission'. So the statement leaves room for the camper to sleep 'without permission' on the understanding that you'll 'probably' be moved, but only if discovered. It is a long way from the Trust stating, 'Wild camping is always OK.' But it doesn't say either, 'Wild campers will be subject to legal action in the civil courts.'

This is supported by statements like this one released by the Trust and occasionally posted on its website:

> The Trust does not generally allow camping on non-recognised sites without permission.

> 'Wild camping', where permitted (for example in the Lake District, in upland areas above 450m = 1,450ft), should be out of sight of the public highway, entail only one-night stopovers with a maximum of two campers, and leave no trace of their presence.

Just to reiterate its support for enjoyment of the wild experience, the Trust explains that this 'probable' removal only applies sometimes, as the 'presumption against' is waived in certain circumstances, eg: in 'upland areas above 450m away from the highway'.

Just like the Forestry Commission, the Trust hosts wild camping days for families, and encourages kids to try it for themselves. In its heavily promoted list of '50 things to do before you're 11¾', number 3 is 'Camp out in the wild':

> The whole point of wild camping is that there's no-one else around so we're not going to recommend a spot. Just follow the wild camping rules – pitch late, leave early, leave no trace that you were ever there (and don't wee within 50 metres of a stream!).

Now I'm very much assuming that the Trust isn't advocating an 11-year-old go wild camping alone. This again may be a tacit acceptance that wild camping is an acceptable pursuit, as long as you accept that you may be asked to leave.

In fact, the National Trust does quite like 'wild camping'. So much so that it promotes and runs 'wild events' across its various woodland estates. You can have fires. And cook. And tie hammocks to trees and everything. The only hook is that you have to do it when Trust wardens are around. And there's a fee.

Trust wardens have a lot of information and are keen to pass on their knowledge about wild camping, foraging etc. Although much of this is done as part of paid advice days, wardens post advice on Trust blog sites. For example, this information from a warden refers to foraging for food in the wild on private land:

If you are on private land for whatever reason, without explicit or implicit permission from the owner, then you are trespassing. This is not a crime, but a civil wrong, so you cannot be prosecuted. You can be sued though.

Where implicit permission is given – eg National Trust land – you are ok.

The fundamental law governing foraging is the common law right to collect the 'four Fs – fruit, flowers, fungi and foliage'.

No one is going to get territorial over blackberries or nettles, but if someone is picking a plant that is noted in the designation of an SSSI then yes, a polite word may be needed. Throughout, common sense is important, both for the forager and for the warden.

National Trust areas are highlighted on OS maps in purple (with an oak leaf in England or castle in Scotland). Forestry Commission areas are highlighted on OS maps with a tree sign with a purple border.

The Trust employs tens of thousands of volunteers. Courses in wild camping and bushcraft skills are in such high demand that the Trust actually charges some of its volunteers to work with wardens for a few days' conservation work, before enjoying a hike and camp.

AN TAISCE

AN TAISCE, the National Trust for Ireland, supports Leave No Trace Ireland, and the principles of sustainable, wild camping promoted by the group. Leave No Trace Ireland is an educational programme based in Westport, County Mayo. It is a network of organisations and individuals that promote the responsible use of the outdoors. Its members and funders include councils, companies and the Department of Community, Rural and Gaeltacht Affairs.

Seven principles are listed as helping reduce damage caused to the environment. These principles include responsible wild camping on durable ground.

Advice under Section 4 of the code states:

In more remote areas:
Disperse use to prevent the creation of new tracks and campsites.
Avoid places where impacts are just beginning to show.
If camping:
Protect water quality by camping at least 30m from lakes and streams.
Keep campsites small and discreet.
Aim to leave your campsite as you found it, or better.

The advice and code is supported by the The National Trails Office, Department of Community, Rural and Gaeltacht Affairs, Outdoor Recreation NI, CaminoWays.com, Catholic Guides of Ireland, Cliffs of Moher

Ltd, Countrywide Hotels Ireland, Cycling Ireland, Dublin Mountains Partnership, Duke of Edinburgh, Explore Ireland Tours, Irish Girl Guides, Irish Orienteering Association, Irish Uplands Forum, Limavady Borough Council, Mountaineering Ireland, Mountain Meitheal Mourne, Scouting Ireland, Sport Northern Ireland, Wexford County Council and Wicklow Uplands Council.

The website http://www.leavenotraceireland.org provides three levels of Leave No Trace training.

OFFA'S DYKE

NATURAL ENGLAND

NATURAL ENGLAND is the public body of England charged with protecting and improving the countryside. It has a statutory duty to help people access nature and enjoy the outdoors.

Guidance notes produced by Natural England for landowners regarding access to common land describe wild camping not as a right, but as a 'de facto' practice. The notes state:

> Almost all common land in England is subject to general public access on foot and a considerable area also provides unrestricted access to horse riders. Wider access rights for a variety of recreational activities have also been granted on certain commons by specific acts of Parliament or agreements with landowners. In addition, de facto access (that which has occurred in practice but which is not underwritten in statute) for activities such as climbing, swimming and wild camping has taken place on many commons for a considerable length of time.

Natural England confirms that the foreshore has special status in law, above and beyond the rights on beaches. Notes on 'Coastal Access in England' state:

> [On] beaches... certain activities may be restricted, such as camping, driving vehicles or lighting fires.

> The foreshore is slightly different. This is defined as the region lying between the high and low tideline, limited on the landward side to the medium line between neap and spring high tides, and is marked on OS maps. This strip usually belongs to the Crown. There is not necessarily any right of public access to it, but in most cases you cannot be barred from walking on the foreshore because there is an absolute right of navigation along it when the tide is in, which prevents the erection of barriers.

What so many of these statements confirm is that wild camping is not a right. But neither is it a wrong. The vast majority of public bodies that control and manage public land do take action to encourage and facilitate it, but perhaps with more caution than is necessary. Just like that lovely wildlife officer in Essex.

PRIVATE
LAND

RIVER DOVEY

WHEN I WAS A KID I watched a TV show called *Out of Town*. It featured a presenter by the name of Jack Hargreaves. He appeared to me to be a fabulously wise character who loved the old farming traditions and skills, and basked in the glory of boys' own adventures in the outdoors. There was not a hint of malice or nastiness in him, even while he was killing a rabbit for the pot or shooting a pheasant.

When I started researching some of the themes for this book, I began re-watching old episodes of his TV programmes on YouTube. They filled me with nostalgia, and memories of my childhood, in grainy images from the 1970s that matched those from my parents' photos albums. It was an impression of how country life existed centuries before pesticides poisoned the birds, tractors replaced shire horses and agricultural policies drafted by gaming estates destroyed so many trees.

Hargreaves and his programmes seemed to represent a beautiful, but hard way of life, and I felt sad that – other than perhaps Ray Mears – there was too little on TV today that truly celebrated the outdoors the way Jack did. I even considered dedicating this book to his memory.

Until, that is, I discovered that Hargreaves was not quite what he seemed. He lived most of his life in London. He ran PR for the Tory party, and he wrote and distributed propaganda for the National Farmers' Union, before becoming their director of communications and setting up their information department. He was what we call today a spin doctor; a gatekeeper. And he was very good at it.

I delved a little further and discovered that Hargreaves was more than a PR man. He was a brilliant media-savvy journalist, a broadcaster, producer, a top TV executive and an entrepreneur. Most importantly of all, he believed the countryside was the

RIVER DOVEY

preserve of the elite circles he moved within, and that the public – the townies – should not be given access over the land.

Despite looking like a humble farmer, Hargreaves was from a wealthy family involved in the manufacture of wool. His parents owned two homes – in London and West Yorkshire – and Hargreaves enjoyed a private education, along with his two siblings.

He made a lot of money from broadcasting. His success was partly based on making great radio shows in the late 1930s and then even better TV in the 1960s and '70s. *Out of Town* was about the farming way of life. But as much as it entertained, it partly helped feed the propaganda of his aristocratic friends that the town and city folk should be kept out.

Much of Hargreaves' skill was in the way he delivered his message to the viewer. His language was seldom polemic and never adversarial. But he is among a short list of TV outdoor pundits who glory and revel in the freedom that they know others can never enjoy. Watch Ray Mears making a wild camp in the New Forest (one of Hargreaves' favourite haunts) and he will often ensure his commentary contains a disclaimer that says,

'I was given special permission to camp here because byelaws don't allow it.'

Hargreaves at one time became the lessee of the Beaulieu Boundary shoot – an area that spanned almost 810ha (2,000 acres) of land around the Beaulieu and its estuary – for which he charged people to take part throughout the year, killing thousands of birds. And as an independent member of the Defence Lands Committee 1971–73, he offered his thoughts and advice to the Nugent Report of 1973, reviewing the use of land owned by the Ministry of Defence. He argued that the best way to preserve the countryside was to keep it for the sole purpose of farming and the landowners, and to keep everyone else out.

He consistently argued that the towns had no entitlement to use the countryside for recreation. But he saw no double standard in that it was a private playground for himself and his friends to fish, shoot and trap.

Hargreaves' case to safeguard tradition and the countryside might be more credible if it wasn't so uniquely elitist; if we hadn't heard it all before, from the Normans and their fondness for private forests in the UK. The irony is that the exact opposite is true in the rest of Europe, especially in France. There is, for instance, an index of French wine growers and farmers known as French Passion. It is a list of almost 2,000 farms where it is free to camp over 24 hours. The farms benefit from selling produce to campers (although purchase is not a condition). Campers benefit from seeing the French countryside and experiencing French farm produce. The web link is http://www.france-passion.co.uk. There is a similar scheme in Italy with more than 500 farms.

There is virtually nothing like it in the UK. But don't let that stop you. Camping and sleeping on private land in Middle England is about asking the question. Whether it's a pub or a farmer's shop, if I become a buyer, the publican or the farmer is usually happy to allow me to pitch a tent for free. I've never been refused a free overnight stay on a pub's land – in return for buying a bar meal.

Hargreaves' argument that tourists and townies should be kept out of the countryside is, in my opinion – like his programmes – based on some old traditions that probably need a review.

The Backpackers Club is part of a future that Hargreaves wanted to resist. Each year it publishes a list of pubs and farms that allow free wild camping. It's available to members only, but the cost to join is nominal and great value.

I rang Hargreaves' old employer – the National Farmers' Union – on two occasions in 2012 to ask if they would consider putting it to their members that the UK should perhaps look to adopt the French model of free camping on farms and vineries, with a view to boosting their farm-shop footfall and sales.

Hargreaves was no doubt turning in his grave. I'm still waiting for the NFU to get back to me.

THE FOUR BEDZONES

There's always some place to go. There's always something to see. There's always something to stimulate your thought, your feelings, your mind. I think trouble begins in our lives when we get too studied in our living existence; where everything gets to be too patterned. TONY CURTIS ON *WOGAN* (BBC TV, 1988)

PAUL YOUNG or Marvin Gaye. What does it matter? Wherever I lay my hat – that's my Home.

At the start of the 21st century there are four bedzones in the UK and the Republic of Ireland. The first is a national zone where wild camping is enshrined as a right: Scotland. 'The last of the free' said the Caledonian chieftain Calgacus, before he went to war with the Roman army in the 1st Century AD.

The second zone, the beaches, is where we started as kids, before we knew the mountains and the limestone caves existed. They told us we could go play below the low-tide mark, on the foreshore. Build campfires, strum guitars, sing songs, kiss and chase love. We fell asleep with the dawn chorus, before the sun and picnic crowds woke us, and then we ran fully clothed into the sea like crazed, immortal gods, with white teeth, bronzed limbs and bad breath.

Then there's the bit between the sea and the hills. The third zone. I call it Middle Earth. It's where we sleep behind the walls, locked out from wilderness. *The Hunger Games* dystopia, under the rooves and the warm duvets of the towns and cities, where we watch ourselves being watched. It's harder sometimes to think of Middle Earth as wild. Down from the hills. Dry-docked from the tidal rivers, beaches and foreshore. But even here our options in Middle Earth

are only limited by how we see the world. There's just so much 'wild' where our tamed and domesticated gardens end, and the alleys and edgelands bleed into the farmers' fields and ditches, the wooded valleys, the lakes, rivers and canals.

We discovered the mountains, the fourth zone, a lot later. Colder and quieter, we'd fall asleep with aching limbs and wake up with hot coffee and a view from on top of the world.

The four bedzones – Scotland, Foreshore, Middle Earth and Mountain – are the four tiers around which I've learned to approach sleeping outdoors. In a very general sense, it goes like this:

1) I will not be breaking the law while sleeping wild in Scotland. I am free.
2) I am unlikely to be breaking the law by sleeping on the foreshore. I am free to night fish, navigate water or to rest while waiting for the tide to return.
3) I will not be breaking the law when I sleep outdoors in Middle Earth if I have the owner's permission, either directly or implied (eg kayaking or fishing with a licence on a canal).
4) I am unlikely to be breaking the law when I sleep on top of a mountain far from a road or buildings.

What follows is a brief introduction to the four zones featured in the 100 wild locations in this book.

WILD SCOTLAND

From Cape Wrath to Gretna; every loch, trail and white-sand beach. The lowlands, peaks and what's left of the forest. It's impossible to overstate how liberating it feels to roll a tent into the wild virtually anywhere without fear of being asked to move or pay. 'Freedom' to sleep and wild camp was restored as a right in 2003 under the Land Reform Act. Thank you, Scotland.

SUTHERLAND

FORESHORE

I'd slept on beaches as a kid, but more recently noticed fishermen camping out in bivvies and tents while fishing for cod around Suffolk. I'd also seen kayakers and canoeists making camp as part of multi-day navigations. When I realised that both 24-hour fishing and 24-hour navigation were rights under the Magna Carta, I made a mental note. The foreshore was communal.

The coast is possibly the most important common ground in Britain and Ireland. Our law has enshrined the right to fish, dig bait and navigate, without having to pay for the privilege, 24 hours a day. This means that while the tide is out, it's perfectly reasonable to camp, eat, light a fire and rest until you're able to carry on with your hobby.

Justifying overnight camping simply means combining night-time with a midnight to 4am low tide, ideally providing sleep between the hours of 6pm and 6am when the water is going out and coming back in.

If you don't do canoes, carry a telescopic rod and reel (costing about £15 online). If you don't do fishing or boats, then try carrying a trowel and you qualify as a bait digger. And anyway, you always need a trowel to bury toilet waste.

SILVER SANDS OF MORAR

MIDDLE EARTH

Middle Earth is the third bedzone where it's perfectly legal to camp. The largest bit of land, wedged in between the foreshore and the mountains, this is where we find almost all of our villages, towns and cities. The corners and boundaries of our hundreds, boroughs, parishes and districts, where the ancient graves, spirits and barrows of an unknown past mix company with industrial estates, brownfields, cement factories, gravel pits, church cemeteries and out of town shopping centres.

It's wrong to say camping here is illegal. Like saying it's illegal to sit down at a table in a restaurant without asking. It's not, it's just polite to ask first. And if the restaurant owner is busy serving other clients, and you choose to sit down first, no offence. Sometimes when you're out camping in the wild, no one comes and asks. But buying a coffee usually entitles you to sit in the chair a little longer. In Middle Earth, buying goods from the farm shop, or a 24-hour fishing ticket, can be enough to warrant an overnight nap, on request. Middle Earth is what we know. It's where 99.9 per cent of us live, just as we have for thousands of years. It's prime real estate between the foreshore and peaks.

What has drastically changed in the last few hundred years is that almost all of us in Britain and Ireland's Middle Earth are now forced to live in towns and cities. That's quite a significant shift in lifestyle, in a relatively short space of time (less than 1 per cent of our human existence dating back 70,000 years). When you feel that overwhelming sense of being pulled towards nature, the sea, the forest, it's the tens of thousands of years of living in wilderness within you that's being sucked back into the whirlpool of a nomadic past. If you doubt it, watch any domesticated animal, however placid, revert to a wild excitement whenever it sees a wood, wild open landscape or waves crashing over a shingle beach – and question whether you can empathise with that reaction.

MOUNTAINS

Mountains are the final zone. As far away from the foreshore as it's possible to get. Mountaineers and ramblers have been enjoying free sleep in the hills for ever. Today, there's still no one up there collecting pitch fees. A mountain is generally considered to be a hill that is higher than 600m/2,000ft. There are 120 in the UK and Ireland. Many landowners consider the minimum necessary height for wild camping to be 450m/1,500ft. Literally hundreds of hills fall within that catergory.

Although not enshrined in law (except in Dartmoor and Scotland), camping on mountains is mostly considered acceptable as part of a traditional and historic use of hills dating back centuries.

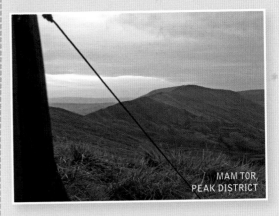

MAM TOR,
PEAK DISTRICT

My 100 camps fall into these four bedzones. The camps are all associated with a single trail, river or canal (marked in bold) that is either a place to sleep or an important link to other sites. Grid reference mapping at the end of each site provides some specific locations that can be placed into a satnav or mapping tool, such as http://www.gridreferencefinder.com. Four symbols throughout the book indicate Wild Scotland, Foreshore, Middle Earth and Mountain. Scotland was where I wanted to make a first bed. A temporal home in the Highlands. Down from there? The law – and moral high ground – are both on your side.

PART
TWO

LOOKING OVER
PILLAR MOUNTAIN
AND ENNERDALE,
CUMBRIA

SCOTLAND

SEE PAGE 5 FOR KEY TO SYMBOLS

1 GLENCOE

I SAT BENEATH the Glencoe peaks in awe. Wedged against a fence post, I leaned both arms on the wire between the barbs, watching the lunar crowns fade and then disappear behind cloud cover, only to reappear like a perfectly timed chorus on an improvised symphony, performed by masters. The ephemeral light around Glencoe is almost as remarkable as its grandeur.

They arrive by coach, car, foot or bike. I can't remember ever seeing so many people stepping outside of themselves, into an out-of-body encounter with a landscape. Modern pilgrims, of sorts. The complicity of human communion and the realisation we share so much in common with nature, and each other, is remarkable to see; a spell only broken by the handheld video cameras that obscure the magic. I realised then why some cultures ban cameras around their churches.

The **West Highland Way** (154km/96 miles) links the town of Milngavie, north-west of Glasgow, to the Highlands at Fort William. It passes close to Loch Lomond and forms part of the International Appalachian Trail. The Way is a combination of old drovers' roads, disused railway, and trade routes. The path follows the eastern side of Loch Lomond, then crosses Rannoch Moor on its way to Glencoe. All climbs and descents are dramatic, in particular the Devil's Staircase – the highest point – 550m (1,804ft) down to Kinlochleven. The Mamore Mountains are reached via an old military road before the path ends around the foothills of Ben Nevis at Fort William.

Several forests include Rowardennan Forest next to Loch Lomond and Garadhban Forest, a place to find shelter from the weather, although this is no place to come poorly equipped or prepared. I chose to carry both a hammock and a small tent.

The Way connects up with five of Scotland's most important routes: Great Glen Way, John Muir Way, Rob Roy Way, Three Lochs Way and the Speyside Way.

PRACTICAL INFO Trek up to the peaks of the Royal Forest along the River Coupall path (56.653490, -4.9266815) to access the western edge of the mountain range in summer; climb the Devil's Staircase along the old military road, now known as the West Highland Way. Leave the trail to find a camp among sheltered rocks and crags (56.678771, -4.9174118).

TRAVEL Trains and buses take you into Milngavie, Balloch, Tarbet, Ardlui, Crianlarich, Tyndrum, Bridge of Orchy and Fort William.

2 JURA

JURA IS PART of the Inner Hebrides, on the west coast, a little north of the Mull of Kintyre and south of the Isle of Mull; wedged between Islay on one side and a fearful whirlpool on the other.

Some say the name is supposed to be an old Norse word for 'deer'. I don't buy that, but I don't particularly care. I like the name, and I like the fact that George Orwell spent some time here writing *1984* during the 1940s, shortly before he died.

Actually, Jura probably comes from the Gaelic word for the yew trees that once covered the entire island. Yews live for thousands of years, and are associated with eternal life, which is why they're so often found planted in churchyards. The 17th-century Scottish writer and explorer Martin Martin claimed islanders here were uniquely healthy and lived a long life, even citing one example of a man called Gillouir MacCrain, claiming he lived to 180. It's likely fiction, although I wonder whether Orwell knew something of Jura's reputation when he accepted the offer to write in the remote farmhouse belonging to his friend.

In the end, he blamed the cold, and a near fatal dip in the Corryvreckan whirlpool, for the tuberculosis that eventually killed him in 1950.

The Jura trees were themselves probably a victim of the elasticity of their wood, which made them perfect for longbows. The oldest yew-tree bow was discovered in Dumfries and Galloway, possibly dating back to 4000 BC, and can be seen in the National Museum of Scotland.

Fields of bracken are all that remain of where the trees once stood. The island has an area of 368sq km (142sq miles) and a population of around 200. There is one hotel, a shop and a church at the village of Craighouse. The Vikings occupied Jura and the surrounding isles until the 13th century, when they became part of Scotland under the Treaty of Perth. They've since been owned by a succession of clans that sound like the Who's Who of Scotland: the Donalds, the MacDonalds, the Macleans and the Campbells.

The Paps of Jura – three mountains in the southern section of the island –

can be seen from all around. Beinn an Òir (785m/2,575ft), Beinn Shiantaidh (755m/2,477ft) and Beinn a' Chaolais (734m/2,408ft) can be accessed from tracks from the east and west. The coastline is a series of cliffs, shingle or sand beaches and caves.

Much of the walking is over wet marsh and peat bog, so the best time to go is September after a dry summer.

Evans Walk crosses the island (10km/ 6 miles from one side to other), following the line of the Glenbatrick River and ending on the north shore at the beach. For wild camping, there are several 'raised beaches' around the coastline. These heather terraces of stone and sand are shelves created over time by the receding waves.

PRACTICAL INFO Camp around the sand and rock over Loch Tarbet (55.989740, -5.8486748); visit one of the wooded beach areas along the coast at Kinuachdrachd Harbour (56.121096, -5.6945443), camp on the heather shore; if kayaking, be wary of the Corryvreckan whirlpool (56.155159, -5.7329750) directly north of Jura's caves on its north-west tip (56.145836, -5.7237053).

TRAVEL A small ferry runs from Islay. A larger ferry runs from Kennacraig on West Loch Tarbert to Islay.

3 GREAT GLEN

THE KNOCK CAME at the door just before 7pm. We were camped in the van at the car park, below the canal locks of Neptune's Staircase. I'd arrived in Fort William to canoe, sail and camp the 60 miles along the **Caledonian Canal** – one side of the Scottish coast to the other. There were four of us. We'd never met, and two of us had never spoken.

Thirty minutes earlier, we had crossed Glencoe in violent winds. Lorries and motorhomes lay strewn on either side of the A82, nose deep in ditches and crumpled steel. Feeling my own van lift up on to two wheels, I'd wanted to stop before a fiercer gust battered the side, and I waited to meet the road gravel and shattered glass cheek-by-jowel. We made it over the crossing at 15mph in what felt like watching 60 instalments of *The Blair Witch Project* alone in a forest at night.

My nerves were so blown that when the knock came again I nearly bounced. Chris

was already up and opening the door. It was a fifth 'friend', not on the trip, but he wanted to offer some advice and goodwill for the journey ahead. I was tired and wanted to go to bed. I'd been up since 5am. But the fifth man was knowledgeable and local. An outdoor expedition leader in his sixties, who had many stories to tell. At first I listened keenly to tales of the Great Glen, the great lochs, the great boats, the great waves and the great lives that had been lost on them.

It was 10.30pm before he left. By then, I wanted to go home. Really. He'd told us that we'd likely capsize; and that if we picked the wrong side of the freezing lochs to go in on, we might not get out for many hours, if at all. It was a wretched night's sleep. We woke the next morning to blue skies, a gentle south-westerly breeze and hot coffee. It was one of the best mornings of my life. And then it got even better; we got on the water.

The canal follows the valley known as Great Glen, which links the west coast of

Scotland to the east, from Fort William to Inverness. This relatively short 97km (60 miles) can be walked, cycled, canoed or ridden on horseback along the canal. The water channel was dug in the 19th century to provide employment and a trade route through the respective lochs along the way: Lochy, Oich, Ness and Dochfour bulge out from forest and rocks, bypassing the respective rivers that run alongside. The canal was a safer route for traders who wanted to avoid losing their goods aboard sailing ships on the open seas.

The Great Glen Way merges with the towpath but frequently leaves to follow forestry tracks, lanes and roads. It covers 127km (79 miles), 30km (19 miles) longer than the canal, and is a better opportunity to explore the valley. Aside from grassy areas around the locks, camping along the canal can be limited. If I were going to do it alone, I'd walk, simply because the choice of places to hammock and tent is so much better: high on the peaks or down, slung from the valley pines.

Among the trail highlights are the peaks overlooking Loch Ness and Creag nan Eun, where the footpath passes into the forest. There are views over the loch from paths that lead up into the snowy peaks at Loch Dubh from south-west of Drumnadrochit.

The Way links with the West Highland Way, the Cape Wrath Trail and the Famous Highland Drove Walk.

PRACTICAL INFO Launch a canoe from the southern end of Loch Ness (57.152793, -4.6704769) in a stiff south-westerly breeze, arriving at dusk to camp at Dochgarroch Lock (57.433055, -4.3023920); if walking or cycling the entire Great Glen trail, time the journey to camp and spend much time around Kytra Lock (57.122573, -4.7223186), beside the incredible Inchnacardoch Forest.

TRAVEL Trains and buses take you into Fort William, Spean Bridge and Inverness.

4 GALLOWAY FOREST

THE FOREST MOVES ON the breeze below Bruce's Stone like a congregation of excited evangelists swaying to the melody of a preacher's hand; the pointed tips of Sitka spruce waving to the souls lost on the wind over the loch below. The boulder is inscribed with the words of victory: Robert the Bruce's triumph over the English in 1307 at the Battle of Glen Trool. Like so many symbols of defiance and war, the stone exudes quiet and calm, those very things displaced by the greed and egos of men. Nothing changes.

Galloway Forest – 780sq km (300sq miles) of wooded area in Dumfries and Galloway – is bordered by Wigtown Bay to the south-west, the River Cree on its western edge, Loch Doon in the north-east and Loch Ken in the south-east. Red deer graze between the valleys and the lowland heather, while crossbills pick over conifer seeds with their crushing pincer-like beaks.

There are three visitor centres to avoid, or not, depending on your mood: one at Glen Trool, another at Kirroughtree, and a final one at Clatteringshaws. People come here mostly to walk, climb or cycle. Although the forest gets plenty of visitors, it's a working area owned by the Forestry Commission, producing 500,000 tons of timber per year.

Galloway Forest is probably the best tree-camping/ hammocking that's easily accessible, close to England and Wales. The Forestry Commission website offers information on formal campsites or the rules on 'wilding': 'Choose a site a long way from roads and do your best to leave no trace of your stay: that means taking rubbish home with you, burying toilet waste and using a stove carefully.' There are some additional rules, such as: 'Camping beside cars isn't wild camping and isn't allowed under the Scottish Outdoor Access Code.'

Night is a uniquely good time to

visit. In November 2009, Galloway Forest became the first in the UK to be designated a Dark Sky Area by the International Dark-Sky Association. The Scottish Dark Sky Observatory, near Dalmellington, is located within the northern edge of the Galloway Forest Dark Sky Park.

The **Southern Upland Way** (338km/210 miles) runs through the forest, coast to coast, passing beneath the Merrick (843m/2,765ft) as it does most of the tops along the way. It links with the St Cuthbert's Way, Annandale Way, Ayrshire Coastal Path; Berwickshire Coastal Path and the Romans and Reivers Route.

> **PRACTICAL INFO** Hammock on the edge of the trees with a view of the night sky around Loch Trool (55.086916, -4.4920349).
> **TRAVEL** Trains and buses take you into Girvan, Barrhill, Patna and Dumfries.

5 SUTHERLAND

A NATIVE SCOTS PINE, trapped by a million pools of water, splinters the sky. The pines are the remnants of the Caledonian Forest, which was hacked back to make way for the Highland Clearances, the forceful eviction of people made legal for the introduction of intensive sheep farming in the 18th century. The wolves disappeared soon after. Sutherland was the last place they were ever seen in Britain.

The name 'Sutherland' comes from Norse rulers of Orkney and Caithness, who considered all below them as south. The west is the best. If you don't believe me, just go online, find a free OS map site and zoom in on that space in the northern corner, somewhere between Scourie and Cape Wrath, and marvel at a feral land where even the sheep can't get.

The options to camp and explore in Sutherland are uniquely plentiful. I'd say the best place in Britain and Ireland. The bogs and marshes leak like sieves dripping with the juices of fledgling life. Walking is a lot of fun, but canoes are a more leisurely way to camp in the deep country. They are an opportunity to carry twice the provisions you might manage in a backpack. More fresh water (if you prefer not to filter your own), more food, more clothes, more

kindling. The Sutherland waterways bypass the occasional deer fences, which can be a pain to get around when walking and camping. Also, unlike the Caledonian Canal, opportunities to moor and pitch tents along the lochs and rivers are more common. Loch Laxford has road access to launch canoes, and several islands to explore and sleep on. The loch is also protected by the mountains if the weather turns. Nearby Loch Crocach is smaller, but more isolated. Even wilder for tents and late-night campfires.

Most of the inland islets have no names marked on national maps. They spread down from Cape Wrath to Lochinver on the Atlantic, and then up from Bonar Bridge on the east coast to Melvich in the north. Ben Hope is the most northerly Munro. Laxford is more typical of the remote seaward islands warmed by the Gulf Stream.

For hikers, the **Cape Wrath Trail** (351km/218 miles) follows down to the Assynt Hills via Cape Wrath, and then Sandwood Bay, Loch Inchard and over the peaks around Achfary Moor. It passes down south into Glenshiel and Strathcarron on its way to the Great Glen.

6 MINCH MOOR

MINCH MOOR NURTURED one of the greatest travel writers and explorers of the 18th century. Mungo Park was born in 1771 on a farm just west of Selkirk.

By the age of 24, he had left to navigate the unmapped parts of Africa's Niger River. He returned two years later to write about his adventures and the local people he met. His stories described the common nature of men, how they shared the same goals, fears and feelings. Park made a second trip to the Niger ten years later, attempting to canoe to the sea. He drowned in rapids after being attacked by natives. A monument to his exploration of pre-colonial Africa is based in Selkirk.

There's a spring next to Minch Moor called the Cheese Well. It was named after the custom of leaving food for the safe passage of fellow travellers from Traquair to Yarrow. Goodwill to travellers was at some stage replaced by a myth of fairies – a superstitious offering to ensure safe

passage over the moor, via the **Southern Upland Way**.

In keeping with the tradition of goodwill, the Mountain Bothies Association has six shelters spread out along the Way's 338km (210 miles). The bothies are based at or close to Laggangarn, Ettrick, Daer Reservoir, Polskeoch, Loch Dee and Traquair. All have limited facilities, but it's worth checking them out and noting their coordinates before leaving home. Just in case. The shelters can become busy in the summer months and are, in my experience, best avoided unless really necessary. Wild alternatives for sleeping around Minch Moor are better. Either find some flat ground around the summit or drop down off the Southern Upland Way into any of the pine woodland scattered about. Much of the ground can be uneven here, which justifies carrying a hammock and a bivvy.

The path guides the walker through many of the areas where Mungo Park grew up – the moor, Yarrow Water, and St Mary's Loch. It is also a coast-to-coast expedition, from the west at Portpatrick, out to the Galloway Forest and Loch Trool, over the Lowther Hills, north of Craik Forest and St Mary's Loch, near Broad Law. It joins with St Cuthbert's Way at Melrose before skimming over the Lammermuir Hills to the east coast to meet the John Muir Way.

The Upland Way diverts around most of the peaks, although that's no reason not to explore the likes of the Merrick (843m/ 2,765ft) by using the connecting paths. The Way links with the Annandale Way, Ayrshire Coastal Path and Berwickshire Coastal Path.

PRACTICAL INFO Hammock in the dense forest around Minch Moor's peak (55.583302, -3.0166700).
TRAVEL Trains and buses take you into Dunbar, Lockerbie, Sanquhar, Glenluce, Barrhill and Stranraer.

walk, cycle, canoe

SLEEPING OUTDOORS requires one of three modes of transport. The first two cost less than a cheap meal for two:

Walking shoes.
A bike.

The last one costs a few hundred pounds and involves some basic training:

A canoe or kayak.

Walking is the easiest and cheapest way to explore the wild. Cycling is the fastest and most efficient. Canoes access the parts where the footpaths and bridleways have been lost or removed.

WALKING

Walking involves minimal outlay, minimal maintenance, and access to the highest, narrowest, most enclosed, most overgrown and rockiest places. The human long-distance walker is one of the most efficient creatures in terms of energy expended to travel for hours and days.

A good way to learn about map-reading, trails and eventually sleeping out in the wilds is to join the Ramblers. Their objective is to protect the countryside, and to ensure that local authorities keep open the paths and increase access for all. They have long campaigned for full access to the outdoors, and they fought hard for the introduction of the Countryside and Rights of Way (CroW) Act 2000. It's seen by some as the first step towards the sort of expansive access available in Scandinavia and Scotland, where the Land Reform (Scotland) Act 2003 awarded walkers the right to access most land. The Ramblers are at the forefront of a campaign to ensure councils are not deprived of central government cash to keep existing footpaths open.

I interviewed the Ramblers' president Kate Ashbrook in 2013. She told me that she had 'great concern' over the future of the trails as more councils were 'neglecting their duties'. I suggested to Ashbrook that sleeping outdoors was an important part of access because overnighting embodied the ability to walk great distances without concern for finding a room. She said the ability to wild camp 'wasn't greatly compromised by landowners'. The problem, she said, was the access in the first place. 'I think wild camping should be allowed,' she said. 'But I don't think it's an issue. No one raises it, and no one really says you can't.'

Ashbrook's point that the access to the trail is more of an issue than the sleeping is why paths and rivers are at the heart of this book. In post-1066 Britain, one cannot really exist without the other. Ashbrook chooses to focus on the path.

CYCLING

If the human walker is an efficient traveller, the cyclist is a superstar. The bike gives us access to the parts others cannot reach. Nothing in the animal kingdom can match a cyclist for space covered in relation to energy expended. No other machine is as efficient as the cycle/human combo. A cyclist is four times faster than a walker and uses five times less energy.

Cycling and camping have been in a partnership for some time. In 1901, six cyclists spent a weekend in tents at Wantage. Those six founded the Association of Cycle Campers, which still exists today as the Association of Lightweight Campers.

An average day's walking for an efficient walker is about 32km (20 miles). A cyclist can do five times that, although 48km (30 miles) is good for me, on any day. I prefer to walk, but if I'm short on time and long on trail, I'll do a bit of both. Cycling through the more mundane sections of a trail, several hours' walking and pushing the bike through the better areas, and then maybe cycling home or into the night, depending on where I'm headed.

Pushing wheels can mean being able to carry more gear. It is not an offence to push a bike over footpaths. It's also more interesting and relaxing. And occasionally footpaths become bridleways and tracks for riding.

My gear can be packed into one bag on the bike and one smaller bag on my back, along with plenty of water bottles.

CANOEING AND KAYAKING

Canoes, and I include those with sails here, provide the most exciting access to the wild for me. Canoe-camping is unique in that more gear can be carried than on a bike or in a backpack. Kayaks – or any shallow-draughted boats, for that matter – have access to areas of foreshore, riverbank and lake that walkers and cyclists can never get to.

A canoe can moor in a section of salty creek that no one has visited for hundreds of years. In Essex, we have the longest shoreline in the UK and thousands of creeks and inlets that can be explored for a few hours at high tide each day.

To find out more, visit the Song of the Paddle and see its camping and outdoor living section: http://www.songofthepaddle.co.uk/forum/forumdisplay.php?17-Camping-amp-Outdoor-Living.

7 LOCH LOMOND AND THE TROSSACHS

LOCH LOMOND is an anomaly within an anomaly. The legislators in England, Wales and Ireland insist there is no right to 'sleep' in the kingdoms they control – only a right to live, breath clean air, eat fruit, drink clean water and to defend oneself from attack. In other words, no one's going to arrest you for eating strawberries washed down with a flask of home-made dandelion soup in the High Street – just as long as you don't doze off on the park bench, after dusk, dreaming of William Wallace.

The Scottish, on other hand, are thoroughly civilised, actively encouraging their citizens to camp out in all weathers by following the specially prepared wild camping code (see www.outdooraccess-scotland.com). The problem for the Scots seems to be when someone commits a criminal offence. In the case of Loch Lomond, that's when folk drive overnight to loch-side car parks to start fires, have barbecues, drink lots of beer and generally make a nuisance of themselves. This activity is known in the courts as 'criminal damage and disturbance of the peace'; but the legislators seem to have confused it with wild camping, so have decided instead to ban wild camping in parts of Loch Lomond.

If you are confused, think phone-hacking. Which means that wild camping is now illegal in one of the only places it is truly legal. Still confused? Me too. So I will take a leaf out of the Nick Davies school of journalism and say simply this. Go and do it. Find a way to navigate around the law, knowing the law by reading the front section

PRACTICAL INFO Paddle out to any of Loch Lomond's islands – Inchconnachan (island) has a collection of red-necked wallabies (56.088655, -4.6137428); trek up to Ben Lomond for views over Loch Lomond and the valley (56.189992, -4.6310806).
TRAVEL Trains and buses take you into Balloch, Helensburgh, Tarbet, Ardlui and Crianlarich.

of this book, and simply keep doing what is right: camp high, far from a road, etc, and follow the camping code.

Loch Lomond and The Trossachs is a forested landscape defined by Scotland's largest body of fresh water, and the Trossachs hills that surround it. The port of Glasgow and Loch Long mark its southern boundary. Loch Tay and the Grampians lie to the north.

Loch Lomond is 39km (24 miles) long and very thin at the top, but sturdy, thick and fat at the southern base – a bit like an effigy of a melting Eiffel Tower, but much prettier. Almost two-thirds is less than 1.5km (1 mile) wide. The most southern parts are 8km (5 miles), separated by a series of islands that rise like ornamental emerald beads on a glass lake.

There are more than 30 islands to explore; more during summer if rainfall has been low. It's possible that some islets were artificially created by early Bronze Age settlers. The largest island, Inchconnachan, is home to a colony of wallabies.

The byelaws to prevent wild camping on busier sections of the loch close to the road are no burden for genuine wild campers, who hike out to the quieter and higher areas. They include the Munros, such as Ben Lomond, Ben Lui, Beinn Challuim and Ben More. The West Highland Way runs along the east of the loch. It links with the Great Glen Way, John Muir Way, Rob Roy Way, Three Lochs Way and many others. The **West Loch Lomond Cycle Path** (27km/17 miles) runs on the west side.

8 LOCH MORAR

THERE ARE MANY STORIES of people who never made it home. Livingstone. Cook. Scott. Sometimes more tragic when they come up just short, only a few miles or a few hundred yards from the road, or the base camp, or the village. But it works the other way round, too. How sad it is when we don't realise what's just a mile or so from home. The wild, within a few hundred yards of the front door.

Loch Morar is hardly on the edge of town. But it's right beside the A830, the main road to Mallaig. The lane along the north shore ends after 4 miles. From there it's a hike or a paddle into the wilderness.

The loch is 18.8km (12 miles) long and the deepest freshwater lake in Britain. At 310m (1,017ft), it is almost 80m (300ft) deeper than Loch Ness. Loch Ness has Nessie; Morar has Morag. Less well-known south of the border, the Morag monster myth has not endured. But then neither have the roads around the loch, which is why it has made it here, into these pages.

There are five islands at the western end of the loch. A day's paddle to the east provides an opportunity to overnight in Oban bothy on the south shore. Trails lead up into the surrounding mountains and hills on An Stac (718m/2,355ft), Cnoc Gorm (527m/1,729ft) and the waterfall at Gleann Cul an Staca.

A full canoeing circuit of Morar and neighbouring Loch Nevis can be completed over three or four days via a land crossing less than a mile wide between South Tarbet Bay on Morar and Tarbet Bay on Nevis, and then paddling around Mallaig and on to the Morar estuary and its white sands – a welcome luxury after the grey stone of the lochs. Both bays can be reached on foot by walking along the **Bracara footpath** on the northern shore of Morar.

PRACTICAL INFO Paddle to the loch's south shore where it meets the River Meoble (56.941697, -5.6457710) and hike up to Meith Bheinn for the best views of the valley (56.926103, -5.5810547) Sleep up high around the peak or return to canoe-camp around the shore.

TRAVEL Trains and buses take you into Mallaig, Beasdale, Glenfinnan, Lochailort and Morar.

SUMMER ISLES

MORE PEOPLE in Britain and Ireland choose to visit woods than beaches. Most of the forests vanished from these islands a long time ago. Chopped down. Destroyed. Pillaged. But beneath the surface, there's another natural plant world.

The Summer Isles are drenched in thousands of acres of sea forest. Weed and algae bulge from the Atlantic blue. The clear waters around these islands are refreshingly warm, heated by hot-water currents known as the Gulf Stream — powerful flows of water that originate from the southern tip of Florida, before crossing the Atlantic to the Scottish west coast where they create a tropical bath, infused with a soft tangle of inquisitive seals, birds, bladderwrack, knotted kelp, seagrass and dulse. (I still wear a wetsuit, just in case someone has turned the heating down over the pond.)

The seaweed can be eaten or explored. A rainbow of oranges, greens and mauves to bathe in, while they lift and dip around the pools and shallows like the ancient land forests that once swung in the Gulf Stream breeze.

One of the Summer Isles is developed. Tanera Mòr has a café and post office, and a single track that navigates the eastern bay anchorage. The new owners say they are making efforts to re-establish native trees. Almost 200,000 have been planted in the last 15 years.

The rest of these tiny islands next to Loch Broom, on the west coast of the Scottish Highlands, involve basic living, which I like.

Canoe-camping is the easiest way to explore the coves and tracks. Arrive on the beach road, around Old Dorney Bay, in Wester Ross, north of Ullapool, to launch in the direction of Isle Ristol, less than a mile offshore.

Horse Island is uninhabited, and supports a herd of wild goats. Isle Martin is the closest to Ullapool. Crofting ended there in the 1960s, but a ferry service still operates for walkers. Priest Island is off the west coast of Wester Ross. There are several caves, one of which (on the south side) is thought to have been home for a Popish priest.

The **Cape Wrath Trail** passes along the mainland shore next to Isle Martin and Loch Kanaird.

10 RIVER SPEY

THE RIVER SPEY is 172km (107 miles) long. Its source is 16km (10 miles) south of Fort Augustus in the Corrieyairack Forest, at Loch Spey. The river flows out into the Moray Firth, and is one of the best salmon rivers in Britain.

Fly-fishing, whisky distilleries and shipbuilding are the industries associated with the river. Vast amounts of trees from Aviemore and Aberlour forests were felled during the 19th century to make wooden-hulled ships, creating the UK's largest shipbuilding centre, at Garmouth.

My favourite overnight stop is at Ben Aigan (471m/1,546ft). It has everything. Peaceful riverside access and wild camping, vast forest to shelter in

if necessary, and views from Ben Aigan's modest peak over Moray, from the Spey Bay coast in the north to the Cairngorms in the south-west.

Tents and bivvies should be pitched above the waterline as it's common for the river to rise fast. Less of a problem by day, a wet bed or worse by night. High ground is plentiful, as are trees for campers who hammock, who I believe have the best of it here. There's good, flat ground all along the Speyside Way. There are occasionally two free 'camping areas' open on the path at Fiddich Park, Craigellachie, and Ballindalloch Station. Toilets and water may be available at both sites, too.

The **Speyside Way** (105km/65 miles) follows the river through Banffshire, Morayshire and Inverness-shire, from the Aviemore hills to Buckpool Harbour. The path passes the Cairngorms with views over white-tipped peaks even in summer, runs along old railway tracks and valley paths, and features a climb to more than 275m (900ft) on Ben Aigan to Red Sheugh.

PRACTICAL INFO Camp on one of the green islets around Drum Wood (57.454463, -3.3563232).
TRAVEL Trains and buses take you into Elgin, Keith, Newtonmore, Aviemore and Broomhill.

SEE PAGE 5 FOR KEY TO SYMBOLS

SOUTHERN ENGLAND

11 RIVER AVON

THEY SAY you can learn about a nation by how it treats its animals. I'd like to make the same argument for trees.

On the River Avon – close to the estuary at Royal Portbury Dock and past the salt marsh, the reed beds and the bearded tits – is a wooded cliff. Rooted into the sandstone and limestone of that riverbank is one of the most critically endangered plants in Europe. The 'true service tree' produces a pear-like fruit that the Romans made into an alcoholic drink called cerevisia, from which the tree gets its name.

The Avon hosts the largest population of true service trees in England at the site, which is within less than a mile of major Roman settlements. The trees' status in the UK is considered 'unknown', and so they have no official protection under British law.

The British and Irish governments of the last thousand years would be imprisoned if we based criminality on the destruction of our trees. If that sounds harsh, type the phrase 'EU forest cover' into Google and then click on images. You will see a series of photo maps that show how 40 per cent of all mainland Europe is bathed in woodland. The British Isles and Ireland are as bald as an upturned satellite dish. Just 10 per cent of our land is covered with trees, and almost 70 per cent of that is in private hands, locked away from view. A national disgrace, bearing in mind how much people enjoy visiting forest.

The Bristol Avon is more than a treasure trove for rare trees. It rises in South Gloucestershire, north of Acton Turville village. It twists 121km (75 miles) through Wiltshire into the sea at Avonmouth, a straight-line distance of just 31km (19 miles). If you know what to look for, it's possible to find rare dragonflies, Slavonian grebes, a large population of Bath asparagus, and the UK's largest colony of wintering avocets.

From Bath to the Severn Estuary, the river is referred to as the Avon Navigation. The river was once crucial to industry and trade, diverted along the New Cut in central Bristol in the early part of the 19th century to create a series of dockside areas and a floating harbour.

There are places to stop and overnight along the river's tidal foreshore between the estuary and Bristol, with access from both sides of the river along either the Severn Way or the River Avon Trail. The Avon Gorge is the wooded section of the river owned by the National Trust. Permission is needed to camp here if you decide to pull up from the foreshore on to dry land or hammock in the trees. There are several overgrown places to wild camp along the freshwater parts of the river, especially into and out of Bath. Frequent pubs along the way will often allow free camping in return for an evening meal bought over the bar.

Walkers, canoeists and cyclists can all get access. The river meets the Kennet and Avon Canal just below the weir at Bath Locks. Together with the River Thames, these three waterways provide an important series of trails. Walkers and cyclists can get from Bristol to London along the River Avon Trail (40km/25 miles), the **Kennet and Avon Canal Walk** (122km/76 miles), and Thames Path combined. They also link up with the Cotswold Way.

PRACTICAL INFO Night-fish and/or sleep on the west foreshore of the Avon (51.490394, -2.6969221) with access to the Old Sea Bank either by canoe, kayak, or the footpath from the adjoining road bridge. Paddle along the Avon through Hencliffe Wood (51.436753, -2.5274400).

TRAVEL Trains take you into Avonmouth, Bristol, Bath, Keynsham, Bradford on Avon, Melksham, and Chippenham. There are buses to Malmesbury.

12 BEAULIEU

WILD PONIES GALLOP through the November mist as the sun warms the icy dawn. Dry needles of white frost rise like fine hairy shoots in late morning, from the uneven ground of crisp leaves and fat-bladed grasses. Fallen trees, their trunks sometimes a metre thick, hang across the river to make good seating. The pea-green ivy with its yellow veins wraps around the horizontal giants like passive, headless, constricting snakes. A comfy place to rest.

In winter, the passing of time in the hidden hollows is shared with nothing more than nature and the occasional kayak. Weeds make a soft, dry bed over the sinking marsh, where the river almost peters out into the forest.

In the distant quiet I first hear, and then see ... pigs. A flash of hairless, multi-coloured skin in pinks, blacks, browns and whites, foraging and rooting for fallen acorns by throwing their sensitive snouts into the peat forest floor with the precision of a prospector sifting for gold. A local told me later that they were not wild, but brought in every autumn by the landowners to prevent the horses eating the sweet oak nuts, which are fatal to them. One's meat is the other's poison.

Beaulieu was the name given to the river by the Norman invaders, and means beautiful place. It was formerly known as the River Exe. It flows south from the middle of the New Forest, near Lyndhurst, to the village of Beaulieu. The last 6.4km (4 miles) from Beaulieu – past the village of Buckler's Hard to the Solent – are tidal. The entire river – even its tidal part – is owned by Lord Montagu of Beaulieu.

Buckler's Hard was once an important shipbuilding centre, responsible for creating warships that fought in the Battle of

a second high tide some two hours later, followed by a period of slack water for about an hour. Then the ebb sets in, and low water is reached in just two and a half hours. This means that as there is a right of navigation, there is a possibility that a traveller can become suddenly stuck in the mud for six hours, necessitating the need for a stopover.

I phoned the harbourmaster at Buckler's Hard Yacht Harbour before a trip in 2014 and was told that there was no need to give notice of a kayak or canoe coming up the river. There was, though, a £5 fee for fishing on the tidal river. I was informed that this tidal fee was indeed 'very rare', but was there because the river is 'privately owned'. I asked if the £5 covered night-fishing and was told it did. The Yacht Harbour website states in the headline on its 'About' page that the river is 'remarkable for several reasons, one being that it is one of the few privately owned rivers in the world'. Fish commonly caught include bass, trout, mullet and flounder.

The **Solent Way** (96km/60 miles) passes Buckler's Hard and Beaulieu, crossing the River Hamble to Portsmouth in the east, and on to Langstone and Chichester Harbour. To the west, the Way crosses coast marshes to Lymington before ending at Milford on Sea, near Christchurch.

Trafalgar in 1805. Saltmarsh Cottage signifies that the tide penetrates deep into the New Forest. At 10am, in November, it is close to low tide; but the water is moving slowly enough seaward for a canoeist or kayaker to make way against the tide.

This is not a waterway blessed with access. Canoes are the best way in, although even the tidal stretches of the river have restrictions. Hidden places are certainly hard to find between the fine stilted houses, marinas and berths. It can be a good idea to camp at night around the mouth of the estuary (eg Lepe) in areas not owned by the Beaulieu Estate. Having said that, unintentionally becoming grounded in a vessel or canoe at dusk by a fast-moving ebb tide might necessitate an enforced stopover, and is unlikely to result in the wrath of the landowners, if it's a genuine error.

The river is unique for many reasons, one in that it has a double tide, and a secondary high water. The flood tide takes six hours coming in; then, after a gentle fall, there is

PRACTICAL INFO Take the shore footpath east of Lepe and consider wild camping along this coast if you intend to explore the river by canoe or kayak (50.784939, -1.3798322). Lunch on the marshes at low tide from a canoe or kayak (50.806998, -1.4295796) with the wooded Keeping Copse in the foreground.
TRAVEL Trains and buses take you into Beaulieu Road Station, Lymington, Ashurst and Brockenhurst.

POOLE HARBOUR

I MET A KINDRED SPIRIT on this path. Actually, I met two, but I'll tell you about the second some other time. I was walking around Poole Harbour in Dorset when I saw an elderly man arrive across the sand, between the yellow gorse bushes, on a push bike. He got off and chained the bike to a small wooden National Trust sign. We were several hundred yards from the Studland Heath road that leads to South Haven Point and the ferry to Sandbanks, a place that for some reason I've always associated with the former West Ham FC manager Harry Redknapp.

The man was in his late sixties. He told me he lived in Bournemouth and that he had visited Studland every week since he was a child. 'This is the best place in the world,' he said, very matter of factly. 'I've travelled a bit. Nowhere compares with this.'

I was on a bike too, and he encouraged me to explore the view, higher up the lanes and footpaths around Brenscombe Hill, the Foreland or Handfast Point and Ballard

Down. He told me how Studland and the southern harbourside around Newton Heath had barely changed since he was a kid. Salt marsh, inlets and brackish lakes. Great Scots pine trees and white-feathered spoonbills. He said that almost every other wild place he could think of had been affected by change over the years, except this one. He told me how lucky he was to be able to still come here. To watch the changing seasons, the red damselfly, the sika deer and the nesting terns.

At 36sq km (14sq miles), Poole Harbour is the largest natural harbour in Europe. It's a port, a playground, and former military hub for the Roman conquest of Britain, and was once an Iron Age settlement. The remains of an Iron Age longboat, from 295 BC, were dug up in the silt off Brownsea Island in the 1960s. The harbour is managed by the Poole Harbour Commissioners. Four rivers drain in, the largest being the River Frome, which flows from the west through Dorchester and Wareham.

Sandbanks is a popular way in. Its status as a residential zone for the wealthy is bleached into the regulations around visitors' car parking. Every road is lined with 'no parking' yellow lines, apart from £10-per-day parking zones along the seafront and two car parks. Vehicles are not even allowed to queue for the ferry. Police signs reinforce the madness of the kings that wear no clothes. The richer the playground, the sillier and more restrictive the rules: if someone arrives to make a queue, everyone else must leave.

The rules of the water that surround the land are not so restrictive. Sand bays are flanked by gorse and birch on the harbour side, muddy pink and shiny mauve heather and watery bog on the sea side. Grassy peninsulas are kept tightly mown by resident deer, rather than salaried gardeners. Anglers fish for dabs and flatfish after digging worms early on the low tide.

The first bay looks out across several of the harbour's islands, which are all reachable by kayak. Brownsea Island has a ferry link in summer. Houseboats and a barge sit around some of the back bays like old squatters at sea. Grassy peat cliffs overhang the foreshore where the rising tide has eroded the shallow cliffs. These overhangs can sometimes reach up to 4.5m (15ft) and make good shelter from wind and rain in bad weather, as long as they don't fall on your head. Some of the better camping is where the cliffs have already collapsed on to the beach.

The most southerly section of the harbour is partitioned from Studland Bay by a peninsula that carries traffic, bikes and pedestrians back over to Sandbanks

HOW TO WILD the car

THE DEVIL: THE CAR. So I know what you're thinking. Can't live with it, can't live without it. Well, that's bollocks. The car is killing us. Polluting our lungs, our lives, our minds, our time. Yep. I'm not kidding.

I'm relatively lucky. I live in Essex. It's a flat county. I work 7 miles from home, which means I can cycle. I get spat at, shouted at, and driven at. A fat bloke that wants to get thin. A cheapskate who won't buy petrol. I'm all those things. But mostly I'm angry. Because I have to breathe in the choking fumes that kill 29,000 of us in the UK each year. Angry with myself as much as anyone else. Because I'm a driver too. Impatient. In a hurry. Not a hypocrite, as such. Just a human being. Always moaning about something. But just wishing we could kill the car.

There's perhaps something more troubling about the car than the toxic fumes.

It's the invisible tin box, with windows, that traps us. Rather than liberating us, the car confines people to a world that is defined by the tin box and the grid network it runs along.

The grid is like an airport travelator that won't let us off. This is because the travelator has a purpose. To deliver us from home to school, school to work, work to the golf club, golf to the shops, the shops to the park, the park to the supermarket and home again. What I didn't realise, until I started exploring the world again, was there are almost no stop-offs into the wild. They just don't exist.

As a sort of starting point, I began looking at trails that crossed through villages. I was shocked how difficult it was to park, especially when there was no public transport either. The alternatives are limited to faraway laybys, pubs, beauty spots and parks used by millions of people each year. Too often these locations are starved of any sense of wonder by the beholder because familiarity very nearly breeds contempt.

on Ferry Road. It's a transit arm that's mostly overlooked by those on their way to the more highly rated areas of Studland Heath, Corfe Castle and the views from Godlingston Hill. The occasional rod angler sits along these north-facing beach bays. At low tide, walk around Jerry's Point, past Bramble Bush Bay, and on to Redhorn Quay. Walk or cycle on the footpath to Shipstal Point and Arne Bay. Heathland meets woodland meets marsh, meets water. Access to the harbour is relatively poor, mainly because there are so few official footpaths. The best access is made at low tide by walking around the stony shore or by kayaking.

The **Castleman Trailway** (26.5km/16.5 miles) is the footpath that enters the back door into Poole Harbour via the rather upmarket, and not at all wild, Upton Country Park, opposite Pergins Island. Castleman is built on the old Dorchester to Southampton railway, along the River Stour valley. It's used by walkers, cyclists and horse riders, and links with the Stour Valley Way (97km/60 miles) into Wiltshire.

It's painful and empty. Not being able to explore beyond your own imagination because the road grid has been placed like a steel mesh above the soft-centred Mother Earth of rivers, woods and soil paths, 99.9 per cent of which are never seen because there's no access within 10 miles. Next time you drive through the countryside, look out of the window and ask yourself: How do I get out there? Where is the bus stop, the parking space and the footpath that will take me to that old oak, or to explore the water in that ditch? Or to listen to the blackbird singing in a particular hawthorn tree? A bird no one has listened to before, and I'd suggest a sound from that particular tree that perhaps no one has heard since motorised tractors were introduced in 1930s. A ditch that hasn't been slept in for more than 300 years. A creek that hasn't been paddled for a century.

The good news is very good indeed. The car, for all its faults and its demons, is more a trap of the mind than the spirit. Start carrying an old bike. From a train station or car park, just cycle the five miles to where the footpath crosses the road. Padlock the bike to a lamppost, and take off with a sleeping bag to where the air is clean, the ditches are wild and the birds sing a lonely, but rarely heard song.

14 RIVER TAMAR

IT WAS ABOUT 4PM on a cold January afternoon when he tapped on my canvas bivvy. The man wore the look of a diligent official who took neither pride nor regret in asking that I leave. I enquired whether he was the landowner. He said he was not, but claimed to be 'his agent'. He rested his walking cane against the trunk of a tree and pulled his hood up over his thick head of hair, while explaining simply that the owner would rather I not rest beside the river.

I politely asked for a name, which he politely gave. But it meant nothing to me. An unknown string of syllables that I'd forgotten as soon as he'd said them, partly because I'd expected him to refuse to say anything; mostly because I wondered how far I would need to paddle before I'd be off the man's land and out of sight of his agent.

I'd left that morning during the early hours of light, pushing out from the mudflats, sea couch, godwits and sandpipers around the Tamar estuary, arriving late afternoon in the freshwater where silver grayling swim among rush pasture and fens. My plan had been to make for several wooded areas on the bank, but as the light began to fade I chose to make for an early bed, before returning on the tide the next morning.

The source of the Tamar is at Woolley Moor, less than 6.5km (4 miles) from the north coast of Cornwall, but the river heads south, entering the sea in Plymouth, on the south Devon side. The Tamar is a busy navigation inland all the way to Weir Quay, near Bere Alston, where the estuary narrows into the tidal river. It's possible to navigate vessels 42km (26 miles) inland to Weir Head, near Gunnislake. **Tamar Valley Discovery Trail** follows much of the river route for 48km (30 miles) through Cornwall and Devon, past Bere Ferrers, Gunnislake and Milton Abbot. There is camping to be had along the way at various quays on request. Some of the quieter, unofficial moorings or hideaways are upstream of Calstock among the fields of daisies and lilies, where their broad leaves carpet the riverbanks. Space is always extremely limited or uneven, so consider carrying either a bivvy or a hammock.

The Tamar Valley Discovery Trail follows much of the river and links with the Two Castles Trail and West Devon Way to form a 145km (90-mile) path known as the West Devon Triangle.

PRACTICAL INFO Walk and camp along the Tamar Valley Discovery Trail, stopping at Blaxton Wood quay (50.44971, -4.1612357) on the River Tavy. It's possible to fish and bivvy 24 hours from the shore around the tidal waters of Kingsmill Lake, west of Neal Point (but please check changes to fishing status) (50.429256, -4.2077997). Access by footpath or canoe and kayak.

TRAVEL Trains and buses take you into Plymouth, Calstock and Gunnislake. Buses run into Bude and Launceston, from where village services run out to the river.

15 RIVER MEDWAY

THE MEDWAY IS HOME to one of my favourite outdoor writers, Marion Shoard. I interviewed her recently for a magazine about her concerns over polytunnels, the plastic arched structures farmers are using to cover the countryside to extend their growing seasons. In between, I asked her why she had recently moved from Surrey to Strood, on the Medway's north shore, 'where thistles run wild'.

'I amble along, endlessly dazzled by the beauty,' she said. 'Endlessly stopping to examine a flower, insect, rock or building. The North Kent marshes are wonderful for birdwatching. If I had more time I'd try to run minibus trips here for older people who can't get out and about. As well as the creeks, shores and saltings, there are woods and stretches of downland turf around here, but also a lot of post-industrial landscapes, which I like. Lots of disused chalk quarries.'

The Romans occupied the lower Medway Valley, and the Domesday Book records show that the Normans held important estates linked to castles at Rochester, Allington, Leeds and West Malling. The 18th-century Enclosures saw an end to the limited common land of the Medway. Fruit-growing and hops have historically made the region profitable, and watermills have

powered industry for thousands of years, to mill corn, smelt iron and pump water.

The Medway (113km/70 miles) feeds into the Thames Estuary at Sheerness, in Kent. About 21km (13 miles) pass through Sussex. The river is navigable for 69km (43 miles) from Tonbridge Wharf to the Thames Estuary. It is tidal from Allington Lock. There are many places to wild camp along the way, especially around some of the ten locks, which are grassy and mostly quiet after dark. Overnighting is available at Marlin Canoe Club campsite (51.223003, 0.42024314), downstream of Yalding Bridge, by contacting 020 8650 0197. Toilets and showers are available on an Environment Agency site nearby by calling 01622 752864.

From Rochester to Tonbridge, the **Medway Valley Walk** (45km/28 miles) follows the river, and then links with the Greensand Way, North Downs Way, Saxon Shore Way and Wealdway.

PRACTICAL INFO Paddle out to Darnet Fort, a popular wild camp for canoeists and kayakers. An old Ministry of Defence (MOD) site, permission may be needed (51.406338, 0.59861412), but no one ever asks in my experience. Trek the Medway Valley Walk and aim to sleep along the quietest and prettiest section of the river – surrounded by hop farms, gravel pits and sluices – from Branbridges (51.208325, 0.39267368) to Tonbridge (51.195514, 0.27666493).

TRAVEL Trains and buses take you into Rochester, Maidstone and Tonbridge.

16 SOUTH DEVON RIAS

THE SOUTH DEVON SHORELINE explores the fringes of four English 'lochs'. They are known collectively as the South Devon Rias: the Kingsbridge, Avon, Erme and Yealm estuaries.

They may be within a few miles of the UK's busiest summer resorts, but overnighting around these waters is the only chance to witness something very few people get to see. All four rias can be explored on foot, but are really best taken on by kayak or canoe. Inside these flooded valleys are wooded hills that were once home to tenant farmers and fishermen. Today, they are locked, silent and deserted.

That's a curse or a blessing. Depending how you look at it. On the downside, the profits generated down the centuries from the salt pans, fisheries and crops have meant the land is now virtually closed to

the public. According to the Domesday Book, this region was one of the most beautiful and profitable assets in England. But gain and desirability can lead to jealous protectionism, and most common land was enclosed by the 18th century. The shutdown is evident today by the almost total lack of footpaths and bridleways. Apart from areas such as Torbay, these waters, creeks and woodlands have remained hidden from view for most of the last 200 years.

The upside? Tidal navigation is enshrined as a right under the Magna Carta and these areas have been virtually untouched by development and tourism, which means if you can find a way in, along a forgotten path or in a canoe, this uniquely untouched piece of coast offers seclusion.

Dartmoor is the water source of the rivers that feed into the South Devon Rias.

KINGSBRIDGE ESTUARY

The slate lies so perfectly broken over the foreshore that it looks like a mosaic of Mediterranean carpet laid by craftsmen. Mounds of black, green and white seaweed are knotted over rocky shores. Cliffs covered in gorse and white flowering hawthorn rise 12m (40ft) above the waterline. Climb over, and beyond the bushes you'll find marshes, reed beds, egrets, and black crows the size of eagles. The wet, grassy fields heave with yellow dandelions where geese graze and butterflies chase April flowers, while cock sparrows chirp dryly and repetitively, the way they did around town houses in the 1970s.

Nine separate creeks flow into the estuary. From Kingsbridge, there is a car park to launch around high tide to Salcombe and its sand beaches. Frogmore and Southpool creeks trail off to the east and both have pubs at the end.

There's a single footpath south of West Charleton that leads across fields on to the foreshore. From here it's possible to explore much of the estuary at low tide to find camping spots around the beaches or

hanging from the salt-beaten branches of trees. Check times and be wary of cut-off. There are several other paths and good estuary views on to the foreshore north of Salcombe and Batson Creek.

RIVER AVON

Flocks of swans sit about the creeks at low tide. They share their place with hundreds of white gulls and egrets, against the backdrop of mud and blue sky, creating an image that this place is somehow holy. Trees hang over the foreshore, the sagginess and fine age of their boughs and branches seeming to mirror the ostentatious swagger of the old, rich houses and estates that rest back from the water's edge. Signs warn that the foreshore is 'private' and that 'netting is illegal'.

The tidal road south-west of Aveton Gifford needs to be walked at a leisurely pace. Just before Stakes Hill is a footpath that follows the line of a creek towards Were Down, through woodland. Not a place to camp, but worth a few hours. There are several footpaths on the other side of the river, north of Buckland, which link with the

South West Coast Path. My advice would be to pitch late and leave early.

RIVER ERME

The River Erme can only be explored by canoe as far up as the weir at Flete. The river is inside the Flete Estate, which has poor and narrow access by road. There is one good footpath near Ermington, either side of the river.

Elvers and young brown trout can be seen in the still, deep waters around the river bends in April. The white water moves fast around the shingle, inlets and sandy islands of yellow dandelion flowers. Kestrels and buzzards hover and glide over the same fields.

The best access and camping is near the sandy river mouth, at low tide, from the **South West Coast Path**, around Wrinkle Wood on the east side and the old Coastguard Cottages on the west. To find the more hidden places along the foreshore, it's really necessary to canoe or kayak in at high tide and then rest and enjoy the sandy shallows and occasional creeks once the waters have begun to recede for six or so hours.

RIVER YEALM

I got talking to a man who rented a house on the River Yealm. He worked from home for a living; canoed and sailed with his family in the estuary for pleasure. He described the creeks 'like something out of *Apocalypse Now*'. There are very few ways into this site other than by canoe. We stood there, the two of us, gaping at the horizon as the sun went down and watching the tide recede on the ebb.

Apparently, a few years ago, a local discovered a footpath between Brixton and South Barton, on the western side of the river, that had been lost over time. It was reinstated by the council and the landowner. It's one of the most beautiful river walks I've taken. There's also some river access around Newton Ferrers and the South West Coast Path.

The Yealm takes its name from the Celtic word for 'kind'. Bridgend Quay is a place to launch on to Newton Creek or to walk around. Leave west out of Noss Mayo, around Noss Creek, on to Passage Road. This single track passes thickets of poplar, maple and ash trees, which rise from the foreshore.

The upper river is inside the Kitley Estate, an area famous for oyster beds. Although access to the creeks is limited, there's a small parking space south of Combe (just a few hundred metres west of Brixton), right next to Cofflete Creek and a disused railway line. Only canoes and kayaks are allowed past Madge Point for 4km (2.5 miles), but stepping outside the foreshore isn't allowed.

If you become stranded by the low tide and need to find a secluded place to sleep until the waters return, Cofflete Creek is about as quiet a place as I've ever come across, much of it surrounded by oak woodland, bluebells and gorse.

Shortaflete Creek – wedged between woodland on either side – is a quiet place to relax for lunch.

PRACTICAL INFO At Kingsbridge, bivvy or hammock around the foreshore and beach under the trees and cliffs around Wareham Point (50.255273, -3.7568951). Around the River Avon, explore the birdlife and wildfowl from the tidal road, footpaths and woodland west of Aveton Gifford (50.306802, -3.8488626).

For the River Erme, fish and camp 24 hours on the sandbanks around Erme Mouth (50.310612, -3.9452934) or else launch a kayak/canoe from Owen's Hill (50.311681, -3.9472032) with tent and sleeping bag and paddle the river at dusk on a full tide.

At the Yealm, paddle a canoe or kayak up the peaceful Cofflete Creek (50.332888, -4.0490413), or take a slow walk from Brixton to South Barton along the waterside footpath (50.336148, -4.0421104) – one of the few paths with water access around any of the rias.

TRAVEL Trains and buses take you into Plymouth, Ivybridge, Totnes and Kingswear.

ON HELFORD EVENINGS I listen to the sounds of the night: water, wind and tricks of the mind.

Round here, I usually prefer to hang. Hammocks strung from the branches of great willows, their weeping leaves draped over the river like tender mobiles on a baby's crib. Strange that such a simple act of defying gravity creates such a feeling of peaceful grandeur; like freewheeling down a hill on a cheap bike. Tonight, however, I chose the floor, a soft, marsh mattress of groundsheet and foreshore between the little egrets nesting high in the trees and the eelgrass spread out diagonally over the mud.

Helford River is a flooded valley at the southern end of Falmouth Bay on the south coast of Cornwall. Its estuary waters cover a 9.5km (6-mile) tidal area from the coast, inland to Gweek, a port since Roman times. At the head of the Helford River is a noisy boatbuilding and repair centre, and then a quieter Gweek seal sanctuary.

Oysters have been harvested here since the third century BC, which is perhaps why the waters are owned by the Duchy of Cornwall, an anomaly that means the tidal fishing rights are retained by the royal family rather than freemen – us, the people. Some areas are also a bass nursery, which makes fishing from a canoe or kayak an offence. Some archaic, communal shellfish collections remain a tradition. Locals gather on the beach on Good Friday as they're allowed to collect cockles.

Wild camping is allowed at Tremayne Quay by the National Trust. The Quay was built in the 19th century in anticipation of a visit by Queen Victoria (which then never happened). Camping is also common at Turnaware Bar and Roundwood Quay in the Fal Estuary below the high tideline, although check byelaws. A report by Natural England – one of the bodies that protects and monitors the area – recently stated that much of the camping was 'associated with anchoring of yachts or motorboats offshore'. The National Trust also manages much of the surrounding woodland, which is inaccessible unless arriving by boat. Spring is the best time to visit, when bluebells, wood anemone and campion flush the woodland floor with flowers of blue, white and pink.

There are numerous creeks feeding into the ria on both sides, most of which are not passable by anything bigger than a canoe or kayak. The inlets mean there are almost 45km (28 miles) of shoreline to explore. For experienced kayakers, the river links into Falmouth Bay and the adjoining River Fal.

A ferry crosses the river to Helford Point every day between April and October. Canoes and small dinghies can be hired from the village boatyard or close to the Helford Passage.

The **South West Coast Path** follows the line of the Helford before crossing it via the ferry, then either west towards the Lizard or east to Falmouth and St Austell. A footpath runs east out of Helston towards Gweek, but other than a short path around the point of Frenchman's Pill, the off-road walking and cycling access is limited.

Good pubs are the Ferryboat Inn, over the Helford Passage, the Gweek Inn and the Shipwrights Arms in Helford.

PRACTICAL INFO Canoe-camp around the muddy creeks and inlets on the foreshore just after high tide (50.089040, -5.1781058).
TRAVEL Trains take you into Falmouth, from where there are occasional buses to Mawnan Smith and Durgan.

THE PEBBLE SHORE of the Lymington River at Brockenhurst reflects the warm colour of autumn trees. Red, orange and amber stones shine like polished marbles from beneath the white-water shallows. Grassy mounds are safe islands for nervous dippers, and lazy ducks. Muntjac deer prance several feet from the ground, their slender legs folded back like ballet performers in flight over an outdoor stage.

The only way to see the New Forest properly is from its rivers and watery paths. Sadly, fences criss-cross the land in an offensive maze of wire designed to keep the waterways private. Even the occasional bridleways have been diverted at obscure angles and out into endless wrong directions away from the rivers.

Once you do manage to reach waterside, it's evident that these routes see limited traffic. Bulrushes the size of lamp posts stand erect like frozen aliens that were about to invade the urban estates.

This forest area was once known as Ytene or 'land of the Jutes', after the Anglo-Saxon tribes that lived there. William I created the 'New Forest' in the 11th century, with a 'new', single boundary. The forest was kept exclusively for hunting deer and theft of the king's venison was punishable by death. The rights of commoners were re-established by The New Forest Act 1877, although most of the land is still owned by the Crown and managed by the Forestry Commission. The 'royal' prerogative still hangs in the air.

Night-time sleep is restricted to the tidal reaches of the rivers and asking for permission from landowners, pubs and farmers. The New Forest Authority has byelaws in place restricting wild camping on most of the land. The justification for this ban is that some campers long ago caused criminal damage.

Some of the hidden areas around streams and thickets of pine, oak and holly make for beautiful daytime 'picnic camps', which rangers will not move in on. Sleeping next to your picnic between the hours of sunrise and sunset is permitted, which means, quite unreasonably, it is possible to sit up all night talking and then fall asleep with the dawn into a plate of cucumber sandwiches.

The broadleaf trees were mostly cut down in the early part of the 20th century to make way for pine and heath, but traditional woodland is finally being reintroduced. The entire forest area is rich in springs and streams for water. Although cycling is popular in the forest, I'm of the opinion you need to either walk or canoe to really settle in.

The cycle network covers several hundred miles, but tends to get busy, and bikes leaving the official waymarked paths in search of solitude risk a fine. Walkers, on the other hand, can go anywhere. It's amazing just how wild the forest can seem even when you're a few hundred yards from the road, hidden from the cyclists and the white gravel paths.

The **Lymington River** is navigable for canoes and kayaks almost all the way to Brockenhurst. To the north-west of the town is one of my favourite walks, through the narrow waterways, wearing thick waterproof boots. The neighbouring Beaulieu (see page 81) is the only lengthy tidal route that enters the forest proper, and offers a few opportunities to overnight along the foreshore mouth of the river, at low tide, in between either navigating or fishing.

> **PRACTICAL INFO** Paddle the river from its estuary at Waterford (50.762381, -1.5350492) to Brockenhurst (50.817205, -1.5490740).
> **TRAVEL** Trains take you into Ashurst, Beaulieu Road, Brockenhurst and Sway. Buses stop at Lyndhurst, Lymington and Ringwood.

19 SCILLY ISLES

I'LL BE HONEST. I love the sea, just not as much as I love mud. At Southend beach as a kid, I waited for the Saturdays and Sundays when the water was out all day. Low tide exposes the black slick that we could sink in up to our knees. We walked a mile offshore, had mud fights, netted shrimps, went crabbing, jumped the warm water creeks, played football and rounders, swam clean, dodged the jellyfish and then collected periwinkles for Sunday-night tea on the way home. Back onshore, we'd wait for the tide to come in. The perfect day was a 5 o'clock high tide, so the sun had all day to heat the mud like a solar-powered electric blanket. I rarely pass an exposed, wet-mud estuary without wanting to be out in it. Wanting to feel salty water pools against bare feet.

The **Scilly Isles archipelago** is the opposite of the Thames microcosm. It's bigger, better, shallower, wilder and warmer. There are 140 islands and islets 45km (28 miles) off Land's End. Just five are inhabited, and all are part of Cornwall. The Duchy of Cornwall owns most, after they were seized during the Norman conquests. The uninhabited areas are managed by the Isles of Scilly Wildlife Trust, which 'leases' the lands from the Duchy for the rent of one daffodil per year. Most properties on the inhabited islands are tenanted rather than privately owned.

Since 1930, the islands have had their own 'county council' known as the Council of the Isles of Scilly. The economy survives mostly on tourism, with agriculture and fishing being the other main trades.

Flower-farming does well as the islands almost never suffer frosts, although the northern isles suffer from harsh winds.

Many of the islands can be walked at low tide. There is a campsite on St Martin's, close to the beach. Wild camping is not allowed, but 24-hour fishing is (which necessitates the need to sleep), as is the right to navigate the islands by canoe or kayak. Navigation of the vast coastline inevitably means vessels running aground at low tide. The waters are shallow, so it is wise to carry a bivvy, warm clothing and food to wait for the tide to return after six hours. Although it is not an offence to sleep while waiting for the tide, anyone camping when the water is in may be asked to move on. Shellfish, mackerel and shrimps can be caught around the rocky areas. Virtually every footpath follows the outline of the coastal edges of the islands.

PRACTICAL INFO Forage on seashells and fish 24 hours around the Eastern Isles, south of St Martin's (49.948536, -6.2625177).

TRAVEL Fly from Exeter, Newquay and Land's End airports or travel by ferry from Penzance. Kayaks and canoes can be taken on the ferry.

20 CHICHESTER HARBOUR

FIELDS OF ONIONS, kale and green leaf are separated from the beach by borders of clover, dandelions and insects. The high tide washes over and up to the sea wall, but there are places to pull back without getting trapped.

This 57sq km (22sq miles) of natural harbour on the Solent is a sunken bowl between West Sussex and Hampshire, below the South Downs. The Romans made a military base here and then built a road to London from nearby Dell Quay. Although the waters are shallow, trade, fishing and oyster-farming have continued for thousands of years until today.

An ancient causeway known as the Wade Way was once the main path on to Hayling Island from the mainland. A channel and canal now means it is not entirely passable on foot, but the path is visible at low tide.

The harbour waters and surrounding land are managed by Chichester Harbour Conservancy, which is regulated by byelaws under an Act of Parliament that stipulated it must conserve, maintain and improve the harbour areas for recreation, natural conservation and natural beauty.

Winter is the best time to visit Chichester Harbour, as the beach areas at Wittering and East Head can become popular in fine months. Canoes and kayaks are suited to exploring the endless narrows that branch off the three main waterways: the Emsworth Channel, the Thorney Channel and the Chichester Channel. There are many footpaths and byways that pass around the

harbour, linking it to the Downs, London, and the south-west and south-east coast.

The beach is mostly flat and stony, so much so I once cycled around almost the entire edge. Dog walkers and runners are the only visitors at dawn and dusk. The creeks, the sailors and their yachts separate the homes and church spires on the other side of the water from the wild. Trees are frozen by the wind, trapped in their twisted shells, even when the wind stops blowing. The natural sea wall provides a kind windbreak for sleepers resting on the southerly parts of Thorney Island. It has the best views, too, and lots of tree shelter.

The **Sussex Border Path** enters and exits the harbour along a 14.5km (9-mile) coastal circuit of Thorney Island. It finishes 220km (137 miles) away to the east, along the south coast at Rye, in East Sussex. It links to the South Downs and the Sussex borders with Surrey, Kent and Hampshire.

The Wayfarers Walk (114km/71 miles) enters north from Inkpen Beacon in Berkshire, where it meets the Test Way. The Lipchis Way connects the harbour's resort town of West Wittering to the South Downs Way and Monarch's Way, via Chichester and Liphook.

> **PRACTICAL INFO** Walk along the isolated beach off Chidham Point (50.814667, -0.88622074) and camp on the foreshore around Farlington Marshes (50.831529, -1.0290104).
> **TRAVEL** Trains and buses take you into Hayling Island and Chichester.

21 HARTLAND

THEY CALL THIS the Shipwreck Coast. Ships navigating in and out of the Bristol Channel have a tiny gap to avoid being blown on to the rocks of Wales and Devon on either side.

I met a camper on the South West Coast Path and he asked where I was stopping next. I explained I was on the way to Hartland. He said when he was there last, he could hardly open the pub door, the wind was so strong. I arrived two days later and saw tree trunks and branches bent horizontal to the land like petrified carcasses being sucked into a vacuum.

Hartland is Devon's most north-westerly point. The name derives from the Old English word 'heort', for a deer.

The **South West Coast Path** leads backpackers through the Hartland peaks, beaches and caves. Pods of dolphins swim past the bay at dusk. The National Trails website suggests that wild camping 'is normally tolerated if you have a small tent,

discreetly pitch it in the evening, pack up early in the morning and leave no trace of your stay'.

Beach camping should be restricted to hours outside of high tides, and great care needs to be taken around many of the cliff top areas as the path is crumbling due to severe erosion. Slate barbs rise from the low tide like shards of layered black glass randomly fallen to Earth into the soft, shallow bed of the Atlantic Ocean. If the weather is particularly bad, there are many large campsites along the path that take in walkers travelling with tents.

Just to the east of Hartland, the rivers Taw and Torridge are major tidal inlets that flush south towards Dartmoor, but both need to be explored by canoe as footpath access is limited. The Tarka Trail (290km/180 miles) follows a small section of the Torridge and links up with the Taw.

PRACTICAL INFO Walk slowly along the cliffs from Clovelly along the South West Coast Path to Embury Beach (50.944238, -4.5441350) via Hartland, stopping to rest or overnight on sandy coves along the way, which change with the tides.
TRAVEL Trains and buses take you into Barnstaple and Okehampton, from where bus services run to Hartland, Westward Ho!, Clovelly, Bideford and Stratton.

GOLF IS MY FAVOURITE pastime when I'm at home. The founding fathers of Royal St. George's chose to set up home on the 'links' ground – an area defined as linking the land to the sea – at Sandwich. For all their prestige, those beaches remain in full public ownership with foreshore rights to fish and navigate the tide around the clock. Apart from a rather expensive toll road for motor vehicles and one or two prohibitive signs, the golfing classes and their private residents work hard to maintain and keep open bridleways and footpaths.

The view from Prince's Street, which gets its name from the equally famous Prince's golf course, is especially good at low tide. The 10km (6-mile) long beach provides a good place for the angler, weary walker or seafarer to bed down for the night after dark.

The white chalk and flint from Cliffs End, south of Ramsgate, down to Dover can be walked along White Cliffs Country Trail. As part of the North Downs formation, the cliffs reach up to 110m (350ft). For many people, they are a symbol of our resistance over the last hundred years to European invasion. Heroic stories of the Second World War will often depict air fighters returning from Germany or France past the iconic coastline.

The mixture of soft white chalk and the skeletal remains of ocean creatures and sediment creates the unique bright tones that light up the beaches, even on a dark day. The **Saxon Shore Way** (262km/163 miles) moves north and south, past the Thames and Medway marshes to Gravesend, and all the way round to the White Cliffs of Dover and the superhighway the North Downs Way (201km/125 miles), before cutting across East Sussex to Hastings.

PRACTICAL INFO Walk the Saxon Shore Way from Stourmouth (51.321386, 1.2378656) out to the coast, and then south towards Folkestone, to meet the North Downs Way at Samphire Hoe Country Park (51.104406, 1.2682995). Sleep on the foreshore and beaches.
TRAVEL Trains and buses take you into Sandwich, Deal and Dover.

23 DARTMOOR – EAST AND SOUTH

THE DARTMOOR PONIES are less intimidating than the hounds of the Baskervilles that hunt the moors of the imagination at night, but no less hardy.

Dartmoor covers 954sq km (368sq miles) and isn't short of visitors across the more popular trails. People are outnumbered, though, by skylarks. They are everywhere, singing in multiple stereo; rising from grass and rock like tiny kites on invisible cords being pulled into a stiff breeze. The moment the line is at its maximum, they sing for glory.

Dartmoor has more Bronze Age settlements than anywhere else in the UK – maybe 10,000 ancient sites, stone circles and pagan tors. Wild living on moors of cowslips, bog, granite and rain-lashed winters can be harsh. Even Dartmoor Prison has a reputation for being escape-proof because of its location. This is the only land in the UK – outside of Scotland – where wild camping is enshrined as a right. Maybe it was the harshness of the landscape that prompted the old barons and lords to forget. And for that we should be grateful. Because spring and summer here are a joy.

The Forest of Dartmoor is the single largest tract of private land, owned by the Duke of Cornwall. The right to camp extends to almost all the upland areas, though more than half of the park is in private hands. Most of the rest is classified as common land. It was tradition on Dartmoor until the 19th century that anyone building a house in a day and having a fire lit in the hearth by nightfall could claim a right to the land.

Dartmoor's highest points are in the north; High Willhays and Yes Tor at 621m (2,037ft) and 619m (2,031ft) respectively.

Ryder's Hill is the highest in the south at 515m (1,690ft). Walkers seem to know every tor and peak. They point and call out the names one by one like proud parents introducing their protégé children to a talent scout. Dartmoor's most famous peak is Hey Tor at 457m (1,499 ft).

High up, the grass masses into a mattress of green and white. It's soft and good for sleeping. Ticks can be problem so it's wise to wear gaiters, apply tick repellent and carry a tick remover.

I met an emergency ranger team on the moor. They rescue about 50 people a year, mostly walkers with sprained ankles or Duke of Edinburgh's Award groups getting lost. I chuckled. One of the rescuers pointed ominously towards the middle of the moor. 'There are no paths out there,' he said. Two unique features make sticking to official footpaths wise. The Ministry of Defence (MOD) uses some areas for tests (red flags are flown to warn the public) and the moor is infamous for its dangerous bogs.

But hundreds of miles of footpaths mean

on Meldon Hill and a little east, south of the river at Cranbrook Castle. There are excellent footpaths all along this northerly section of the Teign, which passes through a series of woods known as Whiddon, Hannicombe, Hore, Bridford, Cod and many more. The River Teign Walk (71km/44 miles) follows much of the river from its source on Dartmoor to the foreshore.

The woodland around the River Bovey is dramatic, especially after rain. Some of the best camping can be had around the woodland north of Lustleigh beside the River Bovey. It's one of the very few areas within the moor where woodland camping is enshrined as a right.

The fallen remains of oak and sycamore trees lay along the banks of the River Dart. Hardier conifers, thin and pine-less, bloom into canopies as they reach the sky, many of the lower limbs choked off by vines and lichen. Once the Dart leaves Dartmoor, the river traffic can be busy below Totnes Weir, but the creeks are peaceful, as are the walks upriver into the moor. Dittisham, Stoke Gabriel and Totnes are good places to launch canoes using the ebb or flood. The John Musgrave Heritage Trail (56km/35 miles) links the South West Coast Path and crosses the river at Dittisham, before leaving the bank at Totnes to the north-east.

Hamel Down (529m/1,736ft) is the highest section on the eastern moor. The Hurston Ridge, south of Chagford Common, reaches 489m (1,604ft). The Two Moors Way provides good access to both.

that sticking to traditional routes is rarely a burden. The longest trails are the 163km (102-mile) **Two Moors Way**, the 57km (35-mile) West Devon Way, the 138km (86-mile) Dartmoor Way and the 79km (49-mile) Dartmoor Ramble. The West Devon Way navigates the western side and links with the Tarka Trail. The Dartmoor Way includes a route for cyclists and walkers. The Dartmoor Ramble visits Belstone, Chagford, North Bovey and Postbridge. The rivers East Dart and West Dart flow through the moor and enter the sea at Dartmouth.

EAST DARTMOOR

The east is dominated by its peaks and four rivers, the Dart, the Teign, the Bovey and the Webburn.

The River Teign is easily navigable all the way into the moor at Piddledown Common and Sharp Tor just north of the river. There are forts here on either side of the river. There's good camping just south of Chagford

SOUTH DARTMOOR

South Dartmoor contains some of the oldest known burial monuments in Britain, dating back to 4500 BC. There are two stone rows, linked to chambers, at Corringdon Ball and Butterdon Hill, Ugborough Common, one of which is more than a mile (1.6km) long. All the peaks in this area are former prehistoric burial mounds.

The River Erme rises on Dartmoor, on the Abbot's Way, just south of where the

River Plym rises. The Erme runs towards an area known as The Meadow, where it is crossed by the Upper Erme stone row, which at 3.3km (2 miles) long may be the longest ancient monument of its kind in the world. It still contains more than a thousand rocks, which lead from the Kiss-in-the-Ring stone circle at the south to a cairn near the top of Green Hill in the north.

The Two Moors Way, out of Ivybridge, leads up to good camping on Brent Moor, just north of the Old Hill Settlements and Bala Brook. Alternatively, follow the River Plym out of Dewerstone Wood along the granite boulders up into the heights of Green Hill (473m/1,551ft) and Ryders Hill (515m/1,690ft). The moss-covered trees and rocks fade against the greenery of the grass sedges to create a velvet coating of smooth carpet that lines the walls and floor of this base camp. The best time to come is in autumn when the golden-brown bracken lies broken across the velvet moss. The river flows out to the city of Plymouth.

Among some of the other highlights to see are the Grey Wethers Stone Circle, Hound Tor, the Beardown Man, the Hawthorn Tree on Saddle Tor, the stone circle cairn on Dartmoor known as both the Nine Maidens and the Seventeen Brothers, and the fields of bluebells at Emsworthy Mire in May.

PRACTICAL INFO Camp and fish under trees along the sand and stone beaches of the River Dart, just south of Totnes (50.417050, -3.6674595).

To the east, walk in Houndtor Wood, along the River Bovey, to Lustleigh Cleave (50.6118, -3.7379), before a short trek south for lunch at Becky Falls (50.6064, -3.7559). Explore stone rows and circle around the River Erme, on Erme Plain, over a southern section of the moor, just to the west of Two Moors Way (50.4743, -3.9209).

TRAVEL EAST DARTMOOR Trains take you into Newton Abbot, Exeter and Yeoford, bus on into villages and towns of the moor. SOUTH DARTMOOR Travel by train to the outskirts of Dartmoor at Ivybridge, Buckfastleigh and Newton Abbot. Bus services run from the towns into Dartmoor proper.

THE HILLTOPS in the north-west are characterised by severe weather, deer grass, blanket bog, moss and lichens. Some of the plants up here are more common in the Arctic. High Willhays (621m/2,037ft) and Yes Tor (619m/2,031ft) are the two highest points in the south of England. Yes Tor is known as the roof of Devon, although slightly lower than Willhays. They are the only summits in England south of the Peak District (and the Black Mountain range on the Welsh/English border) to rise above 610m (2,000ft). Just south of both these peaks are more isolated and quieter camping areas around Dinger Tor, Lints Tor and Great Kneeset.

Care is needed when leaving the main paths, especially when the ground is boggy. Red flags are raised around the areas when live-firing is due to take place by the MOD, which means entry is blocked. The Dartmoor National Park provides an online map of all Range Danger Areas. The map is also shaded purple where wild camping is allowed and pink where it is not.

The **West Devon Way** (56km/35 miles) follows the west edge of Dartmoor over the 29km (18 miles) between Okehampton and Tavistock, and then 27km (17 miles) to Plymouth. It joins with the Tarka Trail at Okehampton.

PRACTICAL INFO Find a wild camp in the north, between Kitty Tor and Lints Tor, one of the quieter parts of north Dartmoor, just north of the hut circles (50.669841, -4.0188928).

TRAVEL Trains and buses take you into Ivybridge, Buckfastleigh, Calstock, Okehampton, Meldon and Exeter.

25 EXMOOR

THE GOAT WAS UNSETTLING.
Nothing ever wakes me. Not even drunken flatmates returning from Gomorrah.

Quite why a wild goat was so damn troubling before 6am was a puzzle. Bleating into my unconscious. I wondered how far away it was and who else was awake. It was enough to get me out, looking over the blackberry bushes down into the bay at Porlock. This place they call Little Switzerland. And then it went quiet. And the sun came up. And I was relieved to be alone in silence again.

These tracks were left over when the Saxon manors were seized. Tree cover accounts for less than 10,000ha (25,000 acres) of broadleaf and conifer, but at least there's no shortage of coastal views. The recently planted pines are most common as the ancient woodlands have been chopped for wood and farming. It began long before the arrival of the Normans,

who implemented 'forest law' as a way to normalise the governance of land and the removal of people. This meant that Exmoor was controlled by a warden of the forest, who would charge the tenant farmers left some limited grazing rights. Poachers and forest lawbreakers suffered harsh punishments here.

The last of Exmoor's trees were removed by the 16th century, although by then it was mostly moorland anyway, with sporadic grazing of animals allowed as forest laws were relaxed. More than 60 per cent of the moor was ploughed in the 20th century for crops and livestock. The remnants of old woodland have been mostly protected since the 1960s.

The Devonshire side – around Lynton – to the west of Porlock is slightly wilder. Bog valleys weave their way around mustard yellow and green semicircular peaks. The Exmoor National Park Authority owns much of the land and doesn't object to wild camping. In a presentation of the Authority's Annual Estate Review 2010/11 to the resources and performance committee on 12 July, 2011, a part of the report read:

> Wild camping or bivying [sic] as part of a long distance walk for example can be desirable for visitors and the Authority will be more tolerant of this type of camping than multiday stays supported by a vehicle... Camping will only normally be allowed by agreement but there may be some locations where 'wild camping' spots could be agreed without a need to confirm permission with us.

The River Exe enters the park from the south, and is navigable almost the entire length from north of Exebridge to south of Exeter. There are more than 965km (600 miles) of path for cyclists and walkers, including the Two Moors Way (145km/ 90 miles) from Cheriton and Tarr Steps, Exmoor, into Dartmoor.

The **Exe Valley Way** (84km/52 miles) trails down from the north-west moor section through the tree-lined valleys, crossing the River Exe several times and following it into the west side of Exmouth on the south coast. The Tarka Trail, the Coleridge Way and Macmillan Way West are other main routes over the moor.

PRACTICAL INFO Walk the Macmillan Way West to Dunkery Beacon (51.162345, -3.5862403) via the ancient Rowbarrows. Wild camp off the path close to Codsend Moor. Walk out of Birchleave Wood, south of beautiful Simonsbath, along the River Barle. Pick up the Two Moors Way (51.137206, -3.7522025) and find a camp along the riverbank of trees.

TRAVEL Trains and buses take you into Minehead, Washford, Watchet and Barnstaple.

26 BODMIN

STARS RADIATE from the night sky over the upland Bodmin plateau. Alone with ponies, mewing buzzards and Neolithic stone circles, I feel strangely comforted by the extraterrestrial bodies of the night, rather than the earthly ones. Perhaps it's because the stars are so far away, in time and space.

The Bodmin that I know is above the last wall, just north of Buttern Hill and south of Davidstow Moor. A stack of stones that looks as ancient as the pagan symbols inside. Moss, wild flowers and lichen climb the haphazard arrangement, which has fallen into a hotchpotch of immovability

cemented by time. I couldn't find a single boulder in that wall that would move or turn.

This crown of land in north-east Cornwall is 388sq km (150sq miles) of granite, moorland and gorse. The name 'Bodmin' comes from the 19th century, a name change over Fowey Moor, which it was historically called after the river that runs through it. It's a lonely place, even by Cornish standards. Raptors call out repeatedly like neglected, hungry children. The ponies are smaller, miniature, unassuming and rarely bothered. Neolithic and Bronze Age stone circles – sometimes no more than 15cm (6 inches) tall – are unmarked and unnoticed a few hundred yards from barely visible footpaths. Always carry a compass here. The moor is good for getting lost as well as for cycling.

The granite tors and rivers provide the most spectacular places to camp. Brown Willy is the highest point at 420m (1,377ft), and Rough Tor stands at almost 400m (1,300ft). Kilmar Tor and Caradon Hill are impressive hills. Much of the open moor is common land used for grazing. The marshier areas of the lowland moor are impossible to pass in winter, but dry out during long summer months.

The paths, tracks and bridleways feed into a substantial network of unmade roads and lanes. Most of these accommodate both walkers and cyclists, although some parts are more suitable to ramblers only.

The **Copper Trail** borders the moor for 97km (60 miles) via St Breward north of Bodmin and the Minions to the south-east. The Camel Trail, on the River Camel, skirts Bodmin and links to the South West Coast Path around the south coast. Several rivers rise on the moor. The Fowey rises at a height of 290m (950ft) and flows into the estuary at the port town it gives its name to. It is navigable to Golitha Falls. There are put-ins along the non-tidal stretch between Bodmin town and Liskeard, and between Golitha Falls and Treverbyn Mill. The River Inny joins with the Tamar, which flows out at Plymouth. The River Camel rises on Hendraburnick Down before it empties into the sea at Padstow 40km (25 miles) away.

RIVER FOWEY

A tall bottle of perfume, the size of my little finger, lay in the stones. I picked it up and saw the slender, rectangular body was ornately melted with narrow, recessed ribs. A tiny black plug sat inside its top, wedged into the perfectly round mouth like an oval cork inside a goldfish's pout. I rolled the glass around in my hand, and a little of the clear, odourless liquid seeped into my palm. The bottle rolled one more time to expose a six letter word: POISON.

I was momentarily overcome with fear, digging my fingers into the sandy shore, rubbing both palms against the shingle and each other, while sensing imaginary pain and breathlessness. Trout and salmon fry zigzagged and darted between the clean shallows of sunlight and the haphazard sprawl of fragmented boulders beyond the orange shale. The fish moved over and beneath the ancient rocks, submerged like a rugged mat-underlay to the Fowey's clear surface, and I momentarily forgot.

I reconsidered the likelihood that I had inhaled toxic fumes, but the moment was gone, replaced by the idea that the bottle was actually full of fresh water. It was a reminder that the wild, even its man-made intermissions, can serve up danger. But I'd moved on. A skylark sang, and I looked for more fish in the shallows under the shadows of the elder bushes.

The source of the River Fowey is on Bodmin Moor, at Brown Willy – the highest point in Cornwall. The river once gave its name to the moor, but that changed in the 19th century when Bodmin town became more influential. Many of the tidal areas are owned by the National Trust.

Outside of the open and highest parts of Bodmin Moor are lanes. Those wedged between the A30 and the river's Golitha Falls are the best access for walkers. This 9.5km (6-mile) route isn't off-road, it's better than that – a narrow, virtually traffic-free country lane, lined with wild flowers and old sycamores. Stunted oaks lean in to the river, covered in ivy, moss and flaked lichen.

Walking north or south, there are plenty of opportunities to cross the river into thickets to find a hidden place to bed down. Further south, fencing occasionally bars access between the road and the river shallows, but moving north the cover of undergrowth turns towards open moor. Coming from the south, canoes and kayaks can stay with the river. Larger craft can only pass the first 11km (7 miles), but canoes get access all the way until the river turns to rapids and white water. Hammocks can be strung on overhanging oaks, but there are also beaches at low tide that will accommodate a small tent or bivvy.

Several creeks empty of water at low tide beneath woodland slopes. Penpoll Creek, south of Lostwithiel, is only navigable two hours either side of high tide, making a canoe camp necessary for two eight-and-a-half-hour slots every 24 hours, if the traveller gets marooned. River Lerryn is also a place to explore on the high tide. Its creeks (known as Manely Pill, Wooda Pill and Mendy Pill) follow wooded areas that run down to the waterside. Footpaths circle around the Lerryn estuary, providing walkers and rod fishermen some access to the shore. Pont Pill passes through woodland and footpaths managed by the National Trust.

The **Saints' Way** follows the south-west part of the river, 47km (29 miles) from Fowey to Padstow. St Neot, Cardinham and Warleggan are three tributary rivers feeding into the Fowey.

27 QUANTOCK HILLS

MY FASCINATION with deer began as a boy, in Richmond Park. My grandfather lived next door, in a block of council flats separated from the estate by a yellow brick wall built higher than some of the trees on the other side. I would climb on to his communal garages, walk along the wall and then sit and spy on the hinds, the squirrels and the magpies. Eventually I'd get bored and jump down and in, from an oak next to the wall. The public entrance to the park was only a six- or seven-minute walk away. But exploring the wall was an adventure.

Walking along the Quantock range, there is that same sense of looking down into another world. I can hear grasshoppers in August. I sit on a flat stone in the heather and stare out among the gorse, looking for

red deer hinds, but only see pine trees and purple flowers. A silver-washed fritillary butterfly flits around a lone thistle, delicate brown wings purring against the purple, spiked flowers. The Gower is out beyond the heat haze, the Bristol Channel, and the ships that passed in the night.

The red deer were introduced into these hills – made famous by poets like Wordsworth – in the late 19th century, for hunting. Centuries before, the hills were strategic locations of war. Bronze Age settlers made their homes here. The Domesday Book refers to the area as Cantoctona, a title that means 'settlement on a circle of hills', taken from the Old English and Celtic. Several of the paths around the hills had military importance during the latter stages of Saxon rule in the 10th century. King Alfred battled the Viking invasion just south of the Quantocks, at Athelney. Many forts were linked along a road known as a 'herepath', which can still be seen between trees along the River Parrett, at Combwich, to Triscombe Stone, and west to the Brendon Hills and Exmoor.

Quantock Forest is a conifer plantation owned by the Forestry Commission, which doesn't officially allow night-time sleeping, but is open to walkers or cyclists day and night. Ash and oak still grow in some parts,

PRACTICAL INFO Walk up in winter for a view over Will's Neck (51.109445, -3.1929454) when the crowds have gone, looking out on to Bagborough Hill. Slide down from the Macmillan Way West into the surrounding woodland for shelter from the weather.

TRAVEL Trains and buses take you into Bridgwater and Taunton. The West Somerset Railway covers the western side of the hills to the coast at Watchet, between Minehead and Bishops Lydeard.

outside the Commission-owned land. Trees are thick throughout the hills, many of them lining the substantial network of trails and bridleways. The village of Aisholt was named after the trees that were cut down in the post-Saxon period.

The most obvious place to camp beyond the forests is along the rocky shoreline where tiny greysand coves provide somewhere to sleep at low tide. The River Parratt is navigable for canoes, and is tidal, passing far inland, beyond Bridgwater. The beach is famous for a creek, the Kilve Pill, that was once an old smugglers' route.

The **Macmillan Way West** (164km/102 miles) follows the middle of the Quantocks like a backbone, on its way between Devon and Somerset. The path crosses the Somerset Levels and joins the South West Coast Path and forms part of the main Macmillan Way from Boston in Lincolnshire to Barnstaple, Devon.

THE WHITE CLIFFS are breathtaking on a clear day; dramatic and romantic in rain. A chalk slice of cake props up the iced topping of the grassy South Downs. When the sun shines, the cliffs reflect brighter-than-marble pillars on a Greek temple. The waves carve at the stone and sandy base, keeping everything that is beautiful in a state of landslip and change. The air hums with spittle and surf and smells of rotten fish carcasses and discarded nets. Ferries sail on the horizon between Newhaven and Dieppe.

I could spend a week bivvying around the Seven Sisters in the company of skylarks, rabbits, chalk and butterflies. But I won't, because there's an entire 160km (100-mile) encampment to explore along the South Downs.

The **South Downs Way** is a pied-piper trail, circling over pastures of grazing cattle, forests and river valleys. In winter, the coast is soggy in salt, tide and fresh rainfall. Ditches, canals and river inlets, engineered by man to drain the land, are at times overwhelmed. Extensive and good footpaths leave the national trail, navigating the South Downs' quietest and wildest sections along its waterways. The Way crosses the tidal Cuckmere, Ouse, Adur and Arun, along which there are small areas of foreshore and beach to camp.

The path has become an important route for cyclists in the south. Linking Winchester to Eastbourne, this is the only national trail where cyclists have a legal right along the entire length. The path, along relatively flat terrain, is a good challenge for beginners. For canoes and kayaks, the rivers provide alternative trails to explore the Downs.

The high ground and woodland provides good shelter. Although much is now fenced and in private hands, there's no shortage of trees for hammocks. High ground on which to 'hide' from fellow walkers is sometimes limited. Campers should avoid National Trust and Natural England land unless there

is permission to sleep, as byelaws restricting sleeping are common in the south. There are very few formal campsites, other than a National Trust camp at Saddlescombe Farm, near Brighton, and a YHA South Downs hostel.

The excellent South Downs National Park Authority actively encourages wild camping on lands not protected (by infrequent byelaws). On its website in May 2013, Trail Officer Andy Gattiker stated:

Responsible wild camping can be a great way to enjoy and really connect with the countryside and we are aware that many people do wildcamp in the South Downs. Although there is no automatic right to wildcamp in England as there is in Scotland, you can still wildcamp anywhere with the landowners' permission. With a bit of forward planning or some polite enquiries along the way a very enjoyable time can be had. If you do get permission to wild camp, be discreet, do not have fires or leave any litter and leave the spot as you found it early the next morning.

It's a good idea to stock up on water, as there are limited streams and freshwater springs. Towns and villages along the way are relatively common.

The Vanguard Way joins with the South Downs Way at Alfriston, from where it trails north to the Ashdown Forest. The Shipwrights Way (80km/50 miles) runs from Alice Holt Forest across the South Downs and down to the sea.

PRACTICAL INFO Leave the South Downs Way where it meets the footpath north-west of Ashcombe Bottom trees (50.895346, -0.056136704) to forage in the woodland. Look for a sleeping spot along one of the highest points in West Sussex, around Graffham Downs (50.939046, -0.70342710).
TRAVEL Trains and buses take you into Eastbourne, Brighton and Winchester.

29 KENNET AND AVON CANAL

SAND MARTINS GLIDED PAST in triumphant waves of playfulness, like fast-flying fish, twisting on invisible surf. Dragonflies hung among the reed banks and we swayed our boats towards them beneath the harsh east breeze.

We were somewhere between Hilperton and Semington, in Wiltshire, when Paul suggested we could spin our kayaks around and paddle back the way we came, to attempt the Thames Estuary, in Essex, in less than a week.

This had never been the plan. We'd parked in Devizes and launched west, hoping to force our way against the prevailing wind. Our plan was to make for the River Avon, on to the Severn Estuary, and from there? Fate would decide. I wearily nodded, 'OK,' only to catch that he was wearing the smile of a man who was more determined than me to keep going – west. 'I was joking,' he said. We moved into a mild curve of the canal and hunched a little lower as the breeze lifted, along with my mood.

The Kennet and Avon Canal is 140km (87 miles) of navigable canal and river between Bath and Reading, linking London to the south-west and the River Severn. The fledgling plan for the waterway was initially challenged after the English Civil War by farmers worried about cheaper Welsh meat and crops. Landowners also made profits from tolls on turnpike roads. But the demand for a water link among merchants who stood to lose goods was too high to ignore. The opening happened in 1810 and from then on most of the barge traffic carried coal and stone. By the early part of the 20th century it had been made redundant by the Great Western Railway,

but recreational boating saw the entire route reopen in 1990.

The canal passes through North Somerset, and Wiltshire, to Reading, in West Berkshire. More than a hundred locks were built to climb the hilly terrain. Caen Hill Locks, at Devizes, are a series of locks that can take almost an entire day to navigate as the waterway rises 72m (237ft) in 3.2km (2 miles).

Navigation and access to the towpath is managed by the Canal & River Trust. Subject to approval from lock masters, the best camping is to be had around the North Wessex Downs, west of Brimpton Lock. The quieter parts are easier reached by canoe or kayak.

PRACTICAL INFO Take the 'three ways bridge' north-west of Semington over the Kennet and Avon Canal (51.346604, -2.1558356). From this point, choose whether to take the footpath north a few thousand yards on to the River Avon, or walk west along the north or south side of the canal. Leave the canal on the footpath east at Warleigh (51.376950, -2.3019173) to forage and walk in the woodland at Bathford Hill (51.389619, -2.2976034) and Warleigh Wood (51.370280, -2.2996634)

TRAVEL Trains and buses take you into Bath, Bradford on Avon, Pewsey, Bedwyn, Hungerford, Newbury, Thatcham and Reading.

The **Kennet and Avon Canal Walk** (122km/76 miles) links the River Thames at Reading with the River Avon at Bath. It also joins the Thames Path to the Cotswold Way National Trails. A 200km (125-mile) canoe marathon from Devizes to Westminster is held each year. Cycling is allowed along the towpath.

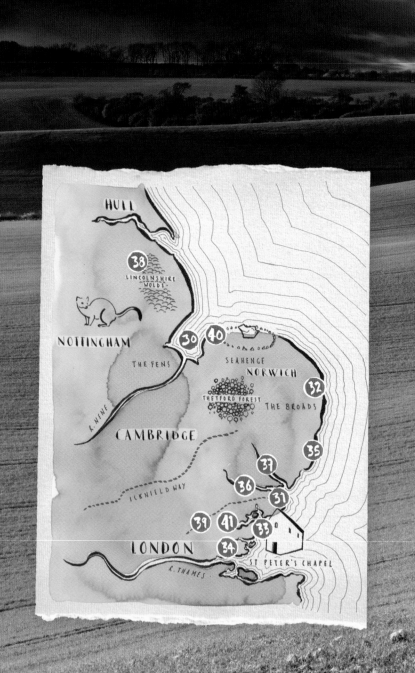

EASTERN ENGLAND

SEE PAGE 5 FOR KEY TO SYMBOLS

I MET A RETIRED FARMER on the sea wall. He described The Wash as a larder that he could live off. He'd been sleeping here, sometimes wild, ever since he was a kid. Samphire (like asparagus) for breakfast, lunch and dinner. Then mussels, winkles and cockles cooked over a campfire.

He had a grey beard and blond strands of hair that hung clumsily from beneath his hat like ribbons. He talked about why the wild was better when he was young, before grazing sheep and cattle were allowed in to flatten the marsh and creeks.

A huge flock of black-headed gulls moved on the shoreline in a single puff of white smoke, twisting and turning on itself in the clean air. Two giant white egret cawed like grumpy crows.

'All the birds have gone,' he said. And I nodded, without knowing why.

He told me to check the tide times before venturing out on to the marsh. The speed of the flood tide here is second only to the Severn; the bore wave can reach up to a metre high in the connecting rivers.

The Wash is a 24km (15-mile) wide rectangular mouth that inhales and exhales with the moon: a hibernating giant next to four guardian rivers – the **Nene**, Great Ouse, Witham and Welland – that suck you in on the flood, from the North Sea, with the waters sometimes washing over the embankments. There are at least three sea walls protecting the arable land from flooding. They were last breached in the 1980s. Drains divide up the fields into mini canals.

The last time I camped there, the ground was sinking and soaking from the November rain. The old farmer told me that, during summer, the marshy banks and islands harden to concrete; so much so that during the Second World War the Ministry of Defence set tank traps to prevent a German invasion. The traps were all silted up, so I couldn't really see them.

I asked him how often he slept out now. Not much, he said. More as a kid, sitting up all night next to the creeks. But the estuary inlets are still hideaways for kayakers and hikers. One night recently he had gone to sleep on a small island that can be walked to just offshore. He took his dog and a shotgun. He said the dog barked all night at noises in the darkness. He gave up and returned home at 1am.

'You know what they say about things going bump in the night,' he said. 'Something just didn't feel right.'

There's a fine network of footpaths and wooded ditches – sometimes more than 15m (50ft) wide – leading into The Wash, which provide places to camp, hide and shelter from the sometimes stiff breezes. It's easy enough finding a flat place, but hammocking is better. Otherwise, below the sea wall along the south-western edge it's quite easy to bed down in the grasses, but keep an eye on that tide or it's a wet bed.

Inland, the salt marshes are a calmer world, domesticated by windmills, church spires and fields dissected by straight roads, ditches and drains. But what man has tamed is very occasionally flooded by nature. As the rivers exhale after rain, they blow out with such force that the power of the ebb spews out its salty spittle at speeds of up to 6 knots.

'The Smeeth' or drove roads provide a more pedestrian chance for exploration. Duck decoys are the only tree cover other than shelter belts. Footpaths linking The Wash are the Macmillan Way (467km/ 290 miles) to the north shore out of Boston to Abbotsbury in Dorset. The Nar Valley Way (55km/34 miles) follows the River Nar and joins with the Peddars Way at Castle Acre.

The Fens Waterways Link Project is a plan to reconnect the cathedral cities of Lincoln, Peterborough and Ely via navigable historic waterways, which includes linking up with Boston, Wisbech and King's Lynn.

The estuary mouth is always guarded: the beaches of Skegness sit to the north, the cliffs of Hunstanton to the south. Boston and King's Lynn are the major towns on the inland corners.

31 WALTON BACKWATERS

THE WALTON BACKWATERS are less marsh, more a reckless mesh of green-brown furrows that succumb to a ride twice a day: 2,833ha (7,000 acres) of creek and islands criss-cross the lagoon. The area can be explored on foot or by boat.

The backwaters are between the Colne and Stour estuaries, 5km (3 miles) south of Harwich and 1km (half a mile) north-west of Walton-on-the-Naze. Along Walton Channel, left after Hedge-end Island, is a dark creek called the Dardanelles, connecting Hamford Water with The Twizzle. Brackish pools, seals and salt marsh make up most of the lagoons, which flower with skipper butterflies and wild sea holly, bindweed, sea lavender, oystercatchers and warblers.

Early summer is the best time to visit, when the mauve sea lavender fixes over

Horsey and Hedge-end islands. At low tide these outcrops can be reached on foot.

I don't think I can get away with any more than two mentions of Arthur Ransome (see Coniston, page 214). Aside from Robert Fisk, Ryszard Kapuściński and Bruce Chatwin, he is my favourite travel writer. Ransome based one of his books, *Secret Water*, here on Hamford Water. Published in 1939, it's not his best – but describes beautifully the adventures of children left on one of the islands.

There are several islets to explore. Skipper's Island, about 500m (1,640ft) offshore, can be reached at low tide via causeways originally laid to graze cattle in the 19th century. Canoeists and kayakers are supposed to get permission to wild camp from the Essex Wildlife Trust on 01206 729678 if there's a chance of running aground at low tide, although if you intend remaining on the foreshore while waiting there is no need. Any of the islets make a place to sleep, but I prefer the north side around Pewit Island. Camping in September is better, when the grass is longer to sleep on.

The backwaters mainline of **Walton Channel** is – at less than 3km (2 miles) – the shortest trail in this book by some way. It is linked to the Blackwater Estuary, Colne Estuary, Dengie Peninsula by sea and shore, and to the Essex Way (130km/81 miles) and Stour Valley Path by land, just north of The Naze, over Hamford Water.

PRACTICAL INFO Walk on to Horsey Island at low tide from the coastal footpath (51.859187, 1.2440296) across the stone path (51.866438, 1.2432957), taking care not to get marooned by the tide unless you are carrying a bivvy or tent. Alternatively, the better option is to canoe or kayak into the hidden creeks around Pewit Island (51.892247, 1.2459166).

TRAVEL Trains and buses take you into Walton-on-the-Naze or Harwich.

32 THE BROADS

THE BROADS in summer are more laid-back than a reclining chair on the Florida Keys. Slow waters ebb beneath willow trees and grassy banks. Long midday shadows lazily move in time with nature's gentle drum, but the best season is winter, when everything stops, the stillness a precursor to a private show of Chinese water deer, voles, barn owls and fat foxes. Jumping rainbow trout intermittently puncture the sound of silence, before the collective voice of nature explodes into a chorus, as sunshine decides to reappear from behind a cloud. Free living just doesn't get better than this.

These waters cover 200sq km (77sq miles) of navigable rivers and lakes astride Norfolk and Suffolk, and attract more than five million people during summer (twice as many tourists as the Florida Keys). Looking for solitude, I set off in February for a four-day canoe trip from the River Waveney. From Suffolk, I navigated out towards Breydon Water at Great Yarmouth, and then north towards Wroxham Broad and Barton Broad.

Don't wait 'til dark to find a pitch. Quite why I stupidly chose to ignore that rule here is beyond me. A phone call to the park rangers before leaving home had clarified

I needed to ask for permission to camp, as most land in The Broads is private. The foreshore is limited to sticky, sinking mud and can be unsuitable to overnighting. The wardens did confirm, though, that the public right of navigation (for which there is a very small but controversial fee) provided permission to park a canoe overnight on any one of almost a thousand free moorings, as long as I slept aboard my craft, on water. There was also the right to fish from many riverbanks and platforms at no cost, day and night.

Before setting off at 9am, I'd advised the rangers of my route and explained that sleeping in the canoe, afloat in the reeds beside a 'wild mooring', was my plan. An alternative was to pull ashore along the New Cut canal, south of Reedham, for a night's fishing. I would sleep in a bivvy once I was overcome by tiredness. There was a grumble of mild disapproval from the ranger, but no rebuttal. I congratulated myself on being so well prepared.

The first six hours on day 1 were fabulous. But as it ended and the winter sky darkened at 4pm, tiredness, cold and hunger crept up on me. My map showed a lonely retreat, the Berney Arms inn, on the River Yare, next to Breydon Water. I decided to press on for another 50 minutes past New Cut for a hot meal, and to camp in the beer garden. The greeting was anything but welcome. The inn was a derelict shell,

temporarily closed by lack of winter trade. Having pulled the canoe ashore, I considered overnighting in the shadow of the ghost pub. But there was something creepy about the uninhabited building. I slid the canoe back across the mud and out on to the estuary, which was just two hours from low tide, and fast flowing at almost 8 knots into the black of Breydon Water.

Speeding along on a night tide in darkness, with just a head-torch, is not wise. Nor is it legal. I quickly realised my mistake and attempted to make for the southerly bank of the sea wall. But by now the tide was so low the mud was exposed and there wasn't enough water to carry me within 200 yards of dry land. Eventually, the only option was to leave the canoe and to drag it, myself and all my gear across the brown, stinking muck. It took 15 minutes to arrive on land, but it felt like a lifetime. My heart was pounding from exhaustion and fear, having twice become stuck, right up to my knees, and only narrowly managing to pull myself free by using the canoe as a lever. It was 5.30pm when I climbed, relieved, into my sleeping bag, and to sleep.

Herring gulls sounded the early morning alarm as the flood tide returned on a blue sky. A dusting of frost sat across the grassy slope. A plume of my breath hung in the still air like a wizard's

party trick. Hot coffee, warmed over a Weber fire cube, ignited the magic of a new day. After a lazy breakfast of muesli bars, I packed up and pushed off for the north, via the River Bure, to Wroxham Broad and on to Barton Broad on the River Ant.

Cold canned fish, pasta and stale French bread provided lunch and dinner most days, but there was no shortage of good food around, with bass fishing and several other pubs open. Although the relative calmness of The Broads makes for good canoe-camping, walking and cycling is a quicker way to cover ground. Footpaths and bridleways make finding a secluded location for night-time fishing and sleeping relatively easy (see page 42 for overnight fishing). The **Angles Way** is a beautiful long-distance path that backpackers follow over several days, which tracks from Great Yarmouth via Breydon Water, alongside the River Waveney, Oulton Broad, Beccles and Bungay, and eventually joins with the St Edmund Way towards Thetford. The Weavers' Way links with it at Great Yarmouth towards Cromer.

For the rest of the trip I camped up several hours before sunset, and then took the opportunity to walk the footpaths short of dark. My second pitch was an unofficial moor in the upper reaches of the Bure, and on the way back my third was among reeds, tied to a mooring platform. I drove home excited by the thought of returning; next

time with company. Winter camping on the tide should never be a lonely adventure. Wilding in The Broads comes with a health warning: it's an experience worth sharing.

Walking or cycling on the Angles Way and the Weavers' Way opens up the entire area by land, which is no bad way to explore. The Angles Way (124km/77 miles) and Weavers' Way (100km/62 miles) combine with the Peddars Way and Norfolk Coast Path to make the 367km (228-mile) Around Norfolk Walk, which trails from Great Yarmouth along the River Waveney to the Suffolk Brecks and links with the Icknield Way.

(see page 42 for overnight fishing)

> **PRACTICAL INFO** Hammock or bivvy along the Angles Way, on the River Waveney; best location is the more than 8km (5-mile) stretch between Oulton Broad (52.473600, 1.7102262) and Beccles Marshes (52.467483, 1.5663053); paddle a canoe or kayak east of Beccles on some of the quietest waters in The Broads (52.464303, 1.4995456); forage on the foreshore at low tide or catch large bass on spinners around the sandbanks of The Narrows, where Breydon Water meets the River Waveney (52.589284, 1.6472248).
>
> **TRAVEL** Trains and buses take you into Norwich, Beccles, Great Yarmouth, Lowestoft, Hoveton and Acle.

I WAS IN an RSPB reserve on Wallasea Island. It was still dark, before dawn, and the farm dogs at the end of the drive were barking in that way that means 'we're not happy and we're a bit mad'. I wondered whether they were chained, or in a cage. Or whether they were able to roam out and down the lane as a pack. I listened hard for the voice of an owner calling them off, but heard nothing. So I sat in the car. Annoyed. Feeling like a coward. But mostly annoyed with the dogs.

Everything about this 'reserve' frustrated me. I like the RSPB. As a charity, it seems to me to be one of the better, more diligent agencies. Working for the interests of the birds and nature, rather than politics and power. Mostly. Until today.

I'd arrived with a kayak and sleeping bag to paddle out into the Dengie Peninsula, and to spend two days photographing seals on the mudflats, and fishing. Before the RSPB bought the land, the entire sea wall was accessible to anglers and boaters down to the foreshore. Now there was fencing all the way along the strip, blocking access to the tides.

The dogs had stopped barking for some time. I slowly edged out of the car, made five or six journeys up on to the top of the wall, and began flinging my gear, including the kayak, over the wire fence and down on to the other side. Within 30 minutes I was afloat. My bad mood drifted off on the salt air as I waited for the dawn. The still water lapped against the sides and I draped my fingers through the weed, and heard an oystercatcher on the shell bank.

Dengie is the tiny village that gave its name to the peninsula. The land mass is an awkward fat, marshy spit, the shape of a blunt wedge. It points towards north London, 80km (50 miles) away, and is roughly 16km (10 miles) long and 11km (7 miles) wide at its widest point. The River Crouch to the south, the Blackwater to the north, and the North Sea to the east define its salt-water borders, around which it's best to either canoe or walk. The eastern part of the peninsula forms the Dengie Marshes. The Saxon chapel of St Peter-on-the-Wall, built in 654 AD, is the only welcoming landmark; a beacon of gentility in a desert of wiry grass and a constant sea breeze. It remains in use today.

The coastal footpath leads into Lower Raypits. A mixture of pasture, sea barley and grass vetchling and intertidal salt marsh, protected from the Crouch Estuary by the sea walls. Thousands of waders – wigeon, teal and pintail – feed and roost here. Great Wakering Common was once part of the salting and creeks, but now provides a place to rest up and watch snipe around brackish lagoons.

The foreshore is divided into sections, defined by the wrecks of boats and barges, small beaches, marshy skies and waders. The stony shore floods at high tide, but the backdrop of soft grass makes for a comfy night mattress. Thickets of shrub and tree sprout among lowly embankments sheltered from the wind, although the hawthorn and blackthorn don't make for good hammocking.

Sales Point near Tip Head, on the most north-easterly edge, is the best place to relax on a calm day. The point is rarely without a breeze. Thousands of waders roost in autumn and winter, their cackling more deafening than a convoy of steel-wheeled carts being pushed over cobbles.

St Peter's Way (66km/41 miles) links with the Essex Way and Three Forests

Way, but more importantly the adjoining lesser footpaths that dissect the peninsula or hug the coastline. I've cycled the entire waterside circuit, but it can be boggy in winter and spring. Canoes or kayaks can launch almost anywhere either side of high tide and provide the best opportunity to get into the tightest stony beaches, particularly around Potton Island. Footpaths line the riverbanks of both the Crouch and the Blackwater, the former leading to the village of Battlesbridge, 22km (14 miles) from Burnham-on-Crouch.

There are occasional farms and vineries between the corridors of quiet. The Limes Farm shop, in Southminster Road, Burnham, sells seasonal fruit and vegetables with seasonal pick-your-own. Clayhill Vineyard encourages visitors to help out for a few hours' picking in summer and autumn in return for a bottle of finest English wine

(and possibly a place to sleep). New Hall Vineyards nearby provides free daily tours and wine-tasting. Shops are rare, so it's best to top up on provisions at Burnham-on-Crouch, the only town.

PRACTICAL INFO Fish and bivvy at night along the foreshore between Holliwell Point (51.629739, 0.92408066) and the mouth of the River Blackwater on Dengie's north shore (51.747901, 0.92006593); in the shadow of St Peter – walk to St Peter's Chapel (51.736331, 0.93938083); kayak around Lawling, Mayland and Cooper's creeks on the south shore of Blackwater to find a night spot on the foreshore to sleep (51.704140, 0.76903611).

TRAVEL Trains and buses take you into Maldon, Burnham-on-Crouch or North Fambridge.

maps

THE POWER OF THE MAP

I walk, cycle and canoe to find sleep. Paths, canals and rivers are the way in to 'Eden'. My backpacking years during the 1980s had taught me always to have a journey mapped out, a planned route on which to go from A to B. But then, once on the road, deviating off was the way to get the most out of life and the trail.

Nowhere in Britain is further than 11km (7 miles) from a road. When I first read that, it depressed me, but it later came to be a personal lifeline. The feeling of isolation and remoteness is entirely linked to your own personal consciousness of the situation, knowing where you are and your ability to return to the town, village or homestead, rather than the distant absence of a fellow human being.

MY FAVOURITE MAPPING WEBSITES

http://www.mapsta.net/uk-os/westox/
(ignore Oxford in title – map covers all of Britain)
http://maps.osi.ie/publicviewer/
#V1,591271,743300,0,10
http://www.paddlepoints.net/Paddlepoints
.aspx?location=uk&zm=5
http://www.gridref.org.uk/
http://www.enetplanet.com/coordinates
_finder.php
http://gridreferencefinder.com/#
http://www.ldwa.org.uk/ldp/members
/search_by_path.php
http://www.summitpost.org/
http://www.ordnancesurvey.co.uk/oswebsite
/opendata/viewer/
http://www.ctc.org.uk/journey-planner
http://itouchmap.com/latlong.html

I like all maps. OS maps, free cycle maps from council websites, Stanford charts, river and canal charts, nautical charts. A map sparks more images in my mind than a hundred metaphors; a mass of ideas, as eyes scan over a sketched terrain.

I used to buy online. Hundreds of them, at 20p per dog-eared edition, £1 for the postage. It was still cheap. Then people started uploading their own GPS-plotted routes to handheld devices.

I rang a tech reviewer at CTC, the national cycling charity. He was testing the latest cycle, byway and footpath satnav equipment. I'd decided it was time to go digital (with a paper map backup). He told me the fors and againsts of the latest equipment. He was good. He knew his stuff; and he loved his gadgets. I pushed him for a definitive verdict. Which one should I get? Garmin Edge? The factory maps? Open-source? Which one plotted the best routes? But he hedged and edged and dodged a straight answer. So I asked again, 'OK. You can have anything you want. Cost is no object?'

I was surprised by his reply. He said, 'I'd go hard copy,' then explained how he downloaded free OS maps from the web, saved them as high-res jpg images, and plotted his own course with a digital marker pen. He would download the map image on to his phone and then print out a second as hard copy, to carry in a plastic carrier. Total cost: zero; apart from the ink for the printer. I've been doing exactly that ever since.

Learning how to read maps is an important part of avoiding getting lost and keeping to the footpaths and rights of way. I keep a key to the map symbols on my phone.

The basics around which a route into the wild are plotted:

1 Footpath – pink short-dashed line (OS Landranger Maps) or green short-dashed line (OS Explorer Maps). Local councils have a duty to put adequate signs in place. Only walkers have a legal right; cyclists are not committing a criminal offence unless byelaws are in place, but may be guilty of civil trespass.

2 Bridleway – pink long-dashed line (OS Landranger Maps) or green long-dashed line (OS Explorer Maps). Walkers, cyclists and horse-riders have legal rights to pass – cyclists must give way.

3 National Trail/Long Distance Route – pink diamond-dashed line (OS Landranger Maps) or green diamond-dashed line (OS Explorer Maps). Walkers, cyclists and horse-riders have legal rights – walkers on all parts, cyclists and horse-riders only in part (check with National Trail website for detail).

4 Traffic-free cycle route – white circles, rimmed in green (OS Landranger Maps) or solid orange circles (OS Explorer Maps).

5 National cycle network – pink square box containing white number of Sustrans-managed track (OS Landranger Maps) or white square box, rimmed in red, containing red number of Sustrans-managed track for traffic-free, and white number in red square for on-road (OS Explorer Maps).

6 Regional cycle network – white, square box containing blue number of managed track (OS Landranger Maps) or white cycle inside blue rectangular box (OS Explorer Maps).

7 Open access land (England & Wales) – area shaded in a yellow tint with a solid rim means walkers are free to roam off footpaths and trails (OS Explorer Maps).

34 THAMES ESTUARY

THE TIMBER AND STONE tracks, 'cockle paths', were built by the Victorians, who had a passion for picking shellfish while watching fat seals chase silver bass across a turgid oxtail-coloured soup. It's the wildest place I know. The Thames Estuary, near Leigh-on-Sea in Essex. Home.

Discarded oyster shells lie broken around the underbelly of the mud. Since they cleaned up the Thames in the 1980s, the bass are a little faster, and the seals a little thinner. Nothing is as it seems. Even the crabs walk on tiptoe in case they're missing something.

Everything changes when the water's in. Towards the west end of Hadleigh Ray – a giant creek that severs Chapman Sands from the mainland – is Two Tree Island. It was once an old landfill; now a nature reserve spliced by a single rippled and cracked tarmac road for men in shorty wetsuits, who tow giant trailers behind Land Rover Discoveries with three kids inside, waiting to jump on their jetskis and go.

The best of the camping over the 346km (215 miles) of Thames is hidden among the salty creeks, for kayakers and canoeists with bivvies. Wild and forgotten. But it wasn't always the case. Sailing barges once navigated the shallows to collect the straw, hay and crops that helped build London. The reed-lined avenues around Canvey, the marshes of Fobbing, Vange, Pitsea and Wat Tyler remain completely unexplored today. These places are the most beautiful. Some of the inlets and marshes can be reached on footpaths at low tide, reaching out from the mainland towards Fobbing Creek, Hole Haven Creek, East Haven Creek, Benfleet Creek and Canvey Point. Do not go alone or without someone with good knowledge of the tides and mud (ideally a local fisherman).

I listened to a retired river pilot remembering when the Thames Estuary froze over in 1963. Looking out beyond the buoys, beyond the white horses on the waves, past the sandbanks along the Ray

Gut, he nodded towards a container ship moving seaward in the mist on the river channel, less than a mile away. He spoke slowly and deliberately through a cockney accent, like a man who wanted to talk himself into riding a dangerous animal. He occasionally looked back at me and smiled – as if to break the ice of that moment. He had the stare of someone asking for permission to continue, which I gave him with mild, but genuine interest.

The wetsuits and onesies were reversing their trailers and jetskis into the water, one after the other, a conveyor belt of live contestants in a reality show of egos. The pilot was oblivious; blind to the weekend's summer ritual, even as they raced off on their machines in sheets of spray and white noise. He told me about the sailors' lives he'd seen lost to the river currents, the old stories of Gravesend, how it got its name from the putrid bodies dumped in the salt shallows after the Great Plague of London. A never-ending stream of tragedy against today's roll-call of giant motorised machines bouncing in on the potholed roads from the towns of Basildon, Benfleet and Southend like a great rip tide of hot air and pleasure meeting a flood of past traumas.

The estuary is where the Thames meets the North Sea. The landscape is best seen at low tide. Today, the mudflats and salt marsh blend in against the rigid backdrop of beaches, B&Bs and tower blocks. The water doesn't become brackish until it gets past Gravesend, where giant mullet fade back to make way for slender roach and dace.

Towards London, the river links to the Mar Dyke, the Ingrebourne River, Grand Union Canal, River Lee and the **Three Forests Way** (96km/60 miles).

PRACTICAL INFO Camp in the seagrass in September on the foreshore along the eastern point of Two Tree Island to forage for blackberries and samphire (51.536921, 0.64437346), access either walking the footpath or launching a kayak/canoe; camp waterside on Fobbing Marsh next to Holehaven Creek while fishing for bass (51.530618, 0.50753060); walk 24km (15 miles) of the south Thames shore in Kent from Yantlet Creek (51.461623, 0.68576059), Isle of Grain, to Gravesend (51.444357, 0.37782498). Sleep on any of the small, deserted beaches along the way, before catching the Gravesend Ferry to Tilbury in Essex, and cycling or walking east to East Tilbury and Mucking marshes (51.487829, 0.43095417).
TRAVEL Trains and buses take you into Leigh, Benfleet, Tilbury, Grays or Purfleet.

35 ORFORD NESS

GRASSLAND AND SHINGLE – like revisiting a scrapyard from my youth. It's hard to explain why I'm drawn to it. Ordinarily special, even more so when the sun shines.

Orford Ness is the largest vegetated shingle spit in Europe, and a favourite of writers like MacFarlane and Sebald. A former MOD test site, the history of this place is wrapped up in modern-day military tests and Cold War duty. Among the remains of former military buildings are the freakish concrete pagodas that can be seen from the mainland. But Orford Ness is more than that. It has a dark wildness.

The 15km (9-mile) stone bank is now owned by the National Trust. The shingle is separated from the mainland by two rivers: the Ore where it meets the sea, and the Alde where it greets the land (at Aldeburgh). At its most easterly point, past the avocets, curlews and gulls, is Orfordness Lighthouse.

A National Trust ferry carries passengers out from Orford Quay to Orford Island. I made my own way across by canoe. The wardens confirmed I could land on the foreshore but warned against stepping foot on the island without a guide or map because of unexploded ordnance. I landed, made tea, and made off, fearing I might forget myself and my passion for trekking in my clumsy size 10s.

There are safe spaces to explore around the shingle peninsula. The sea retreats some way back to provide an opportunity to camp soon after high tide. When the weather whips up it's better to creep across over the shingle banks to camp in the shallows, protected from the wind. These shallow stone valleys hold thousands of gallons of brackish lake waters that characterise the Suffolk and Norfolk shoreline.

The **Suffolk Coast and Heaths Path** (80km/50 miles) tracks the River Ore inland from Orford Ness, en route to Lowestoft and The Broads, or south along the coast to Felixstowe, and the Stour and Orwell Walk (67km/42 miles).

PRACTICAL INFO Launch a canoe/kayak from Bawdsey beach (52.035397, 1.4557992) and paddle up the unique straits of Orford Haven, River Ore and River Alde, past Havergate Island and the old MOD land; walk north-east from Orford along the river path to Sudbourne Marshes (52.141767, 1.5948539) to find flat ground to sleep. **TRAVEL** Trains and buses take you into Woodbridge, Melton, Wickham Market and Saxmundham.

THEY PERCH ON wooden posts along the water's edge, waiting for the fish that swim up to feed. Then they drop. Vertically, like lead-weighted spears falling into the river without a ripple or splash.

The cormorants fish in gangs. Scavengers. The valley is full of them. Partridges, seagulls and metal detector clubs. But it's unmistakably Constable country.

The River Stour is among the longest waterways in the south-east, and one of five estuaries – the others are the Orwell, Deben, Alde and Blyth – on the Suffolk coast. It was once an important trade route into London, with barges moving bricks, grain, flour, manure and coal from the early 18th century until the 20th century.

From the estuary, the hills on either side of the valley act as a giant windbreak that defends the surface of the water. Such gentle calm around a tidal rush. The grass fields spread out like velvet carpets set down for an outdoor gallery of beautifully drawn landscapes, as if reality has copied the artist's hand, only with more care, detail and colour.

The Essex side is quieter, offering better views into its prettier Suffolk neighbour. Towards the A12 the river retains its charm, but loses most of the crowds who parked up their cars between Dedham and Flatford.

Nearer the coast, the sandy foreshore provides good camping on both sides of the river. Swans fly in at dawn to feed on the beaches at Mistley and Manningtree, their beaks and slender necks forming a unique silhouette against the rising sun to the east. Canoes and kayaks have access from Brundon Mill to the sea, more than 40km (25 miles) away. There are platforms and pull-out places en route, some of which pass through private land.

For walkers, the **Stour Valley Path** (96km/60 miles) and the Stour and Orwell Walk (67km/42 miles) navigate the north side of the river, from the tidal edges of Shotley Gate to Newmarket, in Suffolk.

South of the river is the Essex Way. The Icknield Way Trail (235km/146 miles) crosses the Stour Valley Path and runs for 177km (110 miles) between The Peddars Way, at Knettishall Heath near Thetford, and the start of The Ridgeway at Ivinghoe Beacon, Tring, in Hertfordshire.

PRACTICAL INFO Park up at Dedham (51.962439, 0.99396851) and canoe west on the Stour to find the quietest wooded parts of Essex to camp.

TRAVEL Trains and buses take you into Manningtree, Mistley, Harwich, Wrabness, Bures, Sudbury and Stetchworth.

37 RIVER ORWELL

THE ORWELL is an upmarket version of the Côte d'Azur. Grassy pastures and oak trees over sand, like a beach road in the south of France. But it's better than posh camping. There are almost no routes for vehicles along the Orwell's coves. Shadows of low-hung branches stretch across the sleepy folds like clichés on a travel show of popular tourist traps. Only there's no one here.

The river is most famous for the dock at Ipswich, which has been a naval trading post since the seventh century. During the Middle Ages, it was one of the richest ports in the country, dealing in wool with merchants all over Europe. The busiest part of the estuary is now dominated by the port at Felixstowe. Noisy and relatively smelly, although not

excessively so: more a curious mixture of labour, commerce and engineering. Less than half a mile out of the port, the sounds of the lapping tide, frightened wood pigeons and noisy black-headed gulls begin to drown the tone of cranes, as the landscape shifts to salt marsh and the dank wood of birch, holly, ivy, bracken and bramble. Elderberry and deadly nightshade berries shine from the darkest, most ancient trees, reflecting back the sunlight of the river's waves into the canopy.

September is the best time to visit. The water is warm. The trees are still green. Along the shore, the beach is sometimes littered with jellyfish the size of jam-jar lids. They can be easily avoided or returned to the

water (not by hand), depending on how you feel. Large logs are covered in stringy white seaweed parched by the air, salt and sun.

Some of the best beach camping is along a 13km (8-mile) tidal stretch of the riverbank, east of the A14 Orwell Bridge. There are no cars and rarely any people, mainly because the official footpaths often leave the river here. These wooded coves can be canoed and kayaked in the hours before and after high tide, or walked via the sandy foreshore once the flood tide has retreated a little.

The river flows through Suffolk into the North Sea, after joining with the River Stour. The **Stour and Orwell Walk** (67km/42 miles) links with the Suffolk Coast and Heaths Path and follows the Orwell and

PRACTICAL INFO Walk the foreshore at low tide to get access to the beautiful Bridge Wood on the north shore; walk the south shore along the Stour and Orwell Walk from Seafield Bay (51.955684, 1.0710831) to the boatyard at Ostrich Creek (52.033813, 1.1536026), hammocking in oak trees or bivvying on the foreshore along more than 24km (15 miles) of prime riverside.

TRAVEL Trains and buses take you into Felixstowe, Ipswich and Manningtree.

Stour estuaries past the Shotley peninsula to Cattawade. The River Gipping is an extension of the Orwell inland. It can be navigated by canoe or walked along via the Gipping Valley River Path (27km/17 miles). Cross the Orwell at Manningtree to link to the Essex Way (130km/81 miles).

LINCOLNSHIRE WOLDS

BEYOND THE PLANTATIONS, the sycamore and pine woods – where the chalk streams lead up and out and backwards along the fissures – are the Lincolnshire Wolds. The hills are part of a mountain range left over from the Yorkshire Wolds, brutally severed by the Humber Estuary several million years ago.

They've been flattened, which is what I like about them. Their ditches, springs and watery drains remind me of Essex. Thousands of acres of furrows, crops and fields spread out from the hydrated channels in equal order like a replica of my mum's old greenhouse, and the lines of opal and pastel vegetables she grew under glass and polythene.

There's more to the east than nostalgia, crops, hydration and fens. The Lincolnshire Wolds are – at 168m (551ft) – the highest hills in south-east England and East Anglia, covering the land to the coast in the east and the Pennines to the west. Their 558sq km (215sq miles) of sandstone and chalk are hung between four corners: the coast

at Grimsby to the north, Skegness in the south, and then inland between Scunthorpe and Lincoln.

Neolithic communal graves divide up the farms and fields like dividers of ancient magic. The land was once wooded, but all the trees had gone by the 11th century. Most of the Wolds today is either arable land or park, a feature of the various parliamentary Enclosures Acts. Settlements were forcibly abandoned in the 15th century. Mounds are still seen across the landscape where the villages once stood. Just 3 per cent of the land is covered by trees.

Among several important routes is the **Viking Way** (237km/147 miles), which passes from the Humber to Lincoln. The Way is a base from which to find a place to overnight, exploring the alleys and abandoned chalk pits. It's a good idea to set off from the Humber Bridge. Find a secluded place to camp along the path's highest point, in the Wolds, just south of

Caister-on-Sea, around Normanby le Wold or Nettleton Top, and then continue the 48km (30-mile) trek south through the hills, ideally to overnight again in the hollows north or south of Belchford.

The Greenwich Meridian Trail links to the Viking Way. It covers 439km (273 miles) from Peacehaven in East Sussex to Sand le Mere in East Yorkshire, roughly following the line of the Prime Meridian as agreed by the Royal Observatory at Greenwich to be zero degrees longitude. The trail splices vertically through the Wolds' southern section.

PRACTICAL INFO Walk the footpaths south-west and south-east of Chapel Hill (53.070383, -0.19647401) around the rivers and drains crossing the Wold's farmland.
TRAVEL Trains and buses take you into Grimsby, Market Rasen, Skegness and Lincoln.

39 ESSEX WAY

A JOURNEY ACROSS grass, through a working county that I've known since before I knew myself. Blackthorn trees hang heavy with ripe blue-black sloes in October, their lichen-laden silver branches looking older than I remember them last.

The smell comes from silos. Silage: the sweet stench of sweaty, crushed lawns and trapped heat. It's familiar. Addictive. Putrid, in a mercifully recognisable way. Like overdosing on the odour of king prawns grilled in a Chinese takeaway before 9am while walking on the pavement to work.

The **Essex Way** (130km/81 miles) spans the port town of Harwich on the Stour estuary to Epping on the London fringe, via pretty villages and small towns at Willingale, Dedham and Manningtree. They are surrounded by mad horses, fast-flowing rivers – like the Colne and the Stour – and a patchwork of crops, farm animals, and tight hedges that line each field. The foliage and

the occasional oak trees are good places to either bivvy down or hammock. An hour before dusk I look for a bed; walking from the corner of one meadow to the next, the trail ducking under another hedge, emerging into a new field framed by different colours of crops, soils, clipped grasses and livestock. I mostly avoid the cattle, preferring to sleep alone.

The Way crosses St Peter's Way (66km/41 miles), the Three Forests Way (96km/60 miles) and the Essex Clayway (45km/28 miles).

PRACTICAL INFO Take a dip in the cool River Colne north-east of Fordham (51.910910, 0.81827502).
TRAVEL Trains and buses take you into Harwich, Manningtree, Wakes Colne, Kelvedon, Braintree, Chipping Ongar and Epping.

TWISTED, MOSS-LADEN branches spread out like overgrown remnants of a classical arched portico on to Breckland. Forests divide up the hedgerows, grazing sheep and bracken-laden panoramas that make up this ancient trail. The smell of livestock and blossom hangs in the spring air like expensive perfume around the monied wives at a farmers' market, only smothered by a dramatic scent of sea breeze where the Peddars Way crashes into the Norfolk shoreline.

Looking down at the dust and stone path of this 74km (46-mile) Roman road, I defy anyone not to feel the presence of every traveller, drover and pilgrim who has walked this forest-to-sea trail for more than 2,000 years. It's a life-affirming realisation that right here, right now, this brief moment in time is ours.

My favourite stopover point is by the River Nar, at Castle Acre. The Ostrich Inn is good for a pub meal and allows wild campers to pitch in the beer garden for free. The King William IV at Sedgeford does the same sometimes, as does the Gin Trap Inn at Ringstead. Water is available at various streams and rivers, but unless your filter system is extremely efficient (see page 201), consider topping up bottles at farms and pubs. Cycling is allowed along the path, although it's frowned upon on the adjoining Norfolk Coastal Path.

Like most journeys, it's best to start from the beginning, either 6.5km (4 miles) east of Thetford Forest at Knettishal Heath in Suffolk, or north in Holme-next-the-Sea, where the path links with the Norfolk Coastal path. The two trails combined cover 154km (96 miles). The southern end links with the 177km (110-mile) long Icknield Way Path, which leads south-west to Buckinghamshire.

The route is a footpath in its own right, but only one half of a single National Trail:

The **Peddars Way** and Norfolk Coast Path, which opened in 1986. The track is often wide enough to accommodate a one-man tent or bivvy. The trees on the southern section are ideal to tie a hammock. Natural England, the government agency with former responsibility for the path's management, advises walkers and cyclists to either ask permission from landowners before overnighting, or to 'move on' if asked to do so. A lack of campsites, hotels and B&Bs makes free camping more of a necessity than a choice.

There's parking at either end of the Way. Suffolk is perhaps better because the car park is free, although it's rather secluded and I don't ever leave a vehicle overnight.

Numerous points along the path cater for those who want to skip on and off, but the only way to do this trip properly is to arrive by public transport. Buses or trains run into Thetford, from where I either cycle the 6.5km (4 miles) to the trail start, or catch a cab.

Walking from the Suffolk forests in the west and on to village lanes and green trails is a peaceful experience that can easily be finished in three days. Climbing over the mountain-like dunes down to the flat sand and surf feels like the start of a new adventure, rather than the end. Regular buses run from Holme-next-the-Sea into King's Lynn; and home. Otherwise, there's another 82km (51 miles) of truly stunning coastal path to explore.

PRACTICAL INFO Take a dip in the River Thet, south of Brettenham (52.4210, 0.8538); breakfast on the banks of the River Nar, at Castle Acre (52.7005, 0.6905); visit the deer park at Houghton Hall, home of Britain's first Prime Minister, Sir Robert Walpole.

TRAVEL Trains and buses take you into Thetford, Harling Road, King's Lynn, Wells-next-the-Sea; buses only run into Hunstanton.

41 CHELMER VALLEY

THE WARM WIND moves in the bulrushes and dry grasses of the watery shallows when nature arrives for an end-of-year prom in September sunshine. Around the coastal village of Tidwalditun, male dragonflies the size of fat sparrows win the prize for best-dressed guests in their emerald, crimson and gold suits. They hover above the stillness, circling, dipping and darting among the reeds like helicopters from a futuristic sci-fi movie. The female insects flick eggs from their tails under the surface of the rivers Chelmer and Blackwater while on the wing; femme fatale aliens impregnating the silence. But it's an illusory invasion. The visiting swallows have long gone and the air is ripe with the scent of native September fruit. Blackberry vines sag under the weight of their purple-black crop.

Tidwalditun was renamed Heybridge in the Middle Ages after a 'high bridge' was erected over the Blackwater. The adjoining **River Chelmer** was canalised in 1793 to carry goods from Heybridge and Maldon to Chelmsford. The 22km (14-mile) river is still navigable for canoes, kayaks and occasional pleasure boats, but it is best walked.

Willow and poplar trees along the Chelmer Valley footpath mean that hammocks get the best of the hidden camping. Woodland is dense here, particularly between the villages of Little Baddow, Woodham Mortimer and Ulting. These are some of thickest woods in Essex, the dark forest floor smothered in ferns and primroses, shielded from sunlight by a canopy of fir, oak, birch and chestnut.

Anglers camp overnight on the river towpath, inside green tarpaulin tents decked out with camp beds, rods and frying pans. Adolescent pike attack keep nets, biting with such ferocity they gouge holes, mortally wounding the chub trapped inside. Adult pike are commonly caught over 5.5kg (12lb). Barges and houseboats park up, while owners cast hopefully for carp. Byelaws prevent non-anglers from sleeping right on the riverbank without written permission from the Chelmer and Blackwater Navigation Company, but there are day tickets available. There are also plenty of good sleeping spots in the overhanging trees and bushes around the Maldon foreshore that fall outside the restricted areas.

A Camping and Caravanning Club site at Hoe Mill Lock offers an alternative to wild sleeping, and is a favourite among the transient angling, canoeing and cycling communities. There are several pubs and small shops at Woodham Walter and Danbury that will provide water and supplies.

Whether walking, canoeing or cycling, I prefer to start this trip from Chelmsford, making my way along the path towards the coast, rather than inland. Overnighting along the foreshore at either Maldon or Heybridge has the advantage of allowing you to decide on a paid-for breakfast with sea view. The Old Ship at Heybridge, sitting by the canal, is my favourite (ham, eggs, chips and beans). If I walk on the southern riverbank outbound, I try to pick a route home either across the higher ground on the south lanes or along the northern bank.

Like so much of the eastern landscape, Heybridge, Maldon and the Chelmer are connected to a network of salt channels and creeks. St Peter's Way is arguably the most important path, a 66km (41-mile) route that passes from the inlets of the Blackwater Estuary and the Dengie coast to Chipping Ongar, via Hanningfield Reservoir. St Peter's connects with the Essex Way towards the north, and the 96km (60-mile) Three Forests Way joins Hatfield Forest, Hainault Forest and Epping Forest, the latter two inside the M25 London boundary, and the borders of true wild camping: inner-city suburbia.

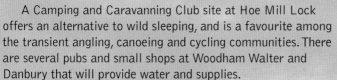

PRACTICAL INFO Walk on to Osea Island (51.730404, 0.73755083) or Northey Island (51.718768, 0.70625975) at low tide along their respective causeways, with a view to sleeping on the foreshore if your return is not possible on the tide.
TRAVEL Trains and buses connect Maldon and Chelmsford to London.

CENTRAL ENGLAND

47

LEEDS & LIVERPOOL CANAL

MANCHESTER

54 SHEFFIELD

PEAK
DISTRICT

55

43

CRESWELL
CRAGS

51

TRENT & MERSEY CANAL

R. TRENT

OSWESTRY FORT

R. SEVERN

SHROPSHIRE
HILLS

53

BIRMINGHAM

48

PETERBOROUGH

MALVERN
HILLS

46

50

GRAND UNION CANAL

OXFORD CANAL

52

56

KING ARTHUR'S
CAVE

COTSWOLD HILLS

OXFORD

42

49

R. THAMES

45

44

42 GRAND UNION CANAL

A REAL-LIFE ADVENTURE park over old England. Two-tone painted signs guide me towards places called Slapton and Tring. Families nestle to picnic contentedly among the grassy locks and tended common land. Anglers sit on stools of contentment, their occasional chores only remarkable because of their ability to do everything in such slow silence, like a stick insect inching its way over a privet stalk.

Black-necked grebes cut across the waters around the Tring reservoirs, where the carp and dace are oblivious to anglers' lines. The lakes bulge from the **Grand Union Canal**, where black terns hover and then dip under the surface of the water, before rising from the droplets of their work with flashes of silver in their tiny beaks.

The Grand Union Canal starts in London and ends in Birmingham. It's the longest canal in the UK (220km/137 miles), with 166 locks. It was nationalised in 1948 and is controlled today by the Canal & River Trust. Commercial traffic died out in the 1970s, before the leisure industry took over.

The towpath can be walked all the way. It's hard to imagine, isn't it? A single path all the way from London to Birmingham:

from Little Venice in Paddington, through Hertfordshire and the Chilterns to Leamington Spa, Warwick and into 'Brum', the place they used to call the workshop of the world.

Hammocking is the best overnight option, strung from the green shelter of willows around the adjoining paths that line the route. Night-fishing and free sleeping on the Waterway Wanderers scheme (see page 42) are best around Napton-on-the-Hill, Stratford-upon-Avon in Warwickshire, and close to bridges 21, 51 and 89, bridge 93/94 at Braunston Junction, Bridge 191 at Trout Road, and Clitheroe's Lock 99 to Bridge 200, at Hayes.

A right turn from the canal at Northampton follows the River Nene out into The Wash. Going north at Norton Junction on to the Leicester Line for 56km

PRACTICAL INFO Divert off the canal along the many hundreds of short footpaths to find sleeping places around adjoining rivers, coppices and scrubland. The footpaths north around the footbridge at Yardley Gobion, north-west of Milton Keynes (52.097115, -0.87001655), lead up to the peaceful River Tove and surrounding countryside, as does the canal footbridge at Lower Shuckburgh (52.261288,-1.2851945), from where footpaths lead both north to a dismantled railway (52.274927, -1.2862677) and south around woodland and small hills.
TRAVEL Trains and buses take you into Watford, Leighton Buzzard, Milton Keynes, Northampton, Coventry and Birmingham.

(35 miles) leads to Leicester city centre, before meeting the River Soar, the River Trent, and the Trent and Mersey Canal.

43 TRENT AND MERSEY CANAL

'**THEY USED** to call her "mother",' said the man. We stood on the bridge next to Canal Street in Burslem, looking down across the Trent and Mersey. Green puddles of water surrounded crumbling brick walls among scrub and yellow florets of nipplewort. A kid rode by to see what we were looking at. He stopped, swung his tiny bike over 180 degrees on the back wheel, and slammed the front down so hard the entire frame rattled until he sat back on its seat.

'What do they call those chimneys?' I asked the man.

'Bottle ovens,' said the kid, and the man nodded, without a smile.

The **Trent and Mersey Canal** was built from here, in Burslem, partly to serve the bottle-shaped kilns that produced pottery – not actual glass bottles, as I'd thought the kid had meant.

The Domesday Book lists Burslem as an important trade route from the Staffordshire moors and Peak District to London. This town went on to become the 'mother of the potteries', a reputation that grew out of the 17th century when the area was known as the Sytch, a stinking black hole of furnaces, rubble and polluted earth. The term 'mother' came from the fact that, in 1910, Burslem merged with five other old towns to become Stoke-on-Trent. Today, Burslem is more famous for Robbie Williams and more visited as a historical break for the barge and holiday community. The canal is relatively clean, lined in June with flowers of purple marsh woundwort, common spotted orchids and hawthorn trees.

The towpath follows the 150km (93 miles) between the River Trent, at Derwent

Mouth Lock in Derbyshire, to the River Mersey, in the north-west. It connects the east coast of England, from the Humber, to the west coast at Liverpool, bringing together England's four great rivers, the Trent, Mersey, Severn and Thames. The entire canal can be walked, canoed or cycled, taking you across Cheshire, Staffordshire and Derbyshire. Paddlers must navigate or portage around 75 locks. Walkers and cyclists pass 230 bridges.

The Waterway Wanderers scheme (see page 42) covers much of the path and includes beautiful sections of the adjoining Caldon and Coventry canals to sleep and camp along. Among the quieter areas of the main canal for overnight fishing or camping are bridge 62 to bridge 71 (Colwich Lock Bridge near the Wolseley Centre); bridge 74 to bridge 75 (just before Great Haywood Marina); Lock 25 to Lock 26 (around Sandon); bridge 111 (Stoke Basin) to bridge 117 (Summit Lock, around Stoke-on-Trent); and bridge 161 (Crows Nest) to Lock 67 (Booth Lane Top Lock). There are so many more.

PRACTICAL INFO Spend a day and night exploring the wilds around the multiple waterways and footpaths where the Trent and Mersey meets the Trent Valley at Great Haywood (52.803794, -2.0099153). The Staffordshire Way (153km/93 miles) leads off from the canal to explore the adjoining forest at Cannock Chase (52.781170, -2.0237366). A riverside footpath navigates the River Sow from where it meets the canal, which runs alongside the River Trent at this point.

TRAVEL Trains and buses take you into Frodsham, Rudheath, Elworth, Alsager, Kidsgrove, Stoke-on-Trent, Stone, Willington and Long Eaton.

survival

SLEEPING OUTDOORS isn't dangerous, per se. You don't have to worry about burglars or electrical fires, like you do at home. But listen to your instincts. If something feels wrong, it probably is. Move on. Having said this, the mind plays terrible tricks at night. Listening to what goes bump in night can drive some people insane with fear. The mind attempts to create pictures of anything it can't see in an effort to understand. Don't let your mind play those tricks. No one is out in the woods looking for victims at 1am. Make sure you walk or cycle hard in the day, so sleep comes easy.

The word 'survival' in the context of living off the land long term is an absurdity. Successful survival in the world of wild camping simply means staying alive. In certain circumstances, when fate or stupidity (or both) conspire, you might require three things: preparation, determination, and possibly most important of all, luck. Most of us have the latter in bundles. That's why we're here. Pure luck. An incalculable sum of a trillion trillions to one chance.

Wild campers learn to be better survivors. They carry in their backpacks the essentials to stay alive: warmth, shelter, hydration and food. There are five things – other than food, water, phone, map, compass – I always carry in case I get stranded. A bivvy, a sleeping bag, adequate clothing, a coke-can stove and a water filter.

The need to survive exposes the lunacy of 'no right' to wild camp. To restrict anyone to not being allowed to camp is essentially saying, 'You have no right to self preservation.' Whether walking, cycling or boating, there are many situations that require the traveller to sleep over.

For a kayaker or a canoeist, the tide might go out. Walkers, particularly when venturing up high, can get lost or injured. A sprained ankle, a long way from the car park, and a little too close to dusk. Alone in rain and wind. It doesn't take very long before the situation becomes extreme. As a survivor you need to be prepared on the track. It isn't often about knowing how to lay traps for rabbits and how to catch fish. Survival is not really about drinking the blood of a badger or wrapping the skin of a dead dog around your head. Because there's usually nothing out there, apart from gorse, rock and wet ground. Extreme stories of 'survival' are fantastic: the plane crash, stuck on a raft for months without water. I enjoy them as much as anyone else. But they are fantasies; tales of entertainment, rather than real learning.

Sometimes it's about the common sense things like good health. Wet wipes are good to keep around. A tick remover and mirror, and a basic first aid kit with cream and dressings.

Fear is a survival mechanism. It's not a bad thing. It makes us wary. Sometimes it gets us home. The bumps in the night can be a frightener, but sleep is the greatest antidote. Waking up in the morning is being a survivor.

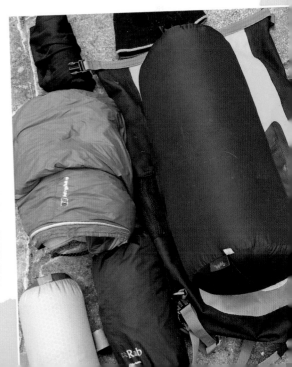

I'M GOING TO BE mischievous and suggest that the River Thames and its path represent two unique opportunities. First, to gape in awe at the opulence of grand houses and finely manicured lawns that stretch out to the emerald and golden riverbank like hanging gardens of the modern-day Babylon. Secondly, a chance to tramp and camp in free splendour between the hours of darkness in one of the richest backyards in the world. Only in Britain.

Everything around the Thames betrays the allure of power, especially around the villages and towns in Oxfordshire, and where the water rises in Gloucestershire. Maybe it's the boat houses and riverside shelters, their red stone walls weathered by white powder, lime lichen and lemon moss in a perfect patchwork of matt green, orange and creeping, milk chalk. Perhaps it's the upmarket Jersey cattle, their soft beige and tan coats melting against the pastures and blue skies. Even the muddy waterside drinking holes seem to me to be more refined than those in other counties. Colours in the shallows of dappled light are as bright as an orchard in early autumn. Red weed blends with the yellow and green leaves fallen from the willows on to the surface of the water.

In late October, the westerly wind still blows warm here. Multi-seated sprint canoes cut and glide through the water, propelled by groups of young men (and some women) in singlets, breaking the silence with their egos, splashing oars, testosterone and a youthful passion for the outdoors.

Red kites glide over oaks and the tallest white willows. Male pheasants squawk like farmyard cockerels choking on seed, while the wheat-dappled hens flutter, plump and plain, across the grassy plains. From my hammock, hung in the trees, I can hear a robin.

The Thames is 338km (210 miles) long with 45 locks. It's navigable for almost 225km (140 miles).

The advice from the National Trails office is to get permission before stopping, sleeping or putting up a tent. The river can be walked, cycled or paddled. There are so many good cycling sections; among the best are the 8.7km (5.4 miles) through Oxford and the 9.4km (5.8 miles) from Weybridge to Hampton Court. The Thames Valley Cycle Route is 155km (97 miles) long from London to Oxford, and often follows the **Thames Path** (296km/184 miles).

Other than walking or cycling, canoeing is a good camping option along the entire route. Although house boats are not uncommon on the river, skiff is a craft that can be hired. It's like a canoe fitted with a tent: http://www.skiffhire.com.

A Thames licence is needed for canoes and kayaks, but the British Canoe Union membership covers that (see page 45). Almost all the 45 locks are permanently manned by lock keepers, who are among the nicest and most knowledgeable people I've ever met. They will often allow canoeists to wild camp on the grassy locks as part of multi-day trips. The Environment Agency provides a free information sheet on Thames riverside campsites, just in case.

The Thames river and path links up with virtually every major waterway and path/trail in the south, whether heading north, south or west. The most important are probably the Grand Union Canal, the Ridgeway, the London Loop, the Oxford Canal Walk, the Wey Navigation, the Wysis Way and the River Avon.

PRACTICAL INFO Whether you arrive here on foot or by canoe, stop over along the riverbank at Dorchester on Thames (51.636463, -1.1798132) to explore or camp around the adjoining Dyke Hills around the Roman town's south flank. Cross the river bridge to forage through Little Wittenham Wood (51.632052, -1.1751440) or to take in the valley views from Sinodun Hill and the old Roman fort (51.628002, -1.1790579).

TRAVEL Trains and buses take you into Kemble, Swindon, Abingdon-on-Thames, Oxford, Wallingford, Goring, Reading, Henley-on-Thames, Maidenhead, Windsor, Woolwich, Tilbury and Southend-on-Sea.

45 THE RIDGEWAY

IT WAS MARCH. The air was full of herbs, sodden mud and singing blackbirds. Crawling from my bivvy, I stood up, scraping my head on a hawthorn bush and falling out on to the path; shoeless, into the mud puddle so carefully avoided the night before. It was my last clean pair of socks. I dragged the soles over the thick wet grass beneath the barbed fence, and then stung myself on a dwarf thistle. Still cursing, I punched, stuffed and thrashed my damp bivvy and sleeping bag into the rucksack, wanting to punish someone for something, nothing, anything, before I looked up, and saw... a muntjac deer. Just staring at me from a few yards away, and everything felt OK, even the embarrassment of being caught.

The Ridgeway is supposed to be Britain's oldest road. So what? I say. Thousands of years wide, and 136km (85 miles) long, through Hertfordshire, Buckinghamshire, South Oxfordshire, West Berkshire and Wiltshire. It is spliced in half by the River Thames. The western section follows the peak of the North Wessex Downs. The eastern section follows the Thames for 8km (5 miles) before turning off towards the Chiltern Hills.

Sleeping here, you're sharing something with the old traders. Like most walks that have survived so long, the Ridgeway was a commerce trail rather than just a line to travel. The Enclosure Acts during the 18th century threatened the paths, but the need to keep trade flowing saw them adapt into the single route left here today; a remnant of the multi tracks where cattle and sheep were guided along by drovers, from the Welsh hills and west England to the merchants in London and the surrounding market towns. The old paths were lined with holly, wild orchids, felwort, salad burnet, wild privet, hazel and oak – just as the Ridgeway is today.

I forgot to say, it's not all about trade. The Uffington White Horse and the stone circle at Avebury are Bronze Age relics along the Way. No less impressive than the bluebell woods in the Chilterns of Buckinghamshire, further east on the same path; just a little more famous for their notoriety, and a nice distraction from our historic obsession with work.

Late April is the best time to walk the trail, when the cherry blossom is out, and the breeze dries the ground. The western section provides the easiest camping, hidden beneath trees and shrubs on the wider parts of the path. Sleeping is generally tolerated as long as it's well away from homes and out of view between the hedges and boundary fences. There are occasional water taps along the way.

The National Trails website offers advice on camping, which supports the 'tolerance' of landowners on condition of no fires, ever. The Trails website states: 'The Ridgeway is privately owned and the public right of way along it is for passage only, not for stopping and camping. In practice, however, most landowners do not object if a tent is pitched on the Trail for a night and disappears the next morning as long as no litter is left, no damage done, nor campfires lit. But please do not camp in adjoining fields, woods or gallops without prior permission from the landowner.'

Horse-riders and cyclists can ride from the west as far as the River Thames at Goring, but in practice many cyclists keep going, subject to a little pushing here and there, and a regard for pedestrian safety.

The Icknield Way Path is one of three more footpaths – along with the Wessex Ridgeway and the Peddars Way – that are collectively known, together with the Ridgeway National Trail, as the 'Greater Ridgeway' (583km/363 miles). All four connect Lyme Regis in West Dorset to Hunstanton in Norfolk. The Grand Union Canal Walk (234km/145 miles) also links with them.

PRACTICAL INFO Grim's Ditch is one of my favourite wooded stretches along the Way, thick with beech trees for almost 8km (5 miles), perfect for hanging a hammock. There's an ancient feel about the ditch, which reaches from Nuffield (51.579174, -1.0438818) all the way to the River Thames at Wallingford (51.589422, -1.1226688). To explore some quieter woodlands, divert south off the Ridgeway on to the Icknield Way at Woodhouse Farm (51.583086, -1.0833223), and then turn left to walk through the Wicks, Mongewell, Bixmoor and Ipsden woods.

TRAVEL Trains and buses take you into Swindon, Pewsey, Ivinghoe, Berkhamsted, Cheddington and Luton.

46 MALVERN HILLS

TOLKIEN FOUND INSPIRATION in the grand settings of the Malvern Hills. Heath and flat-top summits strung out over long grass mounds that look like the back of a monster draped in a cloak of stringy turf, scarred by an army of walking ants. The hillsides are steep and narrow, their paths circling patches of broadleaf woodland where dormice and high brown fritillary butterflies flit in between the quiet shades and sunny corners.

The hills are managed common land, governed under an Act of Parliament by a group of managers known as 'conservators'. They are responsible for all areas spread over 13km (8 miles) north to south between Great Malvern and the village of Hollybush.

This is not a place to overnight; byelaws restrict sleeping out. It's a place to daydream, just as Tolkien did. The Worcestershire Beacon (425m/1,394 ft) is the highest point, but it should be part of an overland trip, an extended day visit while overnighting along the Severn Way, less than a 5km (3 mile) walk to the east (see page 162).

An alternative route in and out is the Worcestershire Way (50km/31 miles) to Bewdley via the Suckley Hills. The **Geopark Way** (175km/109 miles) is another, towards either Bridgnorth or Gloucester. The Three Choirs Way (161km/100 miles) connects with the Worcestershire, Gloucestershire, Wysis and Severn Ways and the Wye Valley Walk.

PRACTICAL INFO Arrive early on the longest days in late June at the highest peak, Worcestershire Beacon (52.104191, -2.3385781). Leave after lunch along the Three Choirs Way for the River Severn, less than 8km (5 miles) away, where wild camping it plentiful along the riverbank on either side. The access is better on the east side, but quieter on the west. Stop off for views from the woodland around Old Hills, west of Pixham (52.137344, -2.2557524).
TRAVEL Trains and buses take you into Malvern Link, Great Malvern, Colwall and Ledbury.

47 LEEDS AND LIVERPOOL CANAL

WALKING ALONE in autumn on the Leeds and Liverpool Canal, you feel like you're sharing the track with the ghost of Dorothy. It's a yellow brick road, across an *Alice in Wonderland* landscape of clover, ferns, sunshine and grass. Britain's longest canal is an epic journey. A ride through an epoch of toil – 204km (127 miles), sea to sea.

The canal took 46 years to build, the longest single waterway ever created in Britain. Ninety-one locks and levers funnel cloudy waters over the Pennines, a combination that, throughout the 19th century, exchanged coal and limestone for cash between Leeds, Wakefield, Bradford and Liverpool. The canal still moves purposefully. Old bridges – their pastel-red bricks coated in matt furry moss – cradle the moving water over ditches and rivers and between wading valleys.

The locks are a fusion of black-wet timber and engineered steel. Bingley Five Rise and the Burnley Embankment are considered two of the greatest feats of canal engineering. Between them are vast circles of still water – pools large enough to turn a dozen long boats. Outside of summer, they are empty, like idle lidos waiting for the early-morning bathers. November raindrops cascade out into gentle, rounded ripples, while underwater drains gurgle like boiling eggs in a pensioner's steel pot.

The £20 million Liverpool Canal Link was finished in 2009. It is a triumph, reconnecting the Leeds and Liverpool Canal to the Liverpool Docks system and the tides around the River Mersey.

My favourite parts for overnighting are around the 19km (12 miles) of fresh water at Skipton and Gargrave. Canoes get the best of it – mooring up on the opposite side to the towpath, often with a bivvy on the grassy sections between the water's edge and the farmers' fences. Gargrave has several shops and cafés. The village is historically a resting point for travellers who stop over on their way from Bradford and Leeds, en route to the Lake District and the east coast. Barges still overnight here. They've been doing it for more than 200 years.

The beautiful town of Barnoldswick lies 13km (8 miles) away. Goldfinches prance between the berries of hawthorn trees like ornate birds of paradise in a Thai temple. This is the highest town on the canal, situated between Barrowford Locks and Greenberfield Locks and less than 48km (30 miles) from Leeds, Manchester, Preston and Lancaster.

There are a few campsites along the way; good for wilders in need of respite. Eshton Road Caravan Park, Eshton Road, Skipton is close to the water. Travellers mostly wild as part of a canoe, cycle or hiking trip over the Yorkshire Dales and the Pennines, or between the connecting waters to the Aire & Calder Navigation, flowing east of Leeds to the tidal River Ouse, at Goole. It's difficult sometimes not to feel alone. This is the quietest water on the 3,220km (2,000-mile) canal network.

The Canal & River Trust fishing pass (see page 42) can be used to camp and fish around more than 48km (30 miles)

of water east of Whittle-le-Woods, Chorley, and south of Barnoldswick, Pendle, both in Lancashire. Other rights have been leased to several private clubs, but they rarely allow overnighting, which is a shame.

The **Trans Pennine Trail** (346km/215 miles) follows the canal out of Maghull. Near to Barnoldswick, the canal links with the Pennine Way and Pennine Bridleway. Numerous other long-distance paths leading off the canal include the 64km (40-mile) Burnley Way (64km/40 miles), Leeds Country Way (100km/62 miles) and the Pendle Way (72km/45 miles), all passing through a mixture of forest, river valley, woodland and moorland.

PRACTICAL INFO There are many places just off and along the canal for canoeists, cyclists and walkers to bivvy and hammock. At Old Hall Bridge (53.951780, -2.1401024), divert a little way south along the Pennine Way from where it meets the towpath. The Way leads to quiet lanes, an old Roman road, fort and disused railway line that can be explored via several short footpaths (53.933555, -2.1351242) running north-east.

TRAVEL Trains and buses take you into Leeds, Bradford, Liverpool, Wigan, Chorley, Skipton and Gargrave.

48 RIVER SOAR

THERE WERE MORE than 200 factories around the banks of the **River Soar** by the end of the 19th century. Today, the edges are mostly lined with large yellow buttercups that flower beneath stubby nettles and elder. The river moves over 80km (50 miles) from its source at Wibtoft in Warwickshire to Trent Lock, via Leicester.

Leicester took its name from the early settlers who chose to 'camp' among the blackthorn, ash and spindle. The people were called the Ligor; *castra* was the Latin

word for 'camp' or 'fort'. After 1066, the Normans stole their name and settlement and carved it into the Domesday Book as the more French-sounding Ledecestre.

The creation of the Grand Union Canal, and its link to the Soar, heralded the rise of the textile factories, and the continued migration of the workers from the fields to the towns. Trade was helped by the fact that the river cut through Leicester bottom to top on an angle, west to east, to meet the River Trent to the north.

Footpaths still line both sides of the water. The trails are mostly quiet in winter, used only by the occasional local who chooses to walk between towns and villages – from Hathern to Kegworth; Barrow upon Soar to Mountsorrel; Sharnford to Broughton Astley.

Canoe-camping is the best way to explore most of the 95km (59 miles) of waterway. The river is popular with anglers, who catch carp, chub, bream, roach and perch. A canalised section runs through the city, with students from the two universities – University of Leicester and De Montfort University – holding a rowing race each year.

The towpaths next to the canal are used for cyclists, ramblers and horse-riders.

PRACTICAL INFO Canoeing and kayaking the prettiest section of the Soar is between Normanton on Soar (52.807068, -1.2477207) and Kegworth (52.839458, -1.2677622). It's less than 5km (3 miles), but lots of places to hang a hammock to relax by day or night (permission may be needed along some parts). The tree-lined east riverbank can be walked by footpath.

TRAVEL Trains and buses take you into Barrow upon Soar, Ratcliffe on Soar, Loughborough and Leicester.

49 COTSWOLD HILLS

I WAS TOLD the view up here was good. From Cleeve Hill Common – 330m (1,082ft) up on the Cotswold ridge – it's possible to see the Severn Vale, Forest of Dean, the Malverns, and even the Brecon Beacons on a good day. What I didn't expect to hear was a golfer. Kicking up the dusty limestone on the highest point on the scarp, I spun round towards the Severn Valley and heard, of all things, not a skylark, but a shout of 'four'.

The Cotswolds are a backdrop of beech woods, sheep tracks and open common around the towns of Bath, Stroud and Cheltenham. History is everywhere: stone circles, Iron Age hill forts, Roman settlements (Bath) and Roman roads (the Fosse Way). Wool production has been important for so long there's even a breed of sheep known locally as the Cotswold Lion.

Sheep-farming was partly to blame for the enclosure of the common land during the Middle Ages, as stone walls and hedgerows were put up. The wool estates spawned settlements like Sherborne Park, Blenheim Palace and Dyrham Park. The Cotswold Hills today are not so 'closed'. The magnificent Cleeve Hill Golf Course, created

on 1,000 acres of common land, sums this up quite well. The club's website reads:

Whilst the course's stunning setting is but a gift of nature, the club's growing reputation is based on a philosophy of encouraging 'no frills' access – free of trivial barriers and unnecessary impediments. Its 'open door' approach to membership encourages people in the community to take up exercise, helps showcase the local countryside to visitors, and at the same time underlines the virtues of comradeship in sport.

I know many golf clubs are casting off the elitist label to chase the green fees, but there's no hint of enclosure in those words.

More importantly, the philosophy of access is enshrined in the estimated 4,777km (2,968 miles) of public rights of way in the Cotswolds, much of it across the richest estates. These paths include two national trails: the start of the 296km (184-mile) Thames Path National Trail and, perhaps more importantly, the 163km (101-mile) **Cotswold Way,** which winds its way around Cleeve Hill.

Sleeping wild along the Cotswold Way in spring is the best way to see the hills. The woods are full of bluebells and the beech tree canopies that radiate green and yellow sunlight from their fledgling oval leaves. There are endless places to camp just off the main trail, especially where alternative paths occasionally divert off to run parallel between foliage, woodland or open fields. It's always polite to check before pitching a tent or bivvy. The reality of finding the actual owner late afternoon or at dusk usually renders attempts to 'ask first' unrealistic. Formal campsites are infrequent, so be prepared to wild camp for a whole week if taking on the full length of the Way. It's a trek worthy of taking time over.

The Cotswold Way passes Sudeley Castle, Hailes Abbey and the scene of the Battle of Lansdown Hill in 1643. It also connects walking routes including the Macmillan Way, Gloucestershire Way, Wychavon Way and Wychwood Way.

PRACTICAL INFO Climb over Cleeve Common along the Winchcombe Way (51.934661, -2.0192957) to The Ring settlement on Cleeve Hill, above the golf club. Come back down on the Cotswold Way via the Roman fort (51.927688, -2.0232010). Look to camp in the wooded hills south of Cheltenham along the Cotswold Way.

TRAVEL Trains and buses take you into Old Sodbury, near Chipping Sodbury, Wotton-under-Edge, Dursley, Stroud, Painswick, Cranham, Leckhampton, Cheltenham, Winchcombe, Stanway and Broadway.

50 OXFORD CANAL

THE OXFORD CANAL community is a combination of holidaymakers, transient travellers and static barges. I met a family near Woodstock who had been living on the water for nine years. They'd spent the last year under a railway bridge. It seemed incredible that someone looking to find peace and quiet on a waterway would decide, of all places, to set up home under a railway line. The husband told me they stopped noticing the trains after only a few months. He carried on talking as another passed over, so I couldn't hear a word he said. Anyway, at least they had shelter, I thought. The rain was hard. We stood there together – he afloat, me on the towpath – watching the puddles rise as a family of swans heckled for bread like stray dogs in an alley. Once the rain stopped, I carried on across the fields. Linnets and skylarks flashed into the sky as white dead-nettles flowered like silk bells on their hairy stems.

The Oxford Canal is 126km (78 miles) long and links Oxford with Coventry via the counties and countryside of Oxfordshire, Northamptonshire and Warwickshire. The canal connects with the Grand Union at Braunston, and both flow west before they split at Napton Junction. This is where the Oxford Canal turns south towards Oxford and the Grand Union turns north-west to Birmingham. The two rival canal companies were once bitter rivals, but the rise of the train after the Second World War saw both routes saved by the leisure barges that now keep them open.

The surrounding land is flat but sometimes tough walking, mainly because there are more rocks than crops in the barren autumn earth. Fields are tightly ploughed to the path edge and hedges, which makes for narrow trails. There are places to hammock in the thickets of ivy, oak and dead trees between canal and farmland. Woodland and old coppices break up the scenery between the occasional road. Blackberry vines hang down from tall elder trees, draping their tips in the still water like tentacles from landed octopi. Fish feed on the surface of the shallow edges.

The **Oxford Canal Walk** (133km/ 83 miles) follows the canal towpath and crosses just one road. There are hundreds of adjoining and linking rights of way for the camper to explore after dusk if the canal path becomes busy in high season.

The Oxford Canal connects with the River Thames at Oxford, and the Grand Union Canal at the villages of Braunston and Napton-on-the-Hill, while the Oxfordshire Way (108km/67 miles) links the Thames Path and the Cotswolds.

PRACTICAL INFO Explore open countryside between a canal section south of Banbury (52.055143, -1.3260627) and the disused quarry at Kirtlington (51.873431, -1.2880611). Lots of tree-lined canal and adjoining riverbank to hammock over this 24km (15-mile) stretch.
TRAVEL Trains and buses take you into Oxford, Lower Heyford, Banbury, Rugby and Coventry.

51 RIVER TRENT

A PAIR OF KINGFISHERS darted into a hole along a steep section of the Trent bank. Grasses hung over the muddy edges like the fringed mop of a schoolboy's forehead. I washed my hands in the water across from where plumes of white smoke rose from the eight cooling towers of the power station at Ratcliffe-on-Soar. The fat tail of steam moved low and east on the prevailing breeze; the same direction as me.

A middle-aged woman walking her dog was in a hurry, but still nodded, 'Morning.' She caught my quiet mood. 'Shame, isn't it?' she said, as she looked up at the chimneys of smoke and mould. And we

both smiled. I think it was the first time I'd spoken to anyone in over 24 hours.

It had taken me just over five days to walk the 113km (70 miles) from the moors of the Dark Peak, around the Kinder Scout plateau (634m/2,080ft), along a combination of paths – the Pennine Way, the Pennine Bridleway and the Derwent Valley Heritage Way – to the River Trent. The Peak District is the highest point of the Trent's catchment and responsible for much of the fast flow after just a few hours' rain.

Stoke-on-Trent, Birmingham, Leicester, Derby and Nottingham define the contrast between the hills and the river valley.

The towns and cities are less a blot on the landscape, more a social partition, with six million people living between pastures, woodland and vale. For all that, even the towering power station seemed more a curiosity than an offence. I inhaled the warm morning air, and caught a fly in the back of my nose.

The source of the River Trent is in Staffordshire, on Biddulph Moor. The 298km (185-mile) waterway trails out to the Humber Estuary and North Sea. For some, it remains the defining boundary between north and south. It is England's third longest river, passing through Staffordshire, Derbyshire, Leicestershire, Nottinghamshire, Lincolnshire and Yorkshire.

The entire valley is farmland – a mixture of cattle, corn, sugar beet and crooked white lines of flowering potato plants. Industry has always been important here; too much so at times. I was told that anglers once caught thousands of salmon each year, but the Industrial Revolution eliminated the oxygen in the water and the life. Improvements since the late 1970s have seen many fish return. Barges and boats still carry sand and gravel. The Trent and Mersey Canal runs parallel to the upper parts of the river around Burton upon Trent.

The valley can be prone to flooding after heavy rain, so weather checks are important for the longer, overnight trips. The combination of interlinking waterways, flooded gravel pits and very occasional local byways offer plenty of opportunities to find an overnight shelter. Adjoining canal towpaths and tracks provide access for walkers and cyclists most of the way, although not always tight to the river itself.

The **Trent Valley Way** follows the river's line. Canoes and kayaks can navigate more than 160km (100 miles) below Burton upon Trent on a combination of canal and river. There are various clubs at Stone, Burton, and Nottingham that offer welcome guidance and advice on journey, stopovers, camping and even possibly an offer of an overnight stay. The Trent is tidal below Cromwell Lock, but advice should be taken from the relevant navigation authority before entering. Fishing the tidal areas for eels and barbell tends to be best after rainfall, and at night.

Routes linking to the Trent include the Cuckoo Way (74km/46 miles), a sometimes overgrown walk – which I especially like for overnighting in a tent. It follows the Chesterfield Canal through Derbyshire, Nottinghamshire and South Yorkshire. The Erewash Valley Trail (43km/27 miles) can also be walked or cycled.

PRACTICAL INFO Canoe-camp and fish by night on the east foreshore, beside the woodland, and along The Cliff, north of Burton upon Stather (53.662846, -0.68961740); explore the network of footpaths around the sand and gravel pits north of Collingham, east riverbank (53.164051, -0.78406334).

TRAVEL Trains and buses take you into Stoke-on-Trent, Stone, Rugeley, Burton upon Trent, Castle Donington, Derby, Long Eaton, Beeston, Nottingham, Newark-on-Trent, Gainsborough.

52 BLACK HILL

THE SCREAMING was annoying. The birds were moving about the canopy of two large oak trees, and then down into the thickets around the water mint. A single magpie was under constant attack from two blackbirds, a male and a female. They seemed to be following me. However quickly I moved up towards Black Hill, they were still there. Then I realised the birds were oblivious to anything other than the frightened trap of their own dispute. I kept moving, faster, past the purple moor-grass and the foxgloves. Looking up towards the upland heath and peaks, wanting to stop and sit and rest, but unnerved by the chatter blistering my ears, as more and more smaller birds kept arriving for the grating exchange.

And then I saw the twist. The magpie had hold of a young blackbird. The victim was almost full size, but still had its adolescent tan feathers. In between chasing off the two parent blackbirds, the magpie would return to re-trap the youngster, to stab down with its giant black beak, a fanatical hunter with a mechanical, upturned anvil thrusting into a tiny feathered ball; again and again. I picked up a stick and spun it across the ground, forcing the magpie off. Not to save the young bird, but wanting to kill it quickly. But it was already dead. Lifeless. Torn. I walked on towards the Olchon Valley, slowly. Now everything was silent. And I hoped the killer crow would return to his meal, rather than go hunt or steal another.

Bruce Chatwin used this place as the setting for his novel *On the Black Hill*. It was a brutal tale. Not of the wild, but of – among other things – the domesticity of a farming family. I looked back several times but never saw the magpie return,

and cursed myself for intervening, knowing I'd made a mistake.

Black Hill rises to 640m (2,100ft), in the Black Mountains in Herefordshire, close to the Welsh border. To the west is the village of Craswall, where the hill is called 'Cat's Back', because that's what it looks like. Most of the area is common land, a mixture of bracken against red sandstone and earth. This is the very edge of proper wild camping territory. The mountains spread across the Welsh and English border, and west to the Brecon Beacons. Bivvies are lighter and easier to pitch, but there's enough flat ground here to justify the comfort of a tent for roomier views over the Olchon Valley or to huddle from the cold morning mists. The best time to visit is a cloudless day and night in September –

but check the weather and take warm clothing. It gets cold up there.

Offa's Dyke Path crosses over Black Mountain, and links with the **Herefordshire Trail** (248km/154 miles) before it circles around the county's castle ruins, rivers and woodland, where former stone quarries lie quietly abandoned.

PRACTICAL INFO Camp down to watch the sun set over Offa's Dyke (52.007710, -3.0853558) and the Black Mountains in Wales from the top of Black Hill in Herefordshire (52.006918, -3.0582333).

TRAVEL Trains and buses take you into Hay-on-Wye, Llangorse, Talgarth, Crickhowell, Cwmdu, all of which are in Powys; Abergavenny in Monmouthshire and Longtown in Herefordshire.

53 LONG MYND

HEATHER REFLECTS a plum haze as the sun rises over the 11km (7-mile) long mountain plateau. A merlin circles down towards the River Onny. The Stiperstones, one of the higher hills, glows like a wall in a school yard from the other side of the valley.

Long Mynd is part of the Shropshire Hill range between Shrewsbury in the north, Ludlow to the south, and the Welsh border over to the west. Iron Age forts are a reminder that camping above 500m (1,640ft) was once a matter of genuine survival. These peaks form a natural border, a historic defence against raids from either side of the boundary line. Today, 19,000 people live here in the 802-sq km (310-sq miles) of relative peace.

The hills have been shaped by centuries of feudal control. Almost 70 per cent of the land is still used for grazing. Former 'squatter' settlements on common land are the remnants of old Roman mining areas, once the largest of their kind in Europe. The Bog Visitor Centre is a former mine once surrounded by 300 buildings and many hundreds more workers. The whinberries collected commercially by the miners' wives are still common in the mountains. Much of the land is now owned by the National Trust.

It's a steep climb up on to the Long Mynd from Church Stretton – the only town near here. Better to hike than bike, although horse-riding and mountain-biking are popular. Spring is so much quieter than summer, but it can get cold after dark, so wear woollen base layers when sleeping. The volcanic rocks and uneven paths provide good walking among more than 3,000

sheep, some wild ponies and red grouse. The Clee Hills near Ludlow are the highest point at 540m (1,772ft).

Several of the peaks above Church Stretton have a few remaining trees to hammock and shelter in when the weather turns. Wenlock Edge has more than 24km (15 miles) of continuous woodland above 300m (984ft). I carry both a hammock and a bivvy here, rather than a single tent, as I like to have the option of sleeping up or down. Isolated pitches are not hard to find on the heath or upland forests.

The rivers are home to otters and freshwater pearl mussels. Native white-clawed crayfish are protected and can't be caught for food.

In the valleys, the rivers Clun, Teme and Onny are mostly lined by elder. The quietest stretches of the rivers Clun and Teme need to be explored by canoe or kayak as the public paths tend to guide walkers away from the waterways. If the water is high enough, it's possible to launch from any of the road bridges (eg Clungunford). The Onny Trail is a good ramble.

The Shropshire Way, the **Jack Mytton Way** and Offa's Dyke Path are three long-distance trails in and out of the area. The Malvern Hills and the Cotswolds are to the south. On a good day it's almost possible to see the Peak District to the north. Birmingham is 48km (30 miles) to the east.

PRACTICAL INFO My favourite walk in the hills is along the brook through Ashes Hollow (52.530217, -2.8309107), with many hidden places on the way up to the Long Mynd to hammock in the trees.
TRAVEL Trains and buses take you into Craven Arms and Church Stretton.

54 DARK PEAK

CROWS BREEZE QUIETLY past as walkers and cyclists crawl along the ridges; diligent but slow progress framed in the outline of their shadows against a backlit skyline.

The Vale of Edale is a super highway, super-junket mass of paths and rivers that momentarily mesh together like fibres on a golden power cable. As you walk the network of pastel trails in autumn, they unravel like copper threads into the Dark Peak's bracken moorland and rocky escarpments.

The walk up is best. Parking is free around Castleton on weekdays, but there's a satisfaction in the leg muscles feeling the longer climb from Hope, the nearby village.

This is one of the busiest tracks in Britain. The late-afternoon hikers look upon wild campers as a curiosity when they set up at sunset. Embankments lower down are an opportunity to explore and stay hidden. Occasional trees are good for whoopie slings and hammocks, and shelter. The wind rubs fast along the ridges. Sometimes when it's raining, the breeze is so fixed it dries the grass before the droplets have had a chance to lick their blades. Snow may cover much of the higher ground in December and January. Sixty minutes after dark – even in summer – the ridges are lonely and still.

The Dark Peak, or High Peak, between Derbyshire and South Yorkshire, takes its name from the wilder landscapes that sometimes outshine the southern White Peak. These upland areas include the moorland of Bleaklow, Black Hill and Kinder Scout (631m/2,070ft). The moors were previously closed to the public. A mass trespass was held at Kinder Scout in 1932 as a protest at the lack of access to countryside across the UK. The action was a partial success in that the moor was opened up to the public, although the land retains some of its forbidden status as an estate for grouse-shooting and sheep.

The Pennine Way curves into Edale on its 435km (270-mile) hike high and north towards Scotland. The **Trans Pennine Trail** (346km/215 miles) links the Dark Peak horizontally to the east coast at Hornsea, East Yorkshire, and the west coast at Southport, Merseyside. Caving and climbing are popular because of the limestone rocks. More than 10 per cent of the land is owned by the National Trust, including the more impressive parts around Derwent Edge, Kinder Scout and Mam Tor.

Outdoor sleeping can be frowned upon, especially in summer when the ground is prone to fire risk. Sleeping out is permissible with owners' permission, but is more likely to be granted outside of the busier months.

PRACTICAL INFO Walk to Kinder Scout (53.392158, -1.8675041) along the Pennine Way, the scene of the mass protest that kickstarted the outdoor access movement; hike to the highest points of Edale Moor to look down into the Vale of Edale (53.380666, -1.8142891).

TRAVEL Trains and buses take you into Hadfield, Glossop, Edale, Hathersage, Buxton, Chinley and Penistone.

55 WHITE PEAK

I 'DISCOVERED' THE THRILL of combining mountain-biking and camping in the Peak District. I can't explain the light-bulb moment. It might have been the hundreds of fellow cyclists I'd passed in the park over that weekend. Maybe it was the access into the hills that rise around the Wild Moor, east of Buxton, and Shining Tor. Maybe the fresh air just went to my head, but I was almost drunk with excitement.

It's slightly damper here in the South Peaks. Moist ferns take root between the crevices of giant branches that have become unwitting bearers of fruit: surrogate crèches covered in a blanket of soft moss around Goyt Forest. Flocks of blue tits flit and jolt into the air in erratic bumpy clouds of dust. As they move above the treetops and past the thickets, grey herons fly along the valley like great predatory hunters swimming in a blue channel of air.

Tors, caves, sinkholes, wet alder woods and oak forest elevate the surroundings from the villages and the lowland farms below. Some cliffs and ledges are more difficult to get to than others, especially when pushing a bike, but where the access is most limited is where campers tend to go undisturbed. Natural caves and disused

mines can provide shelter, but caution and local advice is needed.

The tallest parts are around the Cheshire, Staffordshire and Derbyshire peaks. Shining Tor is the highest point in Cheshire and lies between the towns of Buxton and Macclesfield. This is the Shining Valley – steeped in oak trees that rise from the limestone banks on either side to touch your nose along the footpaths overhead. Cats Tor is just to the north.

Packhorse bridges guide the traveller, walker and cyclist around the rivers, streams and falls. Bracken stems shine like fluorescent tubes in the low midday sun. The **Limestone Way** (74km/46 miles) passes south through the Derbyshire Dales to Rocester in the Dove Valley.

PRACTICAL INFO Explore the numerous quarries, disused mines and woods, and camp and bivvy along more than 11km (7 miles) of the River Manifold from Hulme End to Ilam Country Park (53.053751, -1.8066502).

TRAVEL Train and bus services take you into Buxton, Matlock, Macclesfield and Cheddleton.

56 RIVER SEVERN

THE WIRY FIGURE of the fisherman waist-deep in water, erect and still like a wooden lighthouse, was the only person I saw as I pushed off the canoe into the surging flood tide before dawn.

The sandbanks around the estuary were peaceful and still on the low water; quieter in the darkness before the dawn chorus of waders. The tide was fast crawling out of the creeks and over the rippled mud. I floated the beam of light from my head torch along the silver-froth flow, and watched the curled piles of lugworm cast slip under, one by one.

Plynlimon, in northern Ceredigion, Wales, is where the River Severn starts. The Celts named it Sabrinn-â after a goddess of the river, from which the English 'Severn' takes its name. A statue to 'Sabrina' stands in Dingle Gardens in Shrewsbury. The estuary, like the river, forms the Welsh/English border. There are three ways to explore and camp along almost all of the 354km (220 miles) of river: canoe, walk or cycle. This trail is so good it's worth doing all three.

I prefer to start inland if walking, finishing at the estuary. The **Severn Way** follows the water from its source and

finishes at the sea, passing Hafren Forest, Llanidloes, Newtown, Welshpool, Shrewsbury and Ironbridge. The trek is relatively flat, so good for cycles. The path often leaves the water, and I like the lift of rejoining it after exploring a canal, village, town or reservoir. It's a great footpath, but shouldn't be kept to religiously. Don't get sucked into finishing the one trail at the expense of missing some of the diversions along the way, like the Malvern Hills (see page 147) and the Wyre Forest.

Wild nights can be more difficult if arriving on foot close to a large town at dusk, so plan to be away from them with some good daylight left. Minimal planning avoids making a mistake. Canoes are less of a problem with access to many more hidden spots, subject to either a low riverbank or a shallow, still shore no more than waist-high. There are shops and cafés at intervals along the way.

The Severn and its path link to several major routes, but possibly the most important connection is with the River Avon Trail from Bristol, which eventually leads on to London and then up into the heart of England via the canal network.

PRACTICAL INFO Fish and bivvy 24 hours along the quietest tidal foreshore areas north and south of Littleton Warth (51.616711, -2.5965500); forage in Wonder Coppice, east of Telford, and explore the dismantled railway line along the northern edge of the trees (52.633652, -2.5538546); spend at least a day exploring the multiple coppice and former deer park areas around Apley Terrace (east riverbank) and Colemore Green to the west (52.576089, -2.4203396). The Severn has many corners to investigate, but don't neglect to leave it to explore and find a bed on silent tracks such as the footpath between the disused canal and the River Salwarpe, south of Hawford (52.237873, -2.2230148).

TRAVEL The nearest train stations at the source of the Severn are at Machynlleth, Pontarfynach and Caersws, and the nearest bus stop is Llanidloes. In the south, trains run into Avonmouth, Severn Beach and Gloucester on the English side of the river, Chepstow, Lydney and Caldicot on the Welsh side.

SEE PAGE 5 FOR KEY TO SYMBOLS

IRELAND

57

MUNSTER BLACKWATER

THEY CALL HER the Irish Rhine. The Munster's peat-coloured water provides the local name: the Blackwater or Munster Blackwater rises in the hills, flanked by a naked pool and a trickling, gravel-bottomed stream. She flows from the Mullaghareirk Mountains in Kerry, through the counties of Cork and Waterford into the Celtic Sea at Youghal Harbour, over the peat-rich soil. The estuary town takes its name from the woodland that once lined the river: 'Eochaill', the Irish phrase meaning 'yew wood'. Peat and yew trees. Only three countries in the world were ever richer: Finland, Canada and Indonesia.

The Blackwater, at 168km (105 miles) long, is among Ireland's best salmon rivers. Munster was one of the original Provinces of Ireland before it was shired into counties by the first Norman Invasion in the 12th century. Before the 9th century, the Blackwater flowed into the sea at Whiting Bay. But a vicious storm broke the riverbanks – taking many lives with it – and the estuary was moved by nature to form a natural harbour at Youghal. The Normans built new settlements and military posts and by the 17th century it was one of Ireland's main ports. Early trade involved bringing in coal from Wales in exchange for Irish timber to use as supports, or pit props, in the mines. The port status declined as ships became bigger and they were unable to get access over the shallow sand bars.

Although there's no single walking trail, hikers have been attempting and managing to follow most of the river from sea to source for centuries. For more than 95km (60 miles), it flows horizontally west to east into Waterford County until it reaches Cappoquin, where it turns south towards the sea. This section can be explored by canoe with a view to camping. The river's last 24km (15 miles) are tidal and navigable. The River Bride is a tidal tributary of the Blackwater, less than 8km (5 miles) south of Cappoquin, and is also navigable for 11km (7 miles).

The **Blackwater Way** (168km/104 miles) follows the river valley into the County of Kerry. It passes stone circles and cairns along forest track, bog, field path and sometimes road.

Fishing is expensive. In 1882, a decision was taken by the House of Lords to agree the claim of the Duke of Devonshire to exclusive fishery rights to the River Blackwater and Youghal Bay out to Capel Island. Both salmon and trout are common. The salmon season runs from February to the end of September.

PRACTICAL INFO Fish and canoe-camp 24 hours around the Munster's sandy foreshore (51.994183, -7.8867674) and (52.008872, -7.8480148); kayak 8km (5 miles) up the tidal River Bride (52.076446, -7.8787422) to find a trees to hammock.

TRAVEL Train and bus services take you into Youghal, Banteer, Mallow, Rathcool and Rathmore.

58 RIVER SHANNON

AS PART OF THE River Shannon navigation, Rindoon was once a strategic imperative but today it lies in ruins, on a peninsula in Lough Ree, County Roscommon.

The town was taken, and then built up, by the Anglo-Normans on their first invasion of Ireland in the 12th century. After it was abandoned in the 14th century, it never recovered. But it remains a marker in the ground at the edge of Norman-held territory, a line that had historical context over the centuries that followed.

The Shannon, like Rindoon, is a marker too. East from west. It's now more a keeper of reeds, ducks, swans and day cruisers than a military campaign. It is the longest river in Ireland and the British Isles – and one of the most beautiful. The river trail spans 360km (224 miles) for the long-distance traveller to explore on foot, bike or canoe. It passes through Lough Ree, as well as Lough Allen, Lough Tap, Lough Boderg and Lough Bofin, Lough Forbes and Lough Derg.

The river's source is in the Cuilcagh Mountain, in County Cavan, from where it surges through 11 counties before emptying into the vast, 100km (62-mile) long Shannon estuary at Limerick. The tidal part of the river ends just to the east of the city. The river was named after a woman searching knowledge, Sionann. Much like the biblical Eve character, she looked for wisdom – in Sionann's case, at Connla's Well – where there were salmon and hazel trees, both signifying knowledge and wisdom. Despite being apparently warned of the danger, folklore describes how she ate the Salmon of Wisdom to become wise. The well then burst and she drowned, flushed out to sea. It's possible that, similar to the Eve story, the myth signifies the transition of man from hunter-gatherer to cultivator, as the former dies a violent death by attempting to take ownership of the land, although there are many other theories.

The Shannon has been an important military line because of its division of the

land between east and west. She follows valleys, climbing no more than 76m (256ft) above sea level, which means there aren't many locks – good news for canoe-campers.

Walkers have the **Lough Derg Way** (68km/42 miles), following the banks of the River Shannon along the towpath, forest tracks and road from Limerick to Killaloe, Ballina. Towards the north are views of Lough Derg from the Arra Mountains. There are numerous towpaths along the Shannon-Erne Waterway. Formal campsites appear occasionally, but wild camping is necessary.

The Royal and Grand canals are just two of many waterways that link the river

to the rest of Ireland. It is joined to the River Erne and Lough Erne by the Shannon-Erne Waterway.

59 RIVER BLACKWATER

THE RIVER BLACKWATER in Northern Ireland is not linked to the southern version. It passes over more than 70km (45 miles) along the border between north and south before draining into Lough Neagh at Maghery. It rises in the west near to the town of Clogher.

The Blackwater Canoe Trail navigates through the counties of Armagh and Tyrone. Wild camping is encouraged en route with the permission of owners. At the time of writing, Copney Campsite is a free wild site only accessible from the river, provided by Outdoor Recreation NI. A spokesperson for the group states on its website:

The campsite will be a great asset for canoeists visiting the Blackwater Canoe Trail, its location half way along the

20km trail is ideally suited to allow their journey to be split over two days therefore making the trail more appealing for a short break.

Wild camping is a really important part of the canoe touring experience, the Copney campsite means canoeists can still have that wilderness experience without the difficulty of having to seek permission from a landowner. This new campsite is a great addition to our unique overnight accommodation offering for canoeists.

The free site is indicative of the attempts within northern and southern Ireland to promote the wilderness and wild camping. Pitches are available on a first-come, first-served basis, in partnership between

Outdoor Recreation NI, Dungannon & South Tyrone Borough Council, and funding from the Department of Culture, Arts and Leisure. Further information on the Blackwater Canoe Trail and campsite is available on http://www.canoeni.com.

The canoe trail starts at Maydown Bridge and leads north. It's possible to turn south from Maydown Bridge to Blackwater Town, but more skill is needed as the river can become either faster-flowing after rain or dry in drought. The canoe trail ends at Maghery Country Park, where it flows into Lough Neagh. Wild camping is permitted on Coney Island, situated in the south-west corner of the lough, about 1km (½ mile) from the country park. From Lough Neagh, canoes can join the Lough Neagh Canoe Trail and then the Lower Bann Canoe Trail situated at the north-east end of the lough.

There is walking access to the river at Derry Caw. In Craigavon, the **Loughshore Trail** (176km/110 miles) takes in parts of the River Bann and River Blackwater.

The Blackwater links to Lough Neagh and many hundreds of miles of river, path and canal, all good for wilding, including the River Bann. The Callan River joins the Blackwater 1.6km (1-mile) upstream from Bond's Bridge. Further on, at a bend on the east bank, is the entrance to the first lock of the Ulster Canal.

PRACTICAL INFO Wild camp on Coney Island (54.516998, -6.5510001) after completing the Blackwater Trail.
TRAVEL Buses take you into Aughnacloy, Caledon and Moy.

60 RIVER BANN

THE RIVER BANN is the longest river in Northern Ireland. Over 129km (80 miles), from the north-west coast to the south-east. Lough Neagh gapes from its middle. The Upper Bann rises in the Mourne Mountains in County Down and ends when it enters the lough at Bannfoot, County Armagh. The Lower Bann starts where it flows out of Lough Neagh at Toome. The 60km (38-mile) river from here is navigable. Waterways Ireland is the navigation authority, and

its staff manually operate the lock gates for a small fee. The river is tidal for 11km (7 miles), from The Cutts at Coleraine to the Atlantic at Portstewart.

The best way to explore the Bann is by canoe or kayak from Lough Neagh to the sea. Wild camping is necessary along the trail because there is limited accommodation. A wilderness campsite is provided by Waterways Ireland at Portna. Details on the canoe trail are available from http://www.canoeni.com.

Lough Neagh belongs to the Shaftesbury Estate and is the largest freshwater lake in the British Isles. There is no navigation authority outside of harbours and no registration or charges to use the waters. The **Loughshore Trail** circles 182km (113 miles) of the lake along quiet roads and track, and is part of the National Cycle Network. The Lower Bann Cycleway runs 72km (45 miles) from, and along, the Toome Canal to the Barmouth at Castlerock. It follows much of the river, but some of the route is on road.

PRACTICAL INFO Canoe camp or kayak from the estuary east of Castlerock (55.167692, -6.7706680) to Lough Neagh (54.752765, -6.4668274). Visit the earthen fort in Mountsandel Wood, on the east banks of the Bann, the earliest known settlement in Ireland, dating back to 7000 BC (55.117214, -6.6659546.)

TRAVEL Trains and buses take you into Ballymoney and Coleraine. Bicycles are free on Translink train services at weekends and on weekdays after 9.30am.

I HAVE GROWN TO LOVE checklists. I began creating them for my solo wild camping trips, something I'd never done in my youth, because the only important things I carried were a passport and cash.

Nowadays I mostly travel with a sleeping bag and bivvy. The bivvy is essentially a waterproof condom that wraps over my down sleeping bag. Back in the 1980s, I only ever bothered with a cheap three-season sleeping bag. Quite how I didn't freeze I just don't know, sleeping out in Sinai Desert for many weeks during January and February.

The bivvy protects my posh and expensive down bag from northern Europe's sometimes damp evenings. If I'm planning on a wooded excursion where the floor is short of flat space, I'll take my DD Hammock and sling the bivvy and bag inside. If on a long expedition, I'll carry my TrailStar or Akto – mainly because they provide more room than a bivvy if the weather turns nasty.

This is my list of essentials, followed by what I personally carry and why:

1 One of the most important pieces of kit, in my opinion, is a GPS locator and message system. If you are OK, you message to say so. If you don't, someone comes to the rescue. The Spot locator seems to me to be as good as anything else out there. I can set it up so my wife or anyone else can follow where I am day or night, and I can message if I have no phone signal.

As well as the GPS locator, there are two other useful pieces of communication. A VHF radio and a mobile phone. Sometimes one of them can be a lifeline. I started carrying a VHF radio for no other reason than it came with a sailing dinghy I bought about 15 years ago. I use a Galaxy SIII as a phone communicator. I'm not sure it provides anything other phones don't, but I always carry a spare charged battery and like to back up my OS maps on there, too.

2 Map, torch and compass and an ability to navigate. No one in the UK is ever more than 11km (7 miles) from a road or a few miles from a water source, and you need to be able to find them. I source my maps for free online, on the OS website or others. Although I print out in black and white because it's cheaper, I then colour in all the important paths and locations with marker pens. I carry my maps in a water-proof Aquapac case. I also download the same printed map on to my phone as a high-res jpg file.

For torches, I carry two cycle headlamp/ bike lamp 1800 LM CREE XM-L T6 LEDs. They last for up to eight hours each on the lowest setting, and about 90 minutes on full beam, which virtually lights up an entire valley for 100 yards. They come with rechargeable batteries.

I carry three compasses, one set into a whistle, one as an app on my phone and one regular compass. I've never needed more than the latter, but I do regularly check its accuracy with the phone app – just in case.

LEFT: Waterproof camera, pen and notebook on cycle cross bar pouch.

GPS LOCATOR

ABOVE: Cooking and chopping items can fit inside a bum belt.
Clockwise from bottom left: water filter; knife and sheaf; flint fire steel and holder; folding saw and sheaf; small axe; metal pegs, folding cutlery; fuel bottle for stove; mug; cotton and cord; lighter. *Centre:* cooking pot (with stove and cooking tablet inside); cotton wool rubbed in Vaseline; waterproof matches; whistle; washing-up liquid; metal scourer.

3 Warm shelter: essentially, I prefer a five-season Western Mountaineering sleeping bag and a waterproof shelter – either a tent, tarp or bivvy, which I choose depending on terrain or length of trip. I probably use the Rab Ridge Raider bivvy more than anything else, just because my trips tend to be mostly one night and because it can be set up almost anywhere, in the smallest place that offers shelter if needed.

If trekking where there are trees, I'll usually take my DD tarp and hammock. This gear is value for money and provides fast and easy shelter when the ground is uneven. There's something quite special about hanging from a tree, too. I tie a cloth around the cord to stop rain leaking inside.

I've always like Hilleberg tents. I use the Akto when I'm on a longer trip and want a little more luxury than the bivvy. It works better when it rains as I can pull my boots

and bag inside the porch rather than leaving them inside waterproof bags.

For a combination of tarp and tent, I use the TrailStar. Lots of room, light, easy to put up and makes use of walking sticks.

4 My clothes combination is designed to keep me dry and warm, without causing perspiration or condensation. Sometimes that's a tough ask, especially if uphill or cycling.

I'm not really so much into micro-light, a phrase travellers use when referring to the bare minimum. But my upper kit for several days will include 1) thin woollen base layer x2, 2) a cheap fleece, of thickness depending on season 3) a Pertex jacket with a Primaloft stuffing. I will also carry a lightweight hard-shell trouser and top. Shoes/boots are common sense but I go for Hi-Tec because they're good. I keep all my spare clothing in a dry bag.

CYCLE CAMPING: Sleeping bag inside dry bag on handlebars; bivvy on back rack; waterproofs, mat, change of clothes, food and first aid kit in yellow waterproof rucksack; cooking essentials in bumbag; water on bike; fishing rod strapped to crossbar.

5 Water. There's no logic to it, but in my younger years I'd drink straight from the well, even when backpacking in India. I never used Puritabs and never boiled the water. All throughout my 20s I couldn't understand anyone who wouldn't drink tap water in Spain or Greece. Now I don't even drink from a tap in Kent. As I've got older, I've just become more and more suspicious about water quality, especially in the outdoors, in mountain streams, rivers, anywhere. I've never been ill and I've no reason to doubt the ability of water filters to take out 99.9 per cent, although the issue of chemicals being present in the low-land does bother me. Stupid, because the dogs I've had drink everything and they've barely had a day off work. I carry a Sawyer water filter, which gets used more when I'm carrying powdered food and coffee that both need boiling in water. Other than that, I make sure I'm well hydrated before I leave for a trek. I take two 1-litre plastic bottles for drinking on the move, and a 1-litre bottle for emergencies. I also carry Puritabs.

6 My Fissure Ti-Tri cooking system is one of my favourite pieces of equipment. Although I'm not a micro-light camper, this one is clever because it's made from a coke can and weighs less than a sparrow. It runs on three fuels (alcohol, Esbit and wood). I use it to heat water and/or to start a fire.

7 Food. I like to carry stuff that can mix with water – coffee, powdered milk, couscous. Anything I can add water to, to make a meal.

○ **THIS LIST IS MY STARTING POINT.**
I don't carry everything; I make choices based on the trip.

WEARING
Trousers
Base layer
Woollen hat
Mittens
Woollen balaclava
Socks
Boots/sandals
Gaiters
Fleece (thick or thin)
Primaloft jacket

CARRYING
Dry food, including biscuits
Dry bag (for carrying socks and moving water from the river to the camp)
Silk motorcycle balaclava (winter)
Sealskin socks (for at night)
Water system (hard filter, tablet filter, water filter)
Waterproof trousers and top
Spare base layer top
Spare socks
Phone/charger
Personal locator
FM radio

First aid kit (including Israeli bandage, two first field dressings, antiseptic cream and blister plasters etc), antiseptic wipes, long length of plaster, gauze, scissors, bandage, safety pins, tick removal card with mirror
Spare batteries (kept in my pouch on body for warmth so they will still function when freezing)
Penknife
Laplander folding saw
26cm Wetterlings Buddy Axe
Fire lighter (including steel, vase-lined wool, wet matches – which light when wet – two lighters)

8 Walking poles were a revelation for me. It might be something to do with age, but the more I kept walking unaided, the more I saw people with them. I read lots of reviews and ended up with Pacerpoles. There's not the space here to go into great detail about the benefits. So I'll tell a short story.

I live in Essex in the seaside town of Southend-on-Sea and I work in Basildon, about 11km (7 miles) away. I walked to work on the pavement one day and managed the journey in 2 hours and 20 minutes. I could barely stand up that night because the hard ground had impacted so much on my limbs (I play three rounds of golf each week on grass – around 24km/15 miles – without any problem). When the poles came through, I attempted the same journey and arrived in 1 hour 55 minutes. That night I played a round of golf with the poles, too. I've never looked back. I take them with me on the trail because I can walk further, longer and safer. Sometimes I use them for golf.

9 Knife/axe/saw. I bought most of this stuff second-hand on eBay. Knives have fascinated me ever since I was a kid. Axes a little less so. Saws even less. The practical uses of each or all in the wild are fabulous. The most obvious use for the knife is multi-purpose. Cutting things, removing splinters, sawing small branches, repairs to equipment. The axe and saw are most likely to be carried when I'm on a canoe, and their main function is for cutting wood for fire, especially if it is raining and I need to remove the damp wood.

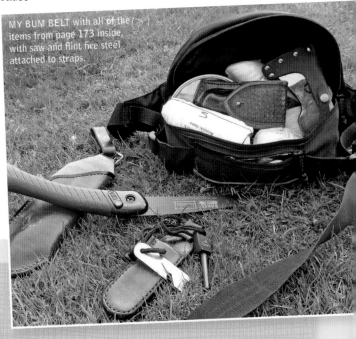

MY BUM BELT with all of the items from page 173 inside, with saw and flint fire steel attached to straps.

Matches/lighter
Stove and fuel (meths best when very cold)
Candle lanterns/UCO 9-hour citronella candles
One pot
Drinking cup
Spork
Water filter and bottles
Stuff sacks (for organising gear)
Dishwashing kit (washing-up liquid/pot scrubber/ dishcloth)
Tent

Western Mountaineering sleeping bag
Exped Down Mat 7 UL sleeping mat
Sealable plastic bags
Hand shovel
Wet wipes (almost as good as a cool shower on a very hot day)
Insect repellent/midge head-cover
Multi-purpose soap

Toilet paper
Toothbrush
Toothpaste
Camera
E-book reader

If I'm walking or cycling, I aim to carry no more than 12kg (26lb) including the bag (excluding water) in my Lowe Alpine TEX Expedition rucksack, but it can be tough to stick to.

GRAND CANAL

GREAT IRISH WATERWAYS are defined by arching stone bridges and grassy towpaths that tiptoe out towards the countryside and beyond. Herons flay their wings in wide circles of calm flight, while swans dip and swoon in regal indifference to the occasional narrowboat. Aside from nature, these trails are barely recognisable from canals in England, just because there are so few people.

Grand Canal opened in 1804 to connect Dublin in the east to the River Shannon in the west. The canal is 131km (82 miles) long, with 43 locks. It begins at the River Liffey, in Grand Canal Dock, and continues through to Shannon Harbour in County Offaly, via blackberry bushes, sycamore trees and cattle farms that line the countryside around Kildare, Caragh, Prosperous, Robertstown, Tullamore and Rahan.

The canal can be canoed or walked. The **Grand Canal Way** is a 117km (73-mile) long-distance trail along the towpath, which is a combination of gravel, grass and hard.

Its route passes through much of Ireland's history, past lock-keepers' cottages and villages that were settled as trade grew up around the canal in the 18th century. There are occasional towns where overnight B&Bs are available, but anyone setting out should expect to have to wild camp at some stage.

The Grand is one of two canals linking east and west Ireland. Its sister canal is the Royal Canal, which opened in 1817, and runs for 146km (90 miles) on a slightly more northerly course from Dublin to the Shannon.

PRACTICAL INFO Start out from Grand Canal Quay (53.341149, -6.2383890) on foot; wooded areas of the canal east of Rathangan make good canoe-camping (53.245264, -6.9154000), but check with local farmers or Waterways Ireland.
TRAVEL Trains and buses take you into Dublin, Sallins, Naas, Edenderry, Tullamore and Banagher.

62 BLACK STACKS

THE BLACK STACKS are the island's highest mountain range. Known as MacGillycuddy's Reeks – after the clan that claims to have owned land in the region for more than a thousand years – these peaks span almost 120km (12 miles) across the Iveragh Peninsula, Ireland's south-westerly region of County Kerry.

Hikers usually walk up from the Hag's Glen, in the north-east, to Ireland's highest peaks: Beenkeragh (1,010m/3,314ft) and Caher (1,001m/3,284ft). The top is Carrauntoohil (1,039m/3,409ft), close to the middle of the mountain range. Like the other two, it can be accessed via the Devil's Ladder and then a right angle north-west to the summit. Although walkers have not traditionally used climbing gear, the Devil's Ladder increasingly requires greater care as loose stones may cause fatal or hazardous slips. There are views over the Hag's Glen, Lough Callee and Lough Gouragh. The Kerry Mountain Rescue Team offers good advice on safety and online mapping for the range: http://www.kerrymountainrescue.ie/routes/devils_ladder.html.

The **Kerry Way** is an alternative for walkers who don't want to hike above 400m while exploring the Iveragh Peninsula. At 214km (133 miles), it is the longest of the Irish Waymarked Trails, circumnavigating the entire peninsula from Killarney. The path passes through the Black Valley, close to the lakes of Killarney, beaches and remote mountain moorland. Much of the off-road trail is isolated, which makes wild camping more of a necessity than a choice. Windy Gap, between Glenmore and Caherdaniel, is the steepest point at almost 400m (1,300ft).

PRACTICAL INFO Walk to MacGillycuddy's Reeks (51.981407, -9.6958580) from Hag's Glen.
TRAVEL Trains into Killarney, buses into Kenmare, Sneem, Waterville and Glenbeigh.

63 MOURNE MOUNTAINS

TIMBER FROM THESE mountain valley estates was used to build ships, including the Belfast-built *Titanic* in 1911. The Mourne Mountains are among the highest and toughest challenges for walkers in the north.

An alternative is the **Mourne Way** (42km/26 miles), an easy track along forest and mountain paths, following the foothills from Newcastle along the wooded banks of the Shimna River beneath Northern Ireland's second highest summit, Slieve Commedagh (765m/2,510ft). The Way traces the east bank of Fofanny Dam Reservoir and then over Butter Mountain (500m/1,640ft), the highest point of the route.

There are many paths to take up into the highest hills if the weather forecast is good and walkers have good mapping skills. The Mourne Wall Challenge follows the Mourne Wall and many of the highest mountains in the north, although some scrambling is needed. There are good views on a clear day of the Isle of Man, Lough Neagh and the Wicklow Mountains.

The tops include:
Slieve Muck (674m/2,211ft),
Slieve Loughshannagh (619m/2,031ft),
Slieve Meelbeg (708m/2,323ft),
Slieve Meelmore (682m/2,238ft),
Slieve Bearnagh (739m/2,425ft),
Slieve Binnian (747m/2,451ft) and
Slieve Donard (850m/2,789ft).

The Trassey Track (850m/2,789ft) – an old smugglers' path across the Mournes, south of Slieve Donard – is a popular route up.

SPERRIN MOUNTAINS

THE SPERRINS rise east to west across 64km (40 miles) of Tyrone and Londonderry. Sawel is the highest peak in the range, at 678m (2,224ft). A 37km (23-mile) section of the **Ulster Way** passes over the range along tracks and roads. It is necessary to leave the Way to climb into the higher parts, although there's no need if looking for quiet – the Glenelly Valley is considered one of the most isolated parts of the north.

The Ulster Way was created in the 1970s, partly inspired by the Pennine Way in England. It fell into disrepair but was revived in the last decade and a new route was officially opened in 2009. The Way's founder, Wilfrid Capper MBE, hiked the entire 1,070km (665 miles) in 32 days during the 1990s, when he was 88 years old. The Way merges with the International Appalachian Trail (450km/280 miles) in the Sperrins. The trail connects west Donegal in the Republic of Ireland to Larne, County Antrim, in Northern Ireland. The path starts at Slieve League mountain and passes the Blue Stack Mountains in County Donegal, rather than following the Ulster Way south.

There are some campsites and hostels along the way, but they are limited and wild camping is often necessary.

PRACTICAL INFO Hike up to Sawel (54.819786, -7.1264958), the highest point in the Sperrins; there is good camping lower down around the Glenrandel River (54.827584, -7.1213400), which flows down from Sawel.
TRAVEL Trains into Londonderry, buses to Strabane, Plumbridge, Claudy and Draperstown.

SLIEVE BLOOM MOUNTAINS

THE SLIEVE BLOOM MOUNTAINS rise from the very centre of Ireland. Although the highest peak, at Arderin, is just 527m (1,729ft), the relative flatness of the surrounding terrain provides views towards the edge of a 360-degree horizon. The range spans from near Roscrea, in the south-west, to Rosenallis in the north-west. There is a series of easy-to-follow trails at Slieve Bloom, Glenbarrow, Clonaslee, Cadamstown, Kinnitty, Glenafelly Forest and Glen Monicknew. The pine forest areas follow tracks out into open bog, moorland, heather ridges and glens. Some of the areas can get wet in winter, so good boots are needed. Red grouse and deer are common.

All paths link with the 60km (37-mile) **Slieve Bloom Way**, which follows waterfalls, streams and upland areas. The high points are Stillbrook Hill (514m/1,686ft), Baunreaghcong (509m/1,670ft) and Wolftrap Mountain (487m/1,598ft).

The Silver River Eco-Walk is available at Cadamstown.

PRACTICAL INFO Wild camp on the top of Arderin – the highest point in the Slieve Bloom Mountains – (53.039871, -7.6543808) during a dry spell in summer, when the mossy ground is less boggy.
TRAVEL Trains and buses into Portlaoise, Tullamore and Birr.

66 THE THREE SISTERS

THREE STORIES for three sisters: Devil's Bit took its name from the chunk Satan chewed from the rocky hills of County Tipperary, and then spat out; an 8th-century copy of four gospels – known as *The Book of Dimma* – was found here in a cave in 1789; almost 50,000 peasants staged a mass protest in 1832 against Church taxes (tithes).

Perhaps more importantly, the slopes of the Three Sisters mountain range are famous for being the source of Ireland's second great river: the River Suir. She joins with two other rivers, the Nore and the Barrow. The trio are known as the Three Sisters – all of which can be explored by canoe or foot around Waterford.

The Suir is only beaten by the Shannon in terms of its length. It flows 183km (114 miles) from Tipperary into the Celtic Sea, passing through Loughmore, Holycross and then forming the border between County Tipperary and County Waterford, just east of Newcastle, before Clonmel, Carrick-on-Suir and finally Waterford. A large Viking settlement was found in 2003 at a bend in the river at Woodstown, just upstream from Waterford.

Countryside along the river provides places to tent or hammock. Parts are a reminder of what Ireland was like more than a thousand years before the Norman Invasion. Otters and hawks between overhanging broadleaf trees; much of the riverbank is overgrown and sometimes difficult to pass.

The East Munster Way and the Tipperary Heritage Way skirt parts of the waterline.

The **East Munster Way** (70km/43 miles) follows the river upstream, west out of Carrick-on-Suir to Clonmel. Walkers sometimes need to cut their way through woodland and forestry tracks, although the towpaths, quiet roads and highland moors are mostly clear. The path climbs out of Kilsheelan into the foothills of the Comeragh Mountains. West of the Comeraghs, it reaches the north part of the Knockmealdown Mountains.

The Tipperary Heritage Way (56km/35 miles) picks up the river valley 13km (8 miles) west of the Comeraghs, at the village of Ardfinnan in County Tipperary, towards the town of Cashel. This area was once considered the most fertile part of the old kingdom. Vikings and then the Normans used the river to access what was known as the Golden Vale. The many historic building and military settlements along the way are a reminder of the various invasions.

As the trail often leaves the river, canoes are a good alternative to walking. The river is tidal for more than 32km (20 miles) between Carrick-on-Suir and the estuary area known as Cheekpoint, east of Waterford. Care should be taken around the fast-flowing waters, but they are among some of the best places to explore at high tide and to camp at low water.

PRACTICAL INFO The narrow and tree-lined River Clodiagh (52.287312, -7.2898579) is one of many small tidal inlets that can be explored by canoe or kayak to find a place to hammock on the foreshore.
TRAVEL Trains and buses take you into Waterford, Carrick-on-Suir, Clonmel, Thurles and Templemore.

67 RIVER BARROW

THE SECOND of the Three Sisters (see page 181) is the original 'wild west'. The River Barrow was a landmark around which the Norman invaders articulated distaste for Irish rebels by regarding them, and the water boundary, as a hostile frontier. The Anglo-Norman barons had landed in Ireland from 1169 onwards. But by the 13th century, the English Crown's control over the lands had begun to wane – partly because of indifference, partly because the old Anglo-Norman lords had made alliance with Gaelic peers, intermarried and become fully integrated into Irish society; detached from the Crown.

By the 15th century, the land directly controlled by 'the English' was limited to the counties of Meath and Kildare. This area was partitioned and 'defended' by fences and ditches, and became known as The Pale, from which the phrase 'beyond the pale' comes. Sir John Davies – the English MP and Attorney General for Ireland – was quoted in the early part of the 17th century as saying, 'Whoso lives by west of the Barrow, lives west of the law.' What followed was more than 400 years of war between those who wanted greater central government control and those who did not.

Today, Beyond the Pale is a seemingly peaceful journey, although there's still some dispute: whether the Barrow or its sister river, the Suir, is the second longest river in Ireland. Unofficially at 192km (120 miles), what's a mere 7km (4 miles) between siblings – even if it is propped by a canal.

The 114km (71-mile) long **Barrow Way** follows towpaths, roads and tracks along the freshwater river and canal between Lowtown in the north and the village of St Mullins in south County Carlow. This is one of the great inland walks in Ireland, from the Celtic Sea at Waterford Harbour to the Slieve Bloom Mountains, passing the towns of Portarlington, Monasterevin, Athy, Carlow/Graiguecullen, Graiguenamanagh and New Ross. Many of the smaller villages and towns were founded by the Normans soon after the invasion. The history, stories, monuments and castles along the route are incredible.

Several important canals built in the 18th century make the Barrow easily navigable for canoes. The canals were links between the port of Waterford and the Grand Canal, which connects the River Shannon to Dublin. The river navigation is made up of three main parts. Firstly, the tidal, which together as the Three Sisters (River Suir and River Nore) provide 88km (55 miles) to explore. Secondly, the freshwater Barrow, 66km (41 miles) inland from St Mullins, County Carlow, to Athy, County Kildare, via 23 locks. Thirdly, the Barrow Line of the Grand Canal, from Athy to the mainline Grand Canal at Lowtown, County Kildare, over a distance of 45km (28 miles) and just nine locks.

PRACTICAL INFO Walkers and canoes can camp around St Mullins Lock (52.495846, -6.9369435), where the river ceases to be tidal and becomes too shallow for boats to pass without the lock system; cross the river at Graiguenamanagh (52.540789, -6.9596672) and walk east for two hours up to Brandon Hill (52.508960, -6.9740868) for wild camping above the wooded Barrow Valley.

TRAVEL Trains and buses take you into Carlow, Bagenalstown, Athy, Monasterevin and Naas.

THE CHANCE TO SLEEP in cordgrass beside basking sharks and seals is a unique experience. Strangford Lough is an adventure; the largest salt-water inlet in the British Isles, spanning an area of 150sq km (60sq miles). The name 'Strangford' comes from the Vikings' Old Norse for 'strong sea-inlet'. The main body of water is known locally as Loch Cuan. A narrow channel links the lough – similar to a Scottish sea loch – to the Irish Sea, in County Down, on the east shore of Northern Ireland. There are bays and mudflats to explore, either on foot or by canoe. Wild camping is allowed around the loch and its many islands.

Walking and cycling trails are all around. The **Castle Ward Boundary Trail** follows 13km (8 miles) from the Shore Car Park, from the water's edge up to Audley's Castle. Separate walks over Delamont Country Park and Killyleagh lead down to the waterside. Waiting for the tide to go out is a good chance to access the quieter parts. A walk at low tide around Rough Island, off the Island Hill & North Strangford Nature Reserve, provides access to the Lough.

Canoes can explore the islands. A bothy is located on Salt Island, just south of Killyleagh – one of 11 canoe launch places on the circular Strangford Lough Canoe Trail. Other access points are at Castle Ward, Island Reagh and Horse Island. A key and payment is required for the bothy, but there's no charge for camping on the other side of the island at North Bay or along most of the shore landing places. Contact Strangford Lough wardens on 07776 462537 or 07900 678411 for more information or advice. For a guide, see http://www.canoeni.com.

PRACTICAL INFO Explore by canoe or kayak and wild camp any one of 40 islands off the coast of Whiterock (54.470087, -5.6222534). Walk the causeway to the 2.5ha (6-acre) Rough Island at low tide (54.546032, -5.6896734); paddle to the bothy on Salt Island (54.376371, -5.6438613).

TRAVEL Trains and buses to Belfast, Bangor, Newtownards, Killinchy, Greyabbey, Portaferry and Strangford.

HOW TO WILD: food and water   200

SEE PAGE 5 FOR KEY TO SYMBOLS

WALES

77

71
SNOWDONIA

79

ST WINEFRIDE'S WELL

R. DEE

72

74
BERWYN MOUNTAINS

87

78

MAWDDACH

69

OFFA'S DYKE

R. SEVERN

80

ABERYSTWYTH

73

75

76
PRESELI MOUNTAINS

BRECON BEACONS

FOREST OF DEAN

70

SWANSEA

GOLDCLIFF

CARDIFF

GOAT'S HOLE CAVE

DURING MY EARLY 20s, my dream was to write for Lonely Planet. I'm not entirely sure why. Maybe I wanted to have a reason to be out, rather than just tramping it on beaches and running away from a static life. A bit like owning a dog to justify walking the parks at dawn and dusk each day.

I also liked the idea of visiting places for free. Of course, the very opposite is true with travel writing. There's always a cost, and you have to go back. To do it all over again; the second time without the burden of work, without the hassle of having to think, to take notes, to take photos... burdened by the yoke of what's out there. Knowing that it can't all be done again, but wanting to, just because there's so much to see. Wales is an exception because it's so small and compact. So much in one place.

I'd climbed Cadair Idris before being commissioned to write this book. I remember standing up on top and looking down at Barmouth, back towards Bala and then up towards the Snowdonian mountains, and seeing a microcosm of the best bits of Britain, the highlights crammed into a few hundred miles of beach, river, mountain, dune and valley. Less a lonely planet, more a friendly garden.

There are several routes up: the **Pony Path**, from the Mawddach Estuary (5km/3 miles), the much steeper Fox's Path, the Llanfihangel y Pennant Path, and the Minffordd Path, from the south. There's a stone shelter on top, welcome if the weather has turned sour, less so on a blue-sky day with views. Trails linking to the main mountain tracks include the Glyndŵr's Way, Wales Coast Path, River Dovey and River Mawddach.

PRACTICAL INFO Trek up to Cadair's highest point on the Pony Path (52.701484, -3.9182138), before coming down to sleep in the Llyn Cau valley (52.694228, -3.9055538).

TRAVEL Trains and buses take you into Tywyn, Machynlleth and Barmouth.

70 BRECON BEACONS

THE CLIMB WAS STEEP, thighs burning, face red hot. The higher I got, the more I inhaled another breath of cooling air. Sheep fed on grass walls, glued to sheets of vertical, flattened green like fluffy albino limpets.

I'd arrived well before dawn, parking in the car park next to Llyn-Y-Fan fishery in Llandeilo, Carmarthenshire. Close to the top, I felt an icy wind. It was May. I met a backpacker on her way down and we chatted. She had spent the night on the top edge. Her face was full of happiness and sunburn. She joked about how cold it had been in the early morning as the dew formed inside her bag, and I imagined what that had been like. Being cold. Alone in darkness. She said her husband didn't worry too much.

Three things struck me as she walked slowly on down, and I carried on up. The solitude. The beauty of the landscape framing her descent. And my own mother's words ringing in my ears: 'Don't go near the edge.'

The **Beacons Way** (158km/98 miles) hugs the steep terrain, almost 1,000m (3,280ft) above sea level. It can be walked in just over a week or visited in shorter sections for overnight expeditions. The first thing about these hill climbs is to go at an easy pace with lots of breaks. Some of the steeper Beacons walks are not for the inexperienced. There should always be room in the backpack for a change of underclothes.

Offa's Dyke links with the Beacons Way on to the easterly section on the English border. The Taff Trail and Usk Valley Walk join a little further to the west. The Taff Trail is 88km (55 miles) of mostly converted railway lines. The Usk Valley Walk is an easy 77km (48 miles) of relatively flat trail, along river and canal.

PRACTICAL INFO Wake up to one of the greatest views in Wales (51.879418, -3.7439454), the scene from the top of the Beacons Way on Fan Foel over Llyn y Fan Fach; overnight on the flat of Corn Du mountain (51.880942, -3.4421539) above the Usk valley before setting off in the morning for the adjoining Pen y Fan, the highest peak in South Wales.

TRAVEL Trains and buses take you into Abergavenny, Pontypool, Llanhilleth, Rhymney, Merthyr Tydfil, Aberdare, Llandovery, Llandeilo and Ammanford.

NORTH SNOWDONIA

TALKING TO PEOPLE as they step down from the Glyders is like peering into souls gorged on sunbeams and energy. Mountain air causes a chemical reaction in the brain that converts overdosing on Welsh wilderness into copious levels of naturally produced serotonin. I can confirm that this continues to happen days after returning to civilisation. No wonder then that, even in the 21st century, mountains remain synonymous with transcendence.

The Glyderau range, part of Snowdonia National Park in North Wales, is a towering enclave of volcanic rock and fauna. It is separated from the park's highest mountains by the Llanberis Pass in the south and Nant Ffrancon in the north, but is still a challenging climb. I should add that extreme caution is needed as the elements can become hostile and potentially life-threatening, particularly in winter.

Despite the harsh environment, springtime blooms with flowers, ferns, mosses, feral goat and mountain hare. Tiny freshwater streams flow into the lakes, which are among the cleanest and most protected in the UK. The subalpine terrain means the peaks are tipped in snow almost into summer. Glyder Fawr is the highest, at just over 1,000m (3,280ft), followed by Glyder Fach, at 994m (3,262ft). Tryfan is possibly the most famous because you must scramble on all fours to reach the 917m (3,008ft) top.

The journey north on the A5 along the Ogwen Valley is one of the most impressive in Wales. When the road meets the shores of Llyn Ogwen, the anticipation of the hike ahead is overwhelming.

The car park at Idwal Cottage, near the western end of Lln Ogwen, is an easy place to get up on to the Glyder ridge.

A popular route is to hike up to the shore of Llyn Idwal and then on towards the steeper Devil's Kitchen path. Care is needed during wet weather, when the rocks get slippery. Once up on the ridge, a network of paths and tracks leads along the top ridge as far as the village of Capel Curig, 8km (5 miles) east, or down and over the other side of the range. There's no shortage of shelves and plateaus to pitch a tent or bivvy, although trees and shrubs for tying a hammock are extremely limited. Try to look for a ridge with shelter. The Castle of the Winds and the Cantilever – a famous overhanging stone that defies gravity – are among two of the highlights around the summit of Glyder Fach.

Snowdon is the highest mountain in Wales (1,085m/3,560ft) and one of three ranges over 914m (3,000ft) high. The northern section can become busy; much of the area is a wilderness with more than 2,414km (1,500 miles) of trail to explore (2,380km/1,479 miles public footpaths, 264km/164 miles bridleways, and off track under Right to Roam). The 11km (7-mile) **Pyg track** is one of the toughest of six paths up to Snowdon. About a mile east of the Pyg track car park, on the A4086, it's possible to access a track up towards Glyder Fach.

PRACTICAL INFO Trek up to the peaks of Glyder Fach (53.105259, -4.0086794) and Glyder Fawr before coming down to find a camp around the waters of Llyn Cwm (53.106521, -4.0376043); scramble on all fours to the top of Tryfan (53.114378, -3.9963627) for views over the Cambrian Mountains.
TRAVEL Trains and buses take you into Porthmadog, Caernarfon, Bangor and Conwy.

72

THE RHINOGS

THE RHINOGS are to hillwalking what a tall hooker is to a rugby scrum: powerful, muscular, strong – like granite. They can be unruly, too. These mountains are made from a sedimentary rock structure known as the Harlech Dome, a mean terrain that must be climbed without the use of tracks. Leaving the footpaths to explore higher views requires the ability to ruck: pushing and scrambling hard against the inclines of boulders and heather bumps while weighed down with the pack from behind.

Rhinog Fawr (720m/2,362ft) and Rhinog Fach (712m/2,336ft) are the goal. They must be climbed one after the other, towering like great pillars on the skyline from beneath the valley floor that separates their presence beneath the Snowdonia peaks to the north, Irish Sea and the Lleyn Peninsula to the west.

The Rhinogs are wilder and quieter than northern Snowdonia. The **Roman Steps** is the best known route up, to Rhinog Fawr from Cwm Bychan. The steps are 2,000 stones, thought to be the remains of a medieval packhorse trail leading to Harlech Castle.

PRACTICAL INFO Climb the Roman Steps (52.843405, -4.0121019) to Rhinog Fawr to find a camp.
TRAVEL Trains and buses take you into Barmouth, Llanenddwyn, Llandanwg and Harlech.

73 OFFA'S DYKE

THE UNEXPECTED, HAPHAZARD moments of human interaction stick in my mind from when I was camping along the ditch that is Offa's Dyke. A night-time encounter with two elderly women grazing their horse on clover in the Dee Valley; helping a kayaker salvage the remnants of his smashed-up craft on the rocky river out of Hay-on-Wye; watching a child hand-feed a collared dove on the stone quay at Brockweir. The magic around the **Offa's Dyke Path's** 285km (177 miles) is less about 'the wilderness' and more about the people along its length. And that's what I like. Having my cake and eating it. But this is no walk in the park.

The 1,200-year-old path takes its name from a giant dyke built by King Offa in the 8th century. Its banks connecting one end of the country to the other, possibly from sea to sea at one time, like some sort of frontier wall. It is the Hadrian's Wall of the west, a symbol of division, along much of the Welsh/English border. The earthen wall towers in places more than 18m (60ft) over the sunken ditch, possibly to stop invaders from Powys. There are brutal tales and stories of revenge carried out by both armies mortally wounding intruders found on the wrong side.

From Chepstow, near the River Severn Bridge, in the south, to the resort town of Prestatyn in the north, the trail weaves its way in and out of Wales and England, over some of the most impressive landscapes in Middle Earth.

There's good cycling along the route, but it's sometimes too much like hard work pushing a bike uphill for hours on end; walking the entire length in 10–14 days is ideal. There are unlimited places to hammock or bivvy, either up high in the hills or in wooded areas. The Wye Valley, Hatterall Ridge in the Brecon Becons,

the Shropshire Hills and the Clwydian Hills are good places to take a rest.

The Dyke links with almost every major track in England and Wales: the Beacons Way, the Gloucestershire Way, the Severn Way, the Shropshire Way, the Wye Valley Walk.

PRACTICAL INFO Wild camp with some of the best views along the path through the forested peaks of the Clwydian Hills between east of Llanferres (53.135830, -3.2551289) and the River Wheeler (53.219885, -3.3535767).

TRAVEL Trains and buses take you into Chepstow, Monmouth, Abergavenny, Hay-on-Wye, Kington, Knighton, Montgomery and then in and around the North Wales towns and villages of Llangollen, Llandegla, Clwyd Gate, Bodfari and Dyserth.

BERWYN MOUNTAINS

LESS IS SOMETIMES MORE. The Berwyn Mountain range is lower than neighbouring Snowdonia. That's the hook. Not many people come here. Why would they? There's an ego to feed. No, that's harsh. Let's just say I sometimes prefer the warm-up act over the headline act.

The hills, in north-east Wales, are mostly high moor, rocky peaks and valleys circled by the River Dee to the north, Glyn Way to the south, Snowdonia to the west and the English border to the east. The tops are not as rugged as Snowdonia, but have a uniqueness: Cadair Berwyn (830m/2,723ft), Moel Sych (827m/2,713ft) and Cadair Bronwen (785m/2,575ft).

The mountains are squeezed north-west between the coming together of Glyndŵr's Way and the Offa's Dyke. The Dyke moves north to the east of the mountains, while Glyndŵr's Way follows the southern line from where footpaths and bridleways lead into the peaks. The closest line up is at the southern part of Lake Vyrnwy. There are 24 peaks above 600m (2,000ft). The **North Berwyn Way** (24km/15 miles) is part of old route used for grouse shooting and slate quarrying. It rises from the River Dee past shooting huts and creeks into the high moorland to Moel Fferna (630m/2,067ft).

PRACTICAL INFO Hike and camp on Snowdon's quieter neighbour, the understated Cadair Berwyn (52.879810, -3.3806250).
TRAVEL Trains and buses take you into Gobowen, Llangollen, Carrog, Chirk and Welshpool.

75 PRESELI MOUNTAINS

MY SEVEN-DAY walk along the coast was almost at an end as I tried to shrug off a lonely pining for home. Rain and solitude are incredible forces for pessimism. Low skies crush the mind's spirit like a chaotic series of unopened bills left next to a sink full of saucepans. Solitude allows seeds of doubt to germinate and flourish among the twisted vines of fate. Without company to divide gloom from the glory, even my sunny moments were shaped by the clouds that hung behind them. A dog day.

I'd moved from the coast on to the higher ground of the Preseli Mountains, hoping a change of scenery would be as good as a rest on my way down to Fishguard. The ancient 13km (8-mile) track along the top of the range is known as The Golden Road. I was drawn, if anything, to the name. Like a sentence from a childhood memory of Sinbad films and primary-school storybooks read by diligent teachers with gentle voices. It conjured up magic, mystery and good fortune.

The adjoining mountain paths sway north from **The Golden Road**, along the River Gwaun valley out to the coast. The mid-morning views were poor, nothing past the occasional fields, bogs and unenclosed drabness of rolling moors. Until, through the level haze, a walker from the other direction. As our paths crossed, I first resisted the urge to mumble more than a polite 'hello', but then blurted loudly how it was 'crap weather'. He spun round on his walking sticks, panting, breathing and smiling; beads of sweat on his forehead just below the canopy of his purple hood, bulbous raindrops hanging from the straight tip of his nose, and rounded cheeks that shone like toffee apples.

He was older than me. Late fifties. A part-time teacher from Swansea. He was carrying a small backpack and a tarp. He had parked the east side of Fishguard and was walking a circular route out and overnight, before returning the next day. We sat down on a cold earth bank; slowly talking, sharing hot tea. He told me how the rocks used for Stonehenge probably came from the Preseli bluestone that surrounded us. I listened. A dog day became a good day. We never saw the sun again. But we left in the same direction. Me backtracking down to the coast. Less homesick.

The Preseli Mountains are in north Pembrokeshire, a curtain backdrop against quite possibly the greatest coastal path in Britain. Foel Cwmcerwyn is the highest point at 536m (1,759ft), with views across all of the Pembrokeshire coast, even as far as The Gower, and some days even as far east as the Black Mountains. The Preseli range spans a rough rectangle down to the surf and coastal path at Dinas Island, north-east to the River Teifi estuary, 20km (12 miles) east to Frenni Fach, near Crymych, and then south to the village and castle at Henry's Moat (just north of Llys y Fran Reservoir).

PRACTICAL INFO Forage in Pantmaenog Forest (51.949370, -4.7893953) before climbing to the top of Foel Cwmcerwyn (51.945958, -4.7742462) – the highest point in the Preseli Hills – to sleep in or around the summit.
TRAVEL Trains and buses take you into Fishguard, Clarbeston Road, Clunderwen and Maenclochog.

76 PEMBROKESHIRE COAST

THE PRESELI MOUNTAIN trails eventually file down to the Wales Coast Path, to meet one of the most historic coastal tracks in Britain, the **Pembrokeshire Coast Path**: crashing surf and yellow stone beaches that shine day and night. The path is a tardis of white-flowering sea campion, heather-scented sea spray and deserted, singing coves.

As the crow flies, there are just 40km (25 miles) between the start and finish of this surreal coastal path in South Wales. A space – smaller than the width of Manchester – transcribed into 300km (186 miles) of stone trail that warps itself between the wrinkles of caves and sandy crevices like an infinite stream of silk sheet music pulled from the conjuror's sleeve. You will climb and descend over so many cliff tops, so many times, that the 10,000m (35,000ft) is greater than the climb up Everest, let alone the Preseli range.

Walking the path back to front, from the village of Amroth to St Dogmaels, means catching the prevailing south-westerlies that gulls and kittiwakes glide on so effortlessly. Thousands of people came the opposite way, from the north, during the Middle Ages as part of the final leg of pilgrimage to the cathedral at St Davids.

A marker stone at Carreg Wastad, inscribed with the 'Last Invasion of Britain', recalls the most recent attempt by the French, when they tried to land near Fishguard in 1797.

The south is the most popular section of the path, around the resorts of Tenby and Saundersfoot. The road from St David's Head to St Dogmaels is quieter.

PRACTICAL INFO Many small
beaches, undergrowth, sandy coves and
caves to sleep off the path between the
Trefasser (52.004012, -5.0713062) and
the old fort at St David's Head (51.903189,
-5.3124046); canoe-camp and fish around
the foreshore of the Carew River, Cresswell
River and Beggars Reach (51.719797,
-4.8619652).

TRAVEL For St Dogmaels, catch a train
to either Clunderwen or Fishguard, and then
take a bus. For Amroth, take a train to Tenby
and then a bus. There is also a railway station
at Kilgetty, 3km (2 miles) away, although
buses are more limited.

77 ANGLESEY

THE LAND OF THE DRUIDS. Anglesey is Wales' largest island, situated off the north-west coast. The isle is another in a long list of lands where the resident tribes and their rulers have resisted occupation and changes to their way of life. It was the Romans that eventually broke the power of the Celtic Druids. General Gaius Suetonius Paulinus attacked their stronghold at Anglesey in AD 60. It was only Boudica's infamous revolt against the supposed theft of her kingdom in Anglia by the invaders

that saw the armies retreat. But it was a short-lived reprieve, with the island under Roman rule less than 20 years later. The native groves and shrines were destroyed and the Romans introduced mining and commerce to maximise their income from the territory. Today, most of the island is used for grazing land.

The island is connected to the mainland by two bridges. This mainland connection doesn't really detract from the nature of separation I can feel along the edges.

The **Anglesey Coastal Path** navigates almost the entire coastal circumference. The 200km (124-mile) route passes dunes, farmland, foreshore, woodland and coastal heath, and only rarely leaves the sea.

The Wales Coast Path (1,400km/870 miles) links Anglesey to Bridgend, Cardiff, Carms, Ceredigion, Gwynedd, Swansea and more.

PRACTICAL INFO Walk more than 30km (20 miles) anticlockwise along the coast path, from just south of the Menai Strait/Britannia Bridge (53.185465, -4.2218399), to Carmel Head (53.401550, -4.5737457), and find caves, sandy coves and foreshore all the way for camping and foraging.

TRAVEL There are six railway stations on Anglesey: Holyhead, Valley, Rhosneigr, Ty Croes, Bodorgan and Llanfairpwll.

food and water

RICHARD MABEY'S classic book *Food for Free* is fun for grown-up scrumpers. It was published in the early 1970s and is still a bestseller. Mabey lists hundreds of flowers, weeds, buds, nuts, trees, fruits, vegetables, fungi and seafish that can be found in the wild and eaten. His images make identifying relatively easy, although for anyone seriously wanting to try it, I'd suggest a course. There are plenty around in local woodlands. Mabey explains when the plants can be found, describes what they look like, and then provides advice on how to cook or eat everything from dandelions and chickweed to acorns and hawthorn berries to limpets and mussels.

Some hardy types promote the eating of pigeons and squirrels. I've shot and eaten both, but don't consider either a realistic part of my travelling as I don't carry an air gun and I've no interest in trying to set traps. A few packets of dried meals, weighing no more than a few ounces, are good for me. Biscuits are rotten for the teeth, but keep energy levels up. Foraging around the coast for shellfish is quite possibly the closest it gets to self-sufficient living, especially when combined with tidal fishing on a lightweight telescopic rod and simple reel.

Hydration is the most common problem around tidal areas, as salt-water filters are expensive and involve expending almost as much perspiration as they provide hydration. So coastal trips necessitate carrying bottled water. Inland it's a bit different. Water treatment systems help the traveller go further while carrying less weight.

Filters and treatment systems have to cope with two pollutants: living, which is organic and needs to be killed, and inanimate, which is usually chemical and needs to be removed from the water. Although pollution is relatively rare (the health of dogs is testament to that, as they drink everything), it's important to know the risks.

Most living contaminants are not dangerous, but they fall into four main

categories, some of which can be very bad: bacteria, viruses, protozoa and cysts. Man-made chemicals can be a problem, although naturally occurring chemicals like mercury and arsenic can also occur outdoors. Perspective is important; 99.9 per cent of chemicals that humans ingest are natural and not harmful.

Boiling water kills all living contaminants. There are debates over how long to boil, which depends on how murky the water is and what altitude you are at. Some say just bring to a rolling boil and then finish. Others say keep going for 10 minutes. Nothing living can survive a 20-minute boil, but that's overstating it, by a lot. You decide.

If you choose not to boil, filters come in various degrees of fineness. There are those that will only take out the large particles, much like a sock, before the water can then be boiled or sterilised with a tablet. Then there are the filters in between that move all the way to removing viruses and even salt water. The salt filters are expensive and time-consuming to use, and are really more for emergency situations when boating on the open sea. The last alternative to boiling or filters is chemical treatments like iodine and chlorine tablets.

It's really important to know something about the water source before travelling, so just like you might study an OS map before hiking, do a little research on water quality in a given area. The single best way to start is to ring the Environment Agency. Officers are required to give you the most up-to-date information they have on water tests relevant to the region being visited. They can give information on recent local heavy rainfall (or the lack of it), which – depending on other factors, such as inadequate drainage systems, geology or farming practices – might be good or bad. In my experience, officers can be non-committal in offering opinions, but they are required to provide objective information that allows you to make an informed decision for yourself. Environment Agency head office will connect you up with area officers with good contacts in the local community, who can also provide more advice on drinking from local streams, waterfalls and pools etc.

From talking and meeting campers, hikers and cyclists who carry water filters, I'd say most use either a Sawyer or Travel Tap, and are happy with that. Canoeists tend to carry fresh water, as weight is not such an issue on board a boat. Nothing is 100 per cent safe. I mostly carry and drink bottled water, and pack a filter just in case. Childhood was more fun. We feared nothing but the wasps.

CLOCKWISE FROM TOP: fold-up water bottle; water filter; stove and pot; plastic bottle for stove fuel; cotton wool rubbed in vaseline for fire lighter; dry food to mix with water; scourer and washing-up liquid; black food flask that acts as a slow cooker for rice etc.

MAWDDACH

WALLOWING IN THE SHALLOWS of low tide is a treat I rarely tire of. Sitting down in the warm, wet sandy ripples of Mawddach Estuary, looking over the rise of the Rhinogs mountain range, feels better than an outdoor penthouse hot tub spa, with oyster catchers and climate control on remote control. On the view backwards, over my shoulder towards the Cadair Idris, the clouds are motionless; breathless on a skyline of tender breeze. Complete.

If peaks are the main attraction in Wales, the southern shores of the Mawddach Estuary demonstrate that there's no need to go climbing to enjoy. For those who want to, the surrounding hills are served by old mining tracks and drovers'

trails. The River Mawddach rises more than 600m (2,000ft) up, in Snowdonia, just north of the peak Dduallt. One of its main tributaries is the River Eden. Despite its magnificence, the river was, until recently, heavily industrialised – by gold mining in the 19th century, shipbuilding in the 18th and the historic trade in wool before that. It is now mostly a protected area, with SSSI status to protect the wildlife and fauna. There are two RSPB reserves, at Taicynhaeaf and Arthog.

Canoe-camping along the foreshore is the best way to enjoy a night out on either the tidal river or the surrounding beaches and coves. The tide retreats a long way to expose sandbanks. Walking and cycling trails are popular in summer, so are best explored in spring and autumn. The Mawddach Trail follows the disused railway line along the estuary for 15km (9.5 miles) between Dolgellau car park and Barmouth.

The **Mawddach Way** is a longer, two-to-three-day walk through the surrounding woodland and hills, with views of the river estuary. The Way (49km/30 miles) circles around both sides of the estuary, beneath the Cadair Idris mountain to the south and Rhinogs mountain range to the north. The path's most impressive feature is crossing the 1.6km (1-mile) long railway bridge over the estuary into Barmouth. In my opinion, a trip best taken at low tide when the sun is out. The trail is part of the Wales Coast Path (1,400km/870 miles).

PRACTICAL INFO Canoe-camp around the foreshore of the Mawddach Estuary (52.723713, -4.0010834); walk or cycle the Mawddach Trail, stopping to forage in woodland along the south shore of the river (52.728236, -3.9949036).
TRAVEL The train station at Barmouth connects with Shrewsbury. There are regular buses from Dolgellau and Harlech.

79 LLEYN PENINSULA

WHITEWASHED COTTAGES, dolphins and ancient common land are features of this landscape, more reminiscent of a Greek isle than a pilgrim's trail over windswept Welsh cliffs. The views from Yr Eifl and Bwlch Mawr are a highlight. Aberdaron village was once a pilgrims' resting place before they moved on to Bardsey along the coastal path. It became known as the 'island of 20,000 saints' after the 5th-century Christians who hid from persecution, and later attained status as a holy burial site.

Choosing whether to overnight on the foreshore or the mountains is a decision only necessary during the fist part of the walk, as the remaining 96km (60 miles) are mostly below 300m (1,000ft). The village of Clynnog Fawr, 16km (10 miles) outside Caernarfon, is one possible route up on to the mountains of Gyrn Goch, Gyrn Ddu and Bwlch Mawr. The views over the peninsula and Caernarfon Bay are incredible. There is a public right of way south of Gyrn Goch, Gyrn Ddu to Bwlch Mawr, and numerous beaches and coves that make good overnight stops. The very tip of the peninsula is mostly rock face and cliff. The options here are either to ask permission from the landowner, stay at one of the many tent sites or navigate the entire 19km (12-mile) section in a single day. The path is an important part of the **Wales Coast Path,** which stretches for 1,400 glorious kilometres (870 miles) from Chepstow to Queensferry. At Porthmadog, it links to the Meirionnydd Coast Walk.

PRACTICAL INFO Take in the best sea views over the Lleyn Peninsula at dusk from the top of Yr Eifl (52.974369, -4.4352789), and a chance to camp overnight above 500m.

TRAVEL Buses take you into both Porthmadog and Caernarfon. There's a train station at Porthmadog. Caernarfon's nearest station is at Bangor, from where it's possible to catch a bus.

OWAIN GLYNDŴR fought the English in the name of Welsh independence. But it was not always so. He was born into privilege in the 1350s, a part of the new English nobility, a landowner and a squire in Sycharth, in the then Kingdom of Powys.

It's said that the Glyndŵr story arose from a land dispute with Reginald Grey, Lord Ruthin. The dispute escalated with Glyndŵr leading a rebellion for Welsh independence against the English. Although he enjoyed some early territorial success, his army was defeated at Shrewsbury in 1403. Glyndŵr reclaimed more land in 1404, and the first Welsh Parliament was created in 1406. Within a year the English had fought back, establishing control and outposts throughout the land. Glyndŵr and his loyalists lived as guerrillas, before they were eventually forgotten.

Glyndŵr's achievements in securing short-lived independence has made him a Welsh hero to this day. The **Glyndŵr's Way** was named in his honour and runs close to his former home and lands. The 217km (135-mile) trail begins at the middle of Offa's Dyke Path, at Knighton on the Welsh/English border. The town was a fortified boundary in both Anglo-Saxon and Norman times. The Welsh name for the town is Tref-y-clawdd, which means 'town on the dyke'. The path arcs through mid Wales close to the Dyfi Estuary, at Machynlleth, and then crosses Wales again to Welshpool via Llanbrynmair, Llangadfan and Lake Vyrnwy. It also links with the Severn Way (360km/224 miles) and, along with Offa's Dyke Path, the Pembrokeshire Coast Path and the Wales Coast path, is one of the most important walking routes in Britain.

PRACTICAL INFO Rest or camp above the water known as Blue Lake (Glaslyn) along the highest part of the trail – above 500m (1,640ft) – at Foel Fadian (52.541577, -3.7309903); continue along the path east to visit deserted mines and the site of an old Roman fort (52.527319, -3.6878872).

TRAVEL Trains and buses take you into Knighton and Welshpool.

81 **LLANGOLLEN CANAL**

CANOE-CAMPING is my favourite pastime. Paddling across the Pontcysyllte Aqueduct – the highest navigable water in the world – is one of the most remarkable journeys I've ever taken. Just don't capsize and then try to get out on the low side. It's 38m (125ft) to the bottom for anyone clambering over that 36cm (14-inch) wall.

The Llangollen Canal crosses the border between England and Wales, linking Hurleston in south Cheshire with Llangollen in North Wales. The canal carried limestone, coal and grain throughout the 19th century, before rail economy and efficiency took over in the 1930s. The waterway fell into some disrepair but saw a revival thanks to increasing leisure traffic from the 1960s onwards. It's now the busiest canal in Britain. The most photographed section is the Pontcysyllte Aqueduct. Its 19 great stone arches carry the canal 307m (1,007ft) across and 38m (125ft) above the river valley floor.

There are just 21 locks along the entire canal, which makes for great canoeing.

Overnight moorings provide a resting place afloat. Advice and guidance from wardens should be taken if planning on pulling ashore and camping on grassy locks. Out-of-season is recommended. There are many hidden grassy banks where hammocks or bivvies can be set up after dark. Cycling or walking along the towpath is fabulous.

The Canal & River Trust Waterway Wanderers scheme (see page 42) is available at many locations along the canal: providing 24-hour fishing (and sleeping). Some of the most rural areas I like best are: **BRIDGE 10:** Stoneley Green to Bridge 13 Grange. **BRIDGE 22:** Thomasons to Bridge 25 Quoisley. **BRIDGE 33:** Hassells No.1 Lift to Bridge 50 Hampton Bank. **BRIDGE 51:** Lyneal Lane to Bridge 55 Little Mill. **BRIDGE 59:** White Bridge Ellesmere to Frankton Junction. Frankton Junction to Kings House Bridge 49a.

The **Llangollen Canal Walk** (79km/ 49 miles) follows the towpath through Whitchurch, Ellesmere and over the Pontcysyllte Aqueduct.

PRACTICAL INFO Kayak over the Pontcysyllte Aqueduct (52.971490, -3.0878448); hammock among the trees and bluebells along the western section of the canal between Chirk (52.935009, -3.0691767) and Llangollen (52.970812, -3.1581670).

TRAVEL Trains and buses take you into Llangollen, Chirk, Whitchurch, Aston and Nantwich.

SEE PAGE 5 FOR KEY TO SYMBOLS

NORTHERN ENGLAND

I HAD A UNIVERSITY LECTURER who swore and moaned a lot. He had a flat beard, like black felt, and an accent warmer than flat ale. It was a nice combination, as long as no one upset him.

Roger came from Yorkshire and he liked to dress his wisdom in metaphors. His favourite analogy was about teacher and pupil. He wanted us to think for ourselves and go our own unique way, but not until we'd learned the conventional truth; the accepted path. He used maps: 'We're 'ere ta teach yoos ow to read the map. You carn not be doing it yeeuur own way, taking short cuts, until yoo ave luuurned to read the map. Do! I! Make. Mu. Self. Cleuuurr?'

We all replied 'yes', because a failure to reply meant question repeated. We also knew Roger wanted us to leave the 'conventional map' behind once we'd graduated out of our first year, which we quite liked.

Before he died in 1991, Alfred Wainwright left us a map across north England. It was a trail called the C2C (Coast to Coast). Wainwright was from the north, too. He was also grumpy. I wonder sometimes whether he knew of Roger, or vice versa. His instructions stated that walkers should go off trail, find their own way. Strange really. The train service I caught to Roger's lessons each day was the C2C Fenchurch Street line.

The **Coast to Coast** is a sequence of footpaths, quiet roads and tracks that Wainwright stitched together into a single walk. His book *A Coast to Coast Walk* was first published in 1973, and featured the 309km (192-mile) passage in 12 stages. For some, it's the best walk in Britain, defined by its status as a journey that crosses England, as well as the fact that it passes through what most people think is its finest landscape: the Lakes. It starts at St Bees beach, in Cumbria, and finishes at Robin Hood's Bay, North Yorkshire (or vice versa). The highest point is at Kidsty Pike (780m/2,559ft), but there are more than a dozen major climbs that reach heights well over 500m as the C2C crosses the fells and Pennines. Ennerdale, Helvellyn and Buttermere are my three favourite places to camp along the path, in late summer/early autumn.

Ennerdale is among the smaller Cumbrian lakes, between some of the tallest hills. Less than 800m (½ mile) wide at its narrowest and 4km (2½ miles) long, the water reaches out in the furthest western corner of lakeland, pointing towards St Bees and the coast.

The fells tower almost 900m/3,000ft above the valley to the south-east. Some of the best for wild camping are around Great Gable (899m/2,949ft), Green Gable and Kirk Fell. The tops can be rocky and cold, which makes wilding around Styhead Tarn and Sprinkling Tarn a little more comfortable, and company with fellow travellers likely. Both tarns hold trout that can be caught.

The lack of road access and settlements means that many areas around Ennerdale's water are remote. The forest, water and mountains are managed by a combination of Forestry Commission, United Utilities and the National Trust.

PRACTICAL INFO Launch a canoe or kayak from the shore of Ennerdale Water (54.52418, -3.40925). Carefully walk along the eroded path to Anglers' Crag, with views over the lake (54.5228, -3.3951). Sleep around Iron Crag (54.4963476, -3.3536387). C2C trail highlights: Cleator (54.5071, -3.5256) to River Liza (54.5127, -3.3367).

TRAVEL Trains or buses take you into St Bees, Whitehaven, Eskdale, Whitby, Darlington, Northallerton, Thirsk, Kendal, Oxenholme, Penrith and Windermere.

HELVELLYN

A FRIEND AND I once travelled to see Benazir Bhutto, the former Pakistani prime minister and the first female leader of a Muslim country. Bhutto was at Essex University as part of a talking tour. Phillipe was a Belgian freelance news photographer. He asked me to interview her so he could take some photos, which he thought might sell to magazines or newspapers back in Pakistan. She was kind and obliging, but his photos didn't sell; anywhere. A few years later, she was killed by a bomb on the eve of the national elections in Pakistan. She was favourite to win a third term as prime minister. Only a few months later, I heard Phillipe had died suddenly in hospital with his wife at his side. Pneumonia.

He was in his early forties. She was 54. Life's like that. Risky. Cruel. Temporal. Beautiful. Dangerous. I think that's partly why we travel. To remind ourselves. If a landscape could sum up all of that, it would be Helvellyn.

The poet William Wordsworth wrote about this place. He too was affected by the death of a fellow artist. Charles Gough had attempted to reach the peak with his dog. His body was found three months later, with his pet waiting close by. A plaque marks the spot.

At 950m (3,117ft), Helvellyn is the third highest mountain in England. It offers some of the rarest views in England, east over Red Tarn, north-east over Patterdale, Glenridding and Ullswater; Thirlmere to the west. There are two steep and narrow ridges up: **Striding Edge** and **Swirral Edge**. Both climbs can be dangerous, and there have been several deaths in recent years. A report on the safety of the mountain is posted on Weatherline, the Met Office mountain weather forecast, especially important during winter.

Red Tarn, between Striding Edge and Swirral Edge, is named after the surrounding rocky scree. It's popular with walkers who want to overnight, but there are many more crevices and lowland places to hide if you want to escape alone.

PRACTICAL INFO Sleep in the valley beside Red Tarn (54.5296, -3.0058). Walk to Helvellyn's peak along Striding Edge (54.5261, -3.0027).
TRAVEL See page 211.

84 BUTTERMERE

STANDING ON the mountains looking over Buttermere or Crummock Water is to witness something rare – a textured, emerald jungle that reaches out into the distance like a 1950s airplane scene from Bogart's classic film *The African Queen*. Share the moment with a companion over a coffee, and time will pass quicker than daisy seeds on a brisk, warm breeze. Watch it alone and you can be moved to tears.

It was just after 8am as I came down after a night on Haystacks. I'd reached the waterfall a few yards from Green Crag when my attention was drawn to a guy far below. He was shouting up some sort of order or warning. Quite how he could make himself heard was remarkable. He must have had iron lungs. His vehicle was barely visible on the valley floor. Looking around, I saw a large, dark mist rolling over Scarth Gap, and concluded the shouting was a mountain rescue team alerting me to an imminent danger. It wasn't until I climbed down that I realised he was a farmer calling down his grazing sheep.

As I walked back around the lake to where I'd parked the car the day before, I met a couple in their late thirties. They'd spent the night together on the shore with their dog. The man said he had been sleeping on the beach for fun, for 20 years. His girlfriend told me she had taken a dip in the water that morning. She described how beautiful it had been, swimming in the dawn. I'll never forget the look in her eyes as she spoke; full of contentment and joy. It seemed to me to epitomise everything about the place.

The **Coast to Coast** path leads up between the streams and steep crags. Going up is always so much easier than coming down. My thighs were still burning, like they were ready to explode into wobbling bowls of jelly, incapable of supporting anything but pain.

The Cumbrians chose Buttermere as a stronghold to fight the Norman invaders. The campaign succeeded for almost 50 years, led by a character called Jarl Buthar.

The lake is now owned by the National Trust and links with Crummock Water, north of the village of Buttermere. The valley is patrolled by wardens, who sometimes ask campers to move on.

Hundreds of paths link into the C2C, spreading out into tens of thousands of miles of walkway. They include the Cleveland Way and the Pennine Way.

PRACTICAL INFO Sleep around High Stile (54.5215, -3.2842), walk through Burtness Wood to the shore of Buttermere (54.5300, -3.2690).
TRAVEL Trains or buses take you into St Bees, Whitehaven, Eskdale, Whitby, Darlington, Northallerton, Thirsk, Kendal, Oxenholme, Penrith and Windermere.

85 URRA MOOR

I PITCHED MY TENT the other side of the stone wall, where the sheep sheltered from the late afternoon sun. The views from Urra Moor are not what they used to be, fields of bracken indicating that this was a vast forest before upland sheep grazers cleared out the trees and began burning heather to provide new and tender shoots for game birds. Mesolithic hunters got by on wild cattle and pig. The new sultans of swing preferred red grouse and game. No matter. Not seeing the wood for the trees is sometimes a bonus when below 500m/1,640ft.

The **Cleveland Way** (177km/110 miles) arches its way around the edges of the North York Moors to define two very different landscapes: moor and coast. Sitting in the heather looking down over Robin Hood's Bay, I can see inside both.

Round Hill is the highest point on Urra Moor, at 454m (1,490ft); it's less than 100m from the Way, but it's more of a passing place, in summer, than a stopover. People walk up from the car park a few miles away. The ground around Cringle and Busby moors is kinder, and also forms part of Wainwright's Coast to Coast Walk. Live Moor, Cold Moor and Carlton Moor are better still for camping and sleeping; quieter, in between slow climbs, wild flowers and stepping stones.

PRACTICAL INFO Walk along Urra Moor dyke, the surving earthworks that marked a prehistoric boundary over the moors (54.4111, -1.1047).
TRAVEL Trains take you into Thirsk, Northallerton, Battersby, Kildale, Saltburn by the Sea, Whitby, Scarborough and Filey.

THE MOST BEAUTIFUL trails are sometimes the most popular, carrying walkers from dawn to dusk all year. Busy is not bad. I liked 'busy' when I first started sleeping in hills. I knew if I got into trouble, someone would be along soon after first light; usually a dog walker.

My favourite 'busy' hike is around Cat Bells above Derwentwater, over the **Cumbria Way** (112km/70 miles), moving on and down south towards Coniston Water, and north to Carlisle and the Caldew Valley. Derwentwater is south of Keswick town, fed and drained by the River Derwent – which gives the lake its name. There are several islands and marinas, including Lord's Island, St Herbert's Island and Otter Island.

St Herbert's Island is named after a 7th-century priest who lived in solitude. 'Beauty is meaningless until it is shared,' Orwell wrote in *Burmese Days*. It makes me think about that old lonely priest.

Boats ferry passengers about, although it rarely obscures the calm. Once up into the fells, it's the views over Derwentwater to the east that draw most of the attention. I could quite happily sit here day and night, resting, watching and listening. Yachts, kayaks and canoes cut across the film of the lake. Crows, green moss, white-flowering wood sorrel and sheep fill the gaps between the community of walkers.

On the west side of the valley is Newlands Beck. It's just as dramatic, maybe more so, with the mountain face leaning up towards High Crags and Dale Head; Bassenthwaite Lake on the horizon to the north-east.

I learned an important lesson one day up in these hills. The restorative power of sleep. I'd set off at dawn and walked too far and too long until dusk. So much so that when

I woke on the hillside during the night, just to check how close it was to the new day, I was barely able to move my legs. I wondered how I would ever get back down. I went back to sleep. Less than three hours later, as the sun warmed the casing of my bivvy, I climbed out into the daylight, and could actually put one leg in front of the other. Along with everyone else.

PRACTICAL INFO Sleep on the high ground at Maiden Moor (54.5516, -3.1823); launch a kayak or canoe from Nichol End Beach (small fee) (54.5955, -3.1560).

TRAVEL Trains and buses take you into Delegarth, Kirby-in-Furness, Foxfield, Windermere Allithwaite, Ulverston and Grange over Sands, Kendal, Windermere, Dalegarth, Penrith, Maryport or Workington.

ENGLISH AUTHOR Arthur Ransome based part of the 'Swallows and Amazons' book series around Coniston. His stories involve children who enjoyed sailing, wild camping and other adventures. Arrive on this lake after dusk and it's not unusual to see fathers and sons still living out that fantasy, hammocks slung above canoes, on one of the lake's islands.

After sleep, heat, food, water, shelter and security, storytelling is the most popular form of survival known to man. Stories hydrate and nurture the mind and soul. In *Songlines*, Bruce Chatwin described how aboriginal stories are sung to bring the land into existence; without the story, nothing exists. It's hard to argue with that. Especially when you're out here, on the edge of sleep.

Coniston is 8km (5 miles) long and 805m (½ mile) wide — the third largest body of water in the Lakes. The lucrative textile trade between the 13th and 18th centuries saw the fells adapted for sheep grazing and wool production. The **Cumbria Way** follows the old animal tracks and paths along valleys and over passes. It runs lakeside on the east of Coniston, through Coniston Park Coppice Campsite and Torver Common Wood, beside the water.

Wilding on Coniston's islands requires two necessities: a canoe and permission from the National Trust. If you have neither one nor the other, the better option is finding a flat piece of ground to tent as part of a hike up the Old Man of Coniston, the highest fell around. Rising from the north-west to

803m (2,634ft), the ascent looks out over the lake and valley and is a quiet place around dusk. There are several pathways up from the Cumbria Way, shoreside, just south of the town on the A593 around Spoon Hall.

PRACTICAL INFO Climb the Old Man of Coniston (54.3707, -3.1219) and find a place to sleep coming back down, or launch a canoe from the quieter east shore of Coniston close to parking (54.3524, -3.0612).
TRAVEL Trains and buses take you into Delegarth, Kirby-in-Furness, Foxfield, Windermere Allithwaite, Ulverston and Grange over Sands, Kendal, Windermere, Dalegarth, Penrith, Maryport or Workington.

88

FOREST OF BOWLAND

I TALKED ABOUT the journalistic formula of the '5 Ws' in the first chapter of this book. The 5 Ws I intend to use here relate to the Forest of Bowland because a) I couldn't think of anything poetic to say about heather moorlands and peat bogs jet-streamed over hardened, gritstone fells that bounce along bulbous horizons; and b) for many outdoor campers, walkers, cyclists and canoeists, Bowland epitomises something they hope to see improved:

WHO – public
WHAT – access
WHERE – outdoors
WHEN – ASAP
WHY – it's a God-given right to enjoy the wild (if in doubt, go and either re-watch *The Hunger Games*, or read Marion Shoard).

The Forest of Bowland has long had its own rules around storytelling. The 'forest courts' existed until the 19th century, following their introduction after the Norman Invasion. The Duchy of Lancaster still owns much of the land as part of the estates run by the Royal Family. The Bowland Fells – sometimes known previously as the Switzerland of England – formed part of a series of great hunting estates used for grouse, boar and deer. St Hubert has a chapel dedicated to him in Dunsop Bridge in honour of his being the patron saint of hunting and the Forest of Bowland.

Walking and cycling here is remarkable for no other reason than there are so few other people doing it. The hills around the north-west – Ward's Stone, Grit Fell and Black Fell – are perhaps the busiest because of their closeness to Lancaster.

The peaks are rocky, but make for good camping under a blow-up mattress, and even better views on a clear, blue sky. Clougha Pike (413m/1,355ft), Grit Fell (468m/1,535ft), Ward's Stone (561m/1,840ft), Wolfhole Crag (527m/1,729ft), White Hill (544m/1,785ft), Whins Brow (476m/1,562ft), Totridge (497m/1,630ft), Parlick (1432m/,417ft), Fair Snape Fell (510m/1673ft), Bleasdale Moor (429m/1,407ft) and Hawthornthwaite Fell (479m/1,572ft) form an obscure circular route around the outside of the forest that tracks clockwise from Lancaster or anticlockwise from Dolphinholme. There are some limestone caves in the area, including Hell Hole, Whitewell Cave and Whitewell Pot.

Much of the area is now free access under the Right to Roam legislation, which means walkers are allowed to leave designated footpaths and trails. It's not especially a help or hindrance for wild campers per se as the new laws specifically exclude 'camping' (not sleeping) as a 'right'. As 'campers' don't tend to 'sleep' all day,

PRACTICAL INFO Set off late afternoon from Lower Fence Wood (53.927036, -2.5437641) along the footpath north towards the peaks of Mellor Knoll and Totridge. Wild camp up high before heading north-west across the Open Access Land. Pick up the Wyre Way over Blaze Moss, around the Trough of Bowland (53.979311, -2.6041031), before following the Way east and south along the tree-lined river valley to Garstang. There is plenty of good hammocking along the Way. Breakfast at Tarnbrook Wyre Waterfalls (54.0116, -2.5944) after walking down from watching the dawn from Wolfhole Crag (54.01666, -2.5661).

TRAVEL Trains take you into Lancaster, Bentham, Clapham, Giggleswick, Long Preston, Clitheroe or Preston.

the change is good in the sense that there is more access land to walk over in order to work up a good appetite for turning in at the end of the day on any of the peaks mentioned earlier.

If in need of a guide, the Forest of Bowland Walk is a 109km (68-mile) circle from Caton, where it begins and ends, via the River Ribble, Longridge Fell and Beacon Fell. The walk links with the Ribble Way (65 miles), through Lancashire and North Yorkshire, and the **Wyre Way** (72km/45 miles).

89

PENDLE FOREST

AS MUCH AS I LOVE stories, the association between Pendle and the infamous witch trials of the 17th century conjures more sadness than intrigue. Pendle Hill is somewhere to avoid around Halloween, when visitor numbers increase. The 1612 trials involved nine women and two men, who were charged with using their craft to murder ten people. One was found not guilty and the others were all hanged. There are 364 days a year – outside of Halloween – when this place is worthy of more than just a nose around the darkest parts of its history.

Pendle Forest is an open area of countryside in east Lancashire between the River Ribble and the River Calder. It's attached to the Forest of Bowland by a combination of footpaths and quiet roads that lead over or under the A59, north and south of Clitheroe.

Pendle was part of a large land mass between the Ribble and River Mersey that was seized under the Norman Invasion. The area was handed to a succession of families and ended up being owned by the Duchy of Lancaster. At one stage it was a hunting chase. A deer park was created at Ightenhill. Some of the land was later sold off for agriculture and pastoral land for cattle.

The Domesday Book lists Pendle Forest as an administrative part of the

Blackburnshire Forest, which included Trawden, Accrington, and Rossendale. Back in the 11th century, Bowland was the other administrative 'forest' region.

Wild camping here is mostly in the Middle Earth region. Walkers do overnight in and around the hill, which at 557m/1,827ft is above the height generally regarded as being high enough for campers not to cause offence. The tops are, of course, quieter in winter, but can be misty, harsh and boggy, so better in autumn or late spring.

The **Pendle Way** covers 72km (45 miles) of moorland and river track over the three peaks of Pendle Hill, Weets Hill and Boulsworth Hill. The route up from Barley is easy. Secluded parts of the River Calder can be accessed by footpaths west of Whalley. The Ribble Way moves north of the Calder and Clitheroe and passes many places where overnighting among bushes or trees is possible. The Pendle Way links with the Pennine Bridleway and the Lancashire Trail (116km/72 miles) and Leeds and Liverpool Canal Walk.

PRACTICAL INFO Enjoy a late afternoon flask of coffee from Pendle Hill and watch the sunset (53.8685, -2.2985), forage in Fell Wood around Lower Ogden Reservoir (53.8546, -2.2847).
TRAVEL Trains and buses take you into Colne, Brierfield and Nelson to the east; Clitheroe and Whalley to the west.

HOW TO WILD home

DOMESTICITY can become like a prison without the interludes of wilderness. The nights on the trail. And if you can share that with a wife, partner or friend, it's even better.

But wild camping is not a permanent thing. Most of us wouldn't survive a winter. It's a beautiful, spiritual pause. An unofficial 'holi day' – an escape in between living; bringing up the family, holding down a job, visiting parents, getting the car serviced, keeping the house clean, unblocking the drains, replacing a light bulb, fixing the dripping tap, oversleeping but still having to fill up with petrol at the service station on the way to work. We work for the privilege to play. Only when I play, I want to stay out all night. To relax out there in Eden because I've earned it; to chill in the wild without having to worry about some landowner or an official saying, 'It's time to go home now. The outdoors has closed for the night.'

No. I'm sorry. I'm not having that. But neither am I making a personal claim over the land. I don't want to take it back from the Saxons, the Normans, the

de Veres, the Windsors, the neighbours, the elite, the factory owners, the lottery winners, the mafia, the farmers, or anyone else who claims it's theirs and not mine. I know my place. I know where I live. And I call it home.

My wife and I had had a row one Sunday morning. It was over nothing. I went out for a few hours to get away from the house; from her. I took my wetsuit, my kayak, a stick of French bread, and headed for the Thames estuary.

That evening I was flicking through some photos I'd taken, in the seaweed and reeds. We were still irritated with each other.

'That's where you're happiest, isn't it?' she said.

'Yeah,' I replied. 'Because I know home is just at the top of the hill.'

Home is where we feel uniquely safe. It's the companionship, and family, and the security that I look forward to after days and nights on the moors, after a couple of days kayaking around the creeks or 72 hours cycling over the South Downs. Home is a sense of ownership. A private place.

I'm sure these feelings fuel some of the concerns landowners have with travellers, wild campers and drifters. The outsiders invading their private space; whether it's a few acres of paddock or a 300sq mile estate. Similar to how some people feel

about immigration, the antipathy towards the wild camper is sometimes a fear of the outsider. The native 'other'. But like most things in life, it's based more on the lack of knowledge than the rational appraisal of a walker, cyclist or canoeist on a sleepover involving a maximum of one night.

There's a lot we 'sleepers' can do to help each other in reassuring landowners. Charity begins at home. When in the wild, that's the temporal home. Collecting litter is the most obvious way to put something back. There's almost no weight to a pink sack full of cans, cartons and plastic bottles. Landowners may not always welcome an idle traveller, but they will rarely fail to appreciate a diligent picker, intent on keeping the outback clean for the sake of others, as well as himself.

Despite this being my 'home' country, some have suggested that if I don't like the occasional restrictions on sleeping in England, I go sleep somewhere else. Scandinavia. Scotland. There's no doubt, a bigger world is out there beyond the rivers and trails of these islands. Sleeping with Bedouins in the Sinai, tramps in the Punjab, backpackers on Goa, Aussies in Bali... There are a lot of temporary 'homes' out there. But we have this one, too.

'Always take time to smell the roses in your own garden,' my dad used to tell me. So here are some more in the north.

'I long to sleep in the long, deep silence, beneath the dizzying volley of stars, with nothing but the sky's infinite expanse for a roof and the warm earth for bed... to doze off in the sorrowful yet serene knowledge that I am utterly alone, that no one pines for me anywhere on Earth, that there is no place where I am missed or expected. To know all that, to be free and without ties, a nomad camped in life's great desert, where I shall never be anything but an outsider, a stranger and an intruder. Such is the only form of bliss, however bitter, the Mektoub will ever grant me. Happiness of the sort coveted by all of the frantic humanity, will never be mine.'

THE NOMAD: THE DIARIES OF ISABELLE EBERHARDT

ENGLAND'S MOST untouched region. The Pennines. Beyond them, the Cheviots are the final frontier: really. A garrison of vistas that merge into Northumberland and Scotland; the scene of many battles between the English and Scottish. I'm sure every piece of high ground in England used to be a fort. But this was surely one of the greatest. To the north, the hills are divided by a series of valleys. The south slopes down to the River Coquet. The Cheviot is the crown, a beacon that towers 815m (2,674ft) over the other great mounds, the wonderfully named Cushat Law, Bloodybush Edge and Hedgehope Hill. Windy Gyle sits astride the border, a climb that can start on one side and end on the other.

Although most of the hills are on the English side, where wild camping is not a right enshrined in law, you can't help but feel entitled to sleep if climbing from the good side: in from the Scots and over the border.

The **Pennine Way** follows the Border Ridge right along the Scottish/English line for 28km (19 miles). There are several bothies in case the weather turns in. Care is needed close to the Ministry of Defence firing range of Otterburn Army Training Estate, an area of 24,280ha (60,000 acres) around the south hills. Notifications about restricted areas are available on the MOD website.

St Cuthbert's Way crosses the Cheviots to the north to link with the Pennine Way.

PRACTICAL INFO Climb to the Cheviot (55.4785, -2.1454) and walk the Scottish/English border along the Pennine Way, sleeping with your head in one and feet in the other (55.5328, -2.233).

TRAVEL Trains and buses take you into Morpeth, Newcastle, Hexham, Chathill, Berwick-upon-Tweed and Haydon Bridge.

91 KIELDER FOREST

THE FORESTS AND MOORS that surround the reservoir at Kielder Water are a man-made triumph. I pinch myself having to say this: 'The largest man-made woodland in England.' It's a statement that means everything and nothing. On the one hand, there is no 'natural forest' in England, so the phrase 'man-made' means zilch. On the other, 'largest forest' – indigenous or not – is perhaps something to celebrate. A vast space of 647sq km (250sq miles), taken up by trees rather than grazing land, or roads, or landfill, or saw mills. Especially as the UK and Ireland have the lightest tree cover in Europe at just 10 per cent, compared with the rest of Europe's kinder 40 per cent forest cover.

Kielder was created from the Sitka spruce trees planted by the Forestry Commission in the 1920s and 30s, with labour provided by the unemployed. What work it must have been – attempting to replant a nation's decimated forest to help restock timber reserves. Almost a century later, close to half a million cubic metres of timber is still produced here each year. Before trees, Kielder had been like most of the rest of England. Yeah. Man-made: open moor for sheep and grouse shoots.

The phrase 'Kielder Forest' refers to the surrounding hills and moors as well as the plantations that bleed into the Cheviots. The **Pennine Way** slides past, just nicking the Kielder Edge before it meshes with Hadrian's Wall.

Kielder Castle, in the North Tyne Valley, was built as a hunting lodge in the 18th century by the Duke of Northumberland. It's an information centre today. Visitors arrive here mostly to walk and cycle.

The trails are endless. Getting lost anywhere outdoors is frightening: on Dartmoor or out on the sands of a great estuary with the tide coming in. Here it's almost a certainty without a map, compass and the skills to navigate. Rookies can keep to the Lakeside Way in Northumberland – at just over 42km (26 miles), it's enough to spread out two energetic days' exploring, sitting, writing, capturing the moment. Horse-riders and cyclists use the trail, too, but it becomes silent between dusk and before dawn.

Although not elevated, the path follows the lake shore. You need to ask permission to camp here. If you can't get it, there are paths and tracks up over the wildest heather moors I've ever walked to Peel Fell (602m/1,975ft) and Knox Knowe Cairn, where sleeping in a tent causes no offence close to the Scottish borders.

Fell-runners can make their way up to Peel Fell, carrying a 9kg (20lb) bag, in less than two hours. For the rest of us, it's a day's walk from the lake path, with time to pick August bilberries and take in the best late-evening views in England by daylight. Sighty Crag to the east may be the most remote location in the UK, as it is considered to be the furthest point from any road. Compass- and map-reading skills are vital in these areas, as even locals get lost.

The forest is best accessed from the Pennine Way, which falls down from the northern Redesdale Forest and skirts the east side of Kielder before meeting the North Tyne river at Bellingham. Footpaths and Sustrans cycle tracks follow the line of the North Tyne up to the Lakeside Way. It links with the North Tyne river, which is navigable for canoes from just south of Kielder Water all the way out to the coast at Newcastle.

> **PRACTICAL INFO** Trek the forest trail along Scaup Burn (55.2999, -2.5474); camp on the most deserted peak in Britain, on the Scottish/English border at Knox Knowe Cairn (55.3177, -2.5496).
> **TRAVEL** Trains and buses take you into Jedburgh, Hawick, Langholm, Longtown, Carlisle, Haltwhistle and Hexham.

92 NORTH PENNINES

MUCH OF THE LAND surrounding the North Pennines is used either for grazing or grouse moor. George Monbiot – the writer and environmental activist – seems to dislike both. I'm offended by the politics of the BBC's *Countryfile*, but not the industrial landscape. Certainly no more than the crashing of metal and the sound of diesel engines when I played in scrapyards.

Industry is wild. Hares, hawkweed, agriculture, bog orchid, edgelands, alleys, drains, sheep, foreshore and mountain. When the rain and wind beats down, the Pennine Way is as depressingly glorious as a Smiths album. And then the sun comes out and the music changes. Perhaps it's the company of the outdoors, the green and rocky towers that rise from the valleys of Lakeland in the west, Kielder Forest and Hadrian's Wall to the north, the Yorkshire Dales in the south; the A1 to the east, like a black hole sucking all the life into London's square-mile vortex; a reminder of why we're up here. On top. Away from it all. Moving forward out of the black, into the rain. And then perhaps a rainbow. A kestrel over a blue moor.

The North Pennines is a range of hills that spreads just west of the River Eden, near Carlisle in the north, diagonally down towards the Yorkshire Dales. Wainwright went coast to coast. I prefer north to south or south to north along and up and down the Pennine peaks. The sense that you're actually going somewhere rather than across, like a crab moving from one rock pool to another.

It's not all open ground. Gulping dales make way for stone villages where mining once powered northern industry. The **Pennine Way** is the natural path to follow as a guide. Just over 400km (250 miles) through the Borders, Northumberland, Durham, Cumbria, and down into North and West Yorkshire and Derbyshire. The alleys and paths that lead off and around into the unknown, cracks and corridors, are unlimited, literally endless; upland rivers, waterfalls, forests, cycleways, byways, tracks that go on and on. Never sideways. Only limited by the inability to sleep out if you've no tent to take shelter or the will to keep going.

PRACTICAL INFO Walk the footpath out of Appleby in Westmorland, along High Cup Gill Beck to High Cup Nick (54.62186, -2.4079) on to the Pennine Way; find a place to overnight along the Way between Maize Beck (54.6299, -2.3943) and Cotherstone Moor (54.5506, -2.0972).

TRAVEL Trains and buses take you into Bardon Mill, Haydon Bridge and Haltwhistle from the north; Stanhope and Wolsingham from the east.

FOREST OF TRAWDEN

THE MOMENTS just before sunrise turn the slopes along the Forest of Trawden into a tranquil place. As the street lights along the Burnley Valley merge into dawn, the shadows of the wooded cloughs, bushed heather and cold-grey, millstone grit rock radiate light, and then life. Woodlice and lizards trade their cracks and crevices for the narrow stalks of sun that reach out into the higher parts. The tundra-like landscape slopes upwards from here into the Peak and Lake districts, but the exchange between township, high plateau and moor was enough for Defoe to crown these hills 'the Andes of England'.

Boulsworth Hill (518m/1,699ft) is among the highest points and good for sleeping out, north of the Peak District, in the southern Pennines section. Farmland and high open moorland surrounded by tree-lined valleys for hammocks.

Black Moor marks the near coming together of three great routes: the Pennine Bridleway, the Pennine Way and the Burnley Way, next to Widdop Reservoir. The **Pennine Bridleway** (330km/205 miles) starts in Middleton-by-Wirksworth, Derbyshire, mostly following the Pennines along old packhorse roads, deserted railway lines and drove roads into Cumbria via Lancashire and North and West Yorkshire. The route is often confused with the Pennine Way. Mary Towneley conceived the idea of the Bridleway when she travelled 402km (250 miles) from Corbridge, Northumberland, to Ashbourne, Derbyshire, on horseback during the 1980s.

> **PRACTICAL INFO** Spend the night up on Lad Law (53.8154, -2.1075) on Boulsworth Hill, for views over Pendle and Calder valleys.
>
> **TRAVEL** Trains and buses take you into Burnley, Nelson, Colne, Cononley and Oakworth.

MY ADULT LIFE is alternately enriched and scarred by teenage memories of Sunday-night TV and, of all things, images of the Yorkshire Dales. Two TV series launched in the 1970s are to blame. *All Creatures Great and Small* by Alf Wight (aka James Herriot), which I loved, and *Last of the Summer Wine*, which, to my shame, I still hate. The populations of the surrounding towns of Skipton and Ripon have grown a little since the 1970s, but the quiet lanes and plains still epitomise gentle panoramas.

To enjoy something slightly more dramatic, the hiker looking for sleep and a camp must trek up into the high Dales, where Compo and Clegg would never dare to step. There's some dispute over who controls these areas. A public inquiry was opened on Tuesday, 4 June 2013, at Castle Green Hotel, Kendal, to allow the planning inspector, Roy Foster, to decide whether Natural England should be allowed to designate the countryside between the western boundary of the Yorkshire Dales National Park and the eastern boundary of the Lake District National Park (M6 Lune Valley corridor) as extensions to the National Parks. Which agency manages what, and into which park it falls, makes little difference to the hiker. They are just names and labels of no real practical purpose for anyone other than pen-pushers and form-fillers.

Camping is best up on top. Get there from any of the towns or villages surrounding the Dales. I most like to camp in North Yorkshire. Just north of Hawes, in Bellow Hill, is a hamlet called Hardraw. There's a small amount of parking to the east and a pub on the Hardraw Beck bridge. The Pennine Way passes through here and leads up towards Cotterdale, Great Shunner Fell and Abbotside Common. Most of the rivers flow out east towards the Vale of York and into the Humber via the Ouse.

The Dales Way (126km/78 miles) peels in from the south-east of Cumbria, across North and West Yorkshire. The Ribble Way (105km/65 miles) rides out from the Dales peaks of Ingleborough, Whernside and Pen-y-Ghent, towards Lancashire.

95 THE WIRRAL

THE BIRTH of the English nation may have had its roots on the modest land mass known as The Wirral. The Battle of Brunanburh, in 937, at Bromborough, involved unified 'English forces' fighting together for the first time against Norsemen and Scottish tribes.

Whether or not the historians are right, it was a short-lived victory for those unwitting nation builders. The Norman Invasion saw much of the Wirral's infrastructure, trade and military destroyed. The area remained heavily populated under the new army. Some parts became defined as forest with exclusive hunting rights for the elite in the early part of the 12th century. But the economy continued to grow around port trade, with neighbouring Liverpool now the important centre. The population had grown to close to a million people by the end of the 18th century.

The Wirral is a peninsula, 24km (15 miles) long and 11km (7 miles) wide, pointing north-west towards the Irish Sea.

It is cut from the Welsh/English border, a defining land tab created by the River Dee to the west and the River Mersey to the east. The Shropshire Union Canal runs from the Dee at Chester to the Mersey at Ellesmere Port and cuts the peninsula from the mainland, making it an island.

The Wirral takes its name from a brown-stemmed shrub – the bog myrtle – that once flourished here; the Old English for a myrtle tree was 'wir', and 'heal' means slope or corner. The unique position and access to water made it an important port in ancient times, and a densely populated settlement during the Middle Ages.

Although the Wirral is a semi-wilderness, the offshore islands in the Dee offer a better chance to escape the lights and rush of modern commerce. The coastal rangers were out when I was last there. They confirmed there was no problem pulling the canoes on to the islands' foreshore once the tide had gone. The rangers were diligent and helpful. They encouraged me to explore and enjoy, and advised that the isles were mostly fabulous for canoes or kayaks, as the tidal currents were not so strong. I was told that 'sleeping', not camping, in a bivvy was OK if I needed to wait for the tide to return at night. Making a fire was out of the question as the entire area is protected habitat under SSSI status.

Little Eye and Hilbre Island are the places worth visiting. Although the main island is inhabited by a few holidaymakers, most of the residents here are seals. For those coming without a canoe, the islands can be walked at low tide over the mud, but check tide times and local knowledge.

The **Wirral Circular Trail** lines much of the coast and history along its 60km (37 miles). The Wirral Way (19km/12 miles) is a short track over the old railway from West Kirby to Hooton; it links with important paths such as the Dee Way.

> **PRACTICAL INFO** Canoe or kayak at high tide to Little Hilbre Island (53.3781, -3.2206) and Hilbre Island (53.3813, -3.2257).
> **TRAVEL** Trains and buses take you into Neston, Heswall, West Kirby, Hoylake and Moreton. Ferry crossings go from Liverpool to Woodside and Seacombe.

96 GOSWICK SANDS

THE CAMPSITE WAS GONE when I last visited. The brightly coloured tents and bleached white vans were always pitched into these dunes for summer, like plastic toys left in a giant sandpit. The sign now almost drowns the peaceful calm: Private Road. One canvas door closes… another opens.

Sustrans Route 1 and the Northumberland Coast Path: this section of path is a well-trodden line over Goswick Sands. The Beachcomber Campsite was formerly carved into the back beach from the no-man's-land of the Northumberland coast, where the purple chives and cordgrass still bend on the wind and spray. This is an area between the dunes and the fields that man cultivated in the Middle Ages for grazing and winter wheat. The Beachcomber Campsite was a sort of shrine. A homage to sleeping out and camping. It was what St Andrews is to links golf. Fascinating how landscapes can shape the mind.

This campsite was, of course, neither 'royal' nor 'ancient'. It wasn't very old either. But it closed in 2012 when the owners retired. I phoned them several times in the months that followed, but

was mostly told the site might reopen next year. For now, the place is quieter and wilder than ever. Shelduck, barnacle geese and curlews fly in, while the dunlin swarm over at dusk like locusts on a biblical flight of fancy. It would seem disconcerting if it wasn't so common.

The coast streams from Berwick-upon-Tweed to the River Coquet estuary, to the east of the A1 road. Its greatest landmark is Lindisfarne, a rugged land

> **PRACTICAL INFO** Sleep along the foreshore (55.7065, -1.900) en route to Lindisfarne.
> **TRAVEL** Trains take you into Widdrington, Acklington, Alnmouth, Chathill and Berwick-upon-Tweed.

mass surrounded by shallow water and crowned by rock. It is known as Holy Island (and sometimes Healing Island because of herbal remedies found close by).

A priory was built here in the 7th century, raided by Vikings in the late 8th century, and then recreated afterwards by the Norman invaders. The castle came much later, in the 16th century. A causeway, which allows crossings at low tide, is an ancient pilgrims' path over the sands. In many ways that's what it still is. A Mecca. A tourist trap. A holiday; for a Holy Day. Nothing changes. We just lose touch with the past.

The path and island see many 'pilgrims' stranded for three hours, despite the warning notices. Marooned walkers take advantage of 'refuge boxes': white wooden shelters on stilts that provide them with cover until the tide retreats.

The **Northumberland Coast Path** is 103km (64 miles) and can be walked in anything from three days to a week. There is so much beach here to camp along: sand and dune to get lost on, especially north of Lindisfarne.

The trail links with the Berwickshire Coastal Path (48km/30 miles) and St Cuthbert's Way (100km/63 miles) towards the Scottish borders, with access to the Cheviot Hills and the Pennine Way.

HADRIAN'S WALL

EMPEROR HADRIAN BUILT this monstrous piece of vandalism across England in the 2nd century AD, from the east at Segedunum, on the River Tyne, to the west at Solway Firth. How the natives must have hated him for it; and then their children celebrated when the invaders left in 5 AD, without instructions on what to do with the damn thing.

It was designed to control the populace. Around 80 milecastles were established as fortified gateways to manage the flow of trade, traffic and people. Like most monstrous structures of the past – particularly those involving extreme feats of engineering and labour to assert power, while extorting money and fear – the ability to resist time fascinates us more.

It's not all bad. The wall reduces the risk of walkers getting lost en route, which may be a practical reason why it's so popular. It is one of England's biggest tourist attractions, although at 118km (73 miles) there's plenty to explore and get lost in, even in summer, as the wall passes through some of the north's best countryside: woodland, streams and shallow lakes.

The wall changes along the way, shaped I'm sure by the reality of changing budgets in the 2nd century AD, the various architects, ditches, mounds, shrubs and the remnants of the military posts. East of the River Irthing, huge square stones up to 5.5m (18ft) wide make up the fortification, while on the other side of the river the wall is much lower, created from turf and earth.

Hadrian's Wall Path covers slightly more ground, 135km (84 miles) from coast to coast, part of which links with the Pennine Way and Cumbria Way.

The Tyneside section of the trail is known locally as Hadrian's Way.

There are several campsites along the way, and really no shortage of places to wild camp after dark – if not on the path, at least close to it. For those determined to sleep in the open without fear of a wake-up call, the Scottish border is at times less than half a mile away, where camping is a right, not requiring permission from landowners.

PRACTICAL INFO Explore Peel Crags early morning (55.0023, -2.3852), late lunch around the waters of Crag Lough (55.0049, -2.37145).
TRAVEL Trains and buses take you into Haydon Bridge, Haltwhistle, Carlise and Newcastle.

98 YORKSHIRE WOLDS

THERE ARE TWO communal graves – Bronze Age barrows – in a field just west of Walkington, on Walkington Wold. The barrows are at the edge of two administrative districts or hundreds, known as Welton and Cave, and offer reasonable views of the surrounding landscape.

During the late 1960s, the site was excavated and archaeologists discovered the headless corpses of more than ten young men. Carbon tests on the bones showed that the Bronze Age graves had been used as an Anglo-Saxon execution cemetery for at least 300 years between the 7th and 10th centuries. The bodies of criminals were placed there as punishment, on the boundary of the district and within the grave of alien spirits.

The execution cemetery is the only known example of martial law from the Middle Ages in north England. The find demonstrates three things: local systems of administration, laws were in place well

before the 10th century, and summary justice often involved the afterlife. Justice meant excluding 'outsiders' – criminals – to the periphery of society: literally on the outskirts of town, and metaphorically within the graves of heathen people from the past. Burying criminals in alien, ancient graves rather than the holy ground of their peers meant they were excluded even in death from society, supposedly left to endure an eternity of torment from the spirits that resided in the heathen graves.

The fertile ground made the Wolds an attractive area for Neolithic settlers. Archaeological finds from all ages are significant. More than 1,500 Bronze Age round barrows have been discovered. Danes Dyke is one of the most significant and visible monuments, a huge ditch and mound that stretches 4km (2.5 miles) across Flamborough Head. The ditch is more than 18m (60ft) wide in places, 6m (20ft) deep, and up to 5.5m (18ft) tall. In many parts it's thick with beech, sycamore, ash and lime trees. Why and when it was created is a mystery: even though it is a defensive structure, the effort that was required to create it has puzzled historians.

The low chalk hills of the Yorkshire Wolds lie just south of Scarborough, defined by a soft peninsula. An overflow of the Lincolnshire Wolds to the south, the hills are surrounded by water: the Humber Gap to the south, the River Derwent to the west and Bridlington Bay to the east, and capped by the rather pointed nose of Flamborough Head.

The Wolds spread across the counties of North Yorkshire and East Riding reaching no more than 248m (814ft) at the highest point at Bishop Wilton Wold. The relatively modest peaks are overshadowed somewhat by the impressive and sudden drop of the cliffs into the North Sea at Bempton, Filey and Flamborough.

Walking the **Yorkshire Wolds Way** (127km/79 miles) over a series of days is probably the best way to take in the area. There are numerous places off or on the path to sleep hidden from view. There are also several official campsites along the way. The path links with the Cleveland Way at Filey.

PRACTICAL INFO See the northern section of Danes Dyke, which stretches across Flamborough Head, from the coastal path that links with the Yorkshire Wolds Way (54.1410, -0.1444).
TRAVEL Trains and buses take you into Kingston upon Hull, Bridlington, Norton on Derwent, Filey, York and Selby.

99 LANCASTER CANAL

CANALS WERE ONCE to the north-west what the M1 has become to Birmingham – a transit highway for haulage. If the world survives the next 200 years to see giant metal plates propelling our goods inside driverless crates along magnetic ley lines in the sky, no doubt motorways will become another addition to the Sustrans Cycle Network. For now, we have the likes of the **Lancaster Canal towpath**, and that's a very good start.

Brent geese glide low in v-formations, like squadrons of young RAF teams performing a fly-past to impress the graceless ducks. Gaggles of seabirds hum and float over the surface of the water at the edge of the canal where it branches out from the tidal edge of the River Ribble, while sparrows flutter in the juniper trees around the wooded ditches from which I hang my hammock to sleep.

The Lancaster Canal is a bridge, an engineering display that links two great sides – the River Ribble to the south, the River Lune to the north – among a network of north-west waterways that once connected industry and trade from Yorkshire and Lancashire to London. The most southerly section, past Preston, is navigable as part of the Leeds and Liverpool Canal. The north canal was connected to the south canal – and the rest of the English canal network – in 2002, when the Ribble Link opened.

Walkers and cyclists can travel on the towpath (91km/57 miles) all the way into the Lake District, at Kendal. The 68km (42 miles) from Preston to Tewitfield, north of Lancaster, is open to canoes and other craft. There are no locks, which avoids the need for portage. The best time to wild camp is in winter, when the fishing is good. The Waterway Wanderers scheme (see page 42) is available at several rural locations, including:

ASHTON BASIN to Bridge 48
BRIDGE 48 to Bridge 66 (Nateby Hall)
BRIDGE 66 Nateby Hall to Bridge 93 (Carr Lane Bridge)
BRIDGE 93 (Carr Lane) to Bridge 118 (Hest Bank)
BRIDGE 126 to Bridge 129b (motorway culvert)
BRIDGE 138 to Bridge 141 (Saltermire Bridge).

The path links with the Lancashire Coastal Way (106km/66 miles) from Merseyside and Cumbria, as well as the Limestone Link, the Lune Valley Ramble and Wyre Way.

PRACTICAL INFO Walk 91km (57 miles) along the towpath (54.0185, -2.8077) to find somewhere to hammock in the trees or bivvy on flat ground.
TRAVEL Trains and buses take you into Preston, Garstang, Galgate and Lancaster.

100 RIVER EDEN

A TRUE STORY. Before starting this journey of 100 camps, I promised myself I'd finish in Cumbria – as a sort of homage to the writings of Wainwright – and specifically around the **River Eden,** for no other reason than when I was last here it seemed a special place, draped in the branches of old trees and the kindness of fly-fishermen and fellow wild campers.

In between, I've read too much about the history of Britain and beyond, and no doubt read too much into it; the transition from Neolithic hunters and nomads to farmers, landowners, domesticators of livestock. The rules and regulations placed over this land and its inhabitants by successive invaders, their kings, their parliaments and their justices. The right to roam, the differences between a pilgrim and a traveller, the similarities between a holy trek that ends at a shrine, and a package holiday that starts in a car and ends in a holy-day resort.

Why Saxon criminals in the Middle Ages were buried with the outsiders and 'demons' inside Bronze Age graves on the edge of

district boundaries; why a fisherman can catch grayling in the tidal Avon in Bristol, but can't do the same in the tidal Avon in South Devon; why a canoeist has a right in law to navigate around the tidal creeks of shallow Essex, but not the fresh waters of the Nene. The relevance of the Magna Carta. The necessity for the Domesday Book to audit a census for the new lords and their estates.

I started out confused. Puzzled why anyone – the RSPB, the National Trust, the Crown Estate, the Duchy of Cornwall, the inheritors of these kingdoms, and lands, and estates – would object so much to a pair of tired legs going to sleep in a little ol' sleeping bag in the bush beside the footpath, or in a tiny green hammock sheet slung between two trees.

The answer is a resounding, 'They don't, really.' And if there is a question mark or a request to 'Move on, please', it's more to do with ignorance than fear, greed and control.

Just before finishing my last trip home from Cumbria, I'd had an unrelated interview with the Bishop of Essex. I'd questioned him over the relevance of the Old Testament stories in the modern world. It was near to Easter, we had a lot of journalists on holiday, and I had some news pages to fill.

The interview was published online in April 2014. Two weeks later, I received a book through the post, sent by the author, Andrew Collins. It was a story entitled *Göbekli Tepe: Genesis of the Gods*, about Collins' attempt to find the location of the Garden of Eden in and around eastern

Turkey and Iraq. He concluded that the garden is a metaphor for the Fall of Man: the transition – based on the knowledge that allowed us to cultivate the land with grains (the forbidden fruit in the story), and in the process moving from the old life as nomadic hunter-gatherers. The story of Eve being tempted to eat from the Tree of Knowledge supposedly signifies humanity giving up the old nomadic way of life for the new cultivated and domesticated land. The forbidden fruit represents the 'seed' to sow the land, a change that occurred 10,000 years ago in the Middle East. It turned the land from being used for communal foraging into one that was sold, bought or stolen, corrupting us and our diets in the process.

Just in case the meaning of the story was lost, the writers of Genesis gave us a backup story: Eve's first children were Cain and Abel. Cain killed Abel. The firstborn of Eve committed the first murder. Cain was a farmer: the domestic cultivator. Abel a nomadic herdsman, the wild wanderer. The settler destroys the wanderer, and in the process – according to a curse sent down by God for killing Abel – is condemned to damnation and a life of strife and suffering in the dirt and dust with the mythical serpent.

It's a human tale. Story-telling hasn't changed since before the beginning of time. Collins concludes in his search for Eden that paradise doesn't exist in a single place. But it's not a figment of our imaginations either; he says it's a feature of our own environment beyond the boundary, the sea wall, the foreshore, up in the mountains.

I haven't said much about the River Eden yet. I've not yet mentioned where to sling the hammock or where to find the kingfishers nesting in the old badgers' setts and the fox holes around the sandy spit. How to access the riverbank and paddle in the safe shallows, where not to swim in the deepening currents; or how to avoid waking on the wrong side of the riverbank surrounded by cattle and dawn shade.

I've left it out, because the answers are out there, beyond the wall. Wainwright wanted us to leave the path, for everything and nothing; Chatwin called it Dreamtime. The sleeping.

PRACTICAL INFO Walk the tree-lined riverside path from Wetheral (54.8813, -2.8286) to Holmwrangle (54.8282, -2.7568) where there are places to hammock. Cross the river at Armathwaite, return to Holmwrangle, and walk back to Wetheral along the riverside path on the other side to complete a 26km (16-mile) round journey. Fly-fish just off the footpath in the river around Lazonby (licence required) (54.7511, -2.6913).

TRAVEL Trains and buses for the River Eden flow into Wetheral, Aiketgate, Lazonby, Langwathby, Appleby in Westmorland, Warcop, Kirkby Stephen and Garsdale.

INDEX

Page references in **bold** refer to the 100 wild camping locations featured in the book.